Penguin Handbooks
The Home Gardener's Cookbook

Gill Coleman was born into an army family and spent her
early years abroad, where she acquired a love of unusual foreign
foods. She obtained a diploma in home economics from the
Atholl Crescent Domestic Science College, and then worked for
a year as a freelance cookery demonstrator before joining
Birds Eye Foods as a home economist. This was followed by a
period of living and working in Greece and the Middle East.
Upon her return to England, she joined *Woman's Weekly* as
Deputy Cookery Editor, helping to produce a wide range of
weekly cookery articles. After four and a half years she left to
have a family, continuing to develop and test recipes on a
freelance basis. Gill Coleman lives with her husband and two
small daughters in a village near Bristol.

Clare Walker was born into a naval family and spent the first
ten years of her life abroad, particularly in Canada. She
began cooking as a hobby while in her early teens, and the interest
never left her. In 1967 she received an M.A. from Glasgow
University, and then began a career as a newspaper reporter,
first on the Dundee-based *Sunday Post*, and finally ending up on
Fleet Street with the *Sun*. She worked on the *Sun* for five
years, largely covering consumer affairs stories, 'retiring' to
have a family and to indulge her passion for cooking to the full.
Clare Walker, her husband Iain and their two young children have
temporarily left their home in Surrey for a two-year stay in
New York City.

The Home Gardener's Cookbook

Clare Walker and Gill Coleman

Penguin Books

Penguin Books Ltd, Harmondsworth,
Middlesex, England
Penguin Books, 625 Madison Avenue,
New York, New York 10022, U.S.A.
Penguin Books Australia Ltd, Ringwood,
Victoria, Australia
Penguin Books Canada Ltd, 2801 John Street,
Markham, Ontario, Canada L3R 1B4
Penguin Books (N.Z.) Ltd, 182–190 Wairau Road,
Auckland 10, New Zealand

First published 1980
Copyright © Clare Walker and Gill Coleman, 1980
All rights reserved

Made and printed in Great Britain by
Hazell Watson & Viney Ltd, Aylesbury, Bucks
Set in Monotype Times Roman

To Iain and Tim,
our favourite guinea-pigs

Contents

Part Two: Fruits

Part Three: Preserving and Miscellaneous

Preface

This book was originally compiled for the benefit of home gardeners with the aim of showing them how to get the maximum enjoyment at the dinner table from the hard work that goes into caring for vegetable plots, fruit trees or allotments.

The return to home-grown produce has quickly caught on in the last few years. Ever-soaring prices at the greengrocer's and the supermarket have forced many people to turn to growing their own food in an attempt to beat inflation. Flower beds and lawns are being dug up to make room for a vegetable patch, and we have even seen Brussels sprouts growing in the front garden amongst the rose bushes!

Allotments are now in such demand that local councils hardly have any to offer. Once they were only too pleased to rent out these odd patches of land for a few shillings a year. Now their annual rental can be as high as £10 and still the waiting lists grow.

In a good year, however, you can end up with a bumper crop which can leave you and the family screaming at the thought of yet another plate of boiled beans or cabbage or yet another apple pie. It was to combat this boredom that we decided to produce this book.

In every chapter we have tried to give a wide range from the simplest, most traditional recipes to the more unusual and exotic dishes. Some recipes will obviously take more time and effort than others. We are both experts at producing dishes with the minimum amount of effort. You have to be when working in the kitchen with a young family under your feet!

We have taken care to spell out every step to avoid any confusion, but we would encourage you to experiment with the recipes by using different fruits and vegetables and new combinations. (At the end of many chapters you will find lists of other recipes in the book which can easily be adapted to the vegetable or fruit just dealt with. We hope you will add to these lists as you experiment.) The results can be most surprising and very satisfying, as we have discovered.

Although we have stuck to our original intention to base our recipes upon the kitchen garden, the book should also appeal to people who don't have a vegetable patch or allotment, but who are buying fruit and vegetables in bulk from the market, or picking their own direct from the farm – a trend which is becoming increasingly popular.

We also believe this book will be invaluable to the ordinary housewife with an eye for a bargain.

There cannot be many people who have not thought on seeing the low price of a certain fruit or vegetable: 'I wish I could buy several pounds of that, but what would I do with it all?' At the height of its season, each fruit or vegetable sells at a bargain price and it is then that the buyer should take advantage of the low cost.

The vegetables and fruits we have chosen to include in this book are those most commonly grown in the British kitchen garden. We have not included the more unusual produce which can be grown in our climate or in the greenhouse, e.g. asparagus, sweetcorn, chicory, aubergines, peaches, grapes, etc.

Yet although this book is centred on garden-grown produce, it is not a gardening book. We do not claim to be expert gardeners, although at the start of each chapter we have included a short section giving gardening tips which we found useful in cultivating our own crops.

In the book you will find many recipes for preserving and bottling your fruits and vegetables, but this is not primarily a preserving book. You will also find short sections on freezing in the chapter introductions, and where a recipe is suitable for freezing we have said so. To get the best use from your freezer we would recommend one of the specialist books on the market.

Throughout our work on the recipes in this book we have been very conscious of economy – economy of money, time and effort. Where possible we have tried not to use too many pots and pans. We have tried not to include too many expensive ingredients, although you will find some recipes using wines (we used home-made ones) or liqueurs and cream. In most cases they can be left out, but please remember to increase the amount of liquid used in the recipe by adding extra (e.g. stock or fruit juice) to counteract the loss of the wine or liqueur.

We were sorely tempted to include one or two successful wine recipes, but as we are mere beginners in this field that would have been presumptuous. If you are looking for a new hobby and new ways to use up your crops (especially fruit which is soft or windfalls) then we can highly recommend home-made wines as well worth the effort.

Metric Conversion Tables

It is important to follow *either* the metric *or* the imperial system, in each recipe, but never to combine the two. The equivalent weights and measures given in these tables are not exact but have been rounded up or down to give convenient working amounts. Weights under 25 g (1 oz) are usually given in tablespoons (tbsps), dessertspoons (dsps) and teaspoons (tsps).

Grams/ Kilograms	Ounces/ Pounds	Millilitres/ Litres	Pints
25 g	1 oz	150 ml	¼ pint
50 g	2 oz	300 ml	½ pint
75 g	3 oz	450 ml	¾ pint
100–25 g	4 oz	600 ml	1 pint
150 g	5 oz	750 ml	1¼ pints
175 g	6 oz	900 ml	1½ pints
200 g	7 oz	1 litre	1¾ pints
250 g	8 oz	1¼ litres	2 pints
300 g	10 oz	1½ litres	2½ pints
350 g	12 oz	1¾ litres	3 pints
400 g	14 oz	2 litres	3½ pints
500 g	1 lb	2¼ litres	4 pints
¾ kg	1½ lb	3 litres	5 pints
1 kg	2 lb		
1¼ kg	3 lb		
1½ kg	3½ lb		
1¾–2 kg	4 lb		
2¼ kg	5 lb		

The levelled metric capacity of the spoons (British Imperial Standard) used throughout the book is approximately as follows:

1.25 ml	=	¼ level teaspoon
2.5 ml	=	½ level teaspoon
5 ml	=	1 level teaspoon
10 ml	=	2 level teaspoons or
		1 level dessertspoon
15 ml	=	1 level tablespoon

Centimetres	*Inches*
½ cm	¼ inch
1 cm	½ inch
2.5–3 cm	1 inch
5 cm	2 inches
7.5–8 cm	3 inches
10 cm	4 inches
12.5–13 cm	5 inches
15 cm	6 inches
17.5–18 cm	7 inches
20 cm	8 inches
22.5–23 cm	9 inches
25 cm	10 inches

Temperature Equivalents for Oven Thermostat Markings

Fahrenheit	Gas Mark	Centigrade	Heat of Oven
225°F	¼	110°C	Very cool
250°F	½	130°C	Very cool
275°F	1	140°C	Cool
300°F	2	150°C	Cool
325°F	3	160°C	Moderate
350°F	4	180°C	Moderate
375°F	5	190°C	Fairly hot
400°F	6	200°C	Fairly hot
425°F	7	220°C	Hot
450°F	8	230°C	Very hot
475°F	9	240°C	Very hot

Part One: Vegetables

General Introduction to Vegetables

The greatest sin to commit against vegetables is to overcook them. This destroys their vitamins as well as their colour and appearance. There can be no excuse for this – one can hardly argue that it is time-saving or cuts corners. On the contrary, it simply increases the fuel bills in the long run.

Recently, British cooks have begun to change their attitudes to the cooking of vegetables and are according more respect to the preparation and presentation of vegetable dishes.

As a general rule, vegetables should be firm and crisp, not soggy or watery. We have drafted a special easy-reference table to show the cooking times and methods for each vegetable and a list of 'do's and 'don't's to give you some guidance in the use of vegetables.

Each chapter in the section is also prefaced with an introduction on the particular vegetable and its basic preparation. We would advise you not to attempt to by-pass any instructions in the recipes as this will not improve the dish and may even detract from it. For example, onions are sautéed in butter to soften them, and in the case of garlic, frying in butter or fat brings out its full flavour.

Preparation

There are seven different ways to cut vegetables:

1. Sliced long or in rounds, thick, medium or thin (as in game chips).
2. Diced – small cubes or even-sized dice, as in a macédoine.
3. Shredded – thin slivers, e.g. cabbage.
4. Chopped – very small dice.
5. Matchstick – thin, even-length strips of vegetables about 5–8 cm (2–3 inches) long.
6. Grated, e.g. carrots in coleslaw.
7. Straws – thicker matchstick strips. Potato straws are the most common.

There are eight different ways to cook vegetables:

1. Boiling – the most popular method, but vitamins are lost in the water.
2. Baking – usually for stuffed vegetables or jacket potatoes. The vegetables are cooked in the oven.
3. Roasting – another oven method using a pan with fat or dripping.
4. Sautéing – frying in shallow fat. The vegetables are usually parboiled first.
5. Deep frying, e.g. chips and fritters.
6. Braising – cooking in stock or gravy.
7. Steaming – the vegetables cook in steam instead of water, thus retaining their vitamins.
8. Pressure cooking – the vegetables cook under pressure much quicker. Careful timing is needed not to overcook them by this method.

'Do's and 'Don't's for Vegetables

Many of the problems arise when vegetables are being boiled, which is the least satisfactory, if still the most popular, way of cooking them.

1. Wash vegetables carefully in cool water and drain before cooking. Do not leave them soaking.
2. Use a vegetable or potato peeler for root vegetables as the most nutritious layer is just beneath the skin, and you lose less vegetable this way. If possible cook vegetables, especially new ones, in their skins and, if necessary, peel them after they are cooked.
3. Do not waste anything. Outer leaves removed in preparation, provided they are not damaged, can be added to the stock pot for making soups or gravy. Damaged leaves and peelings should be put on the compost heap for mulch. Once the cooked vegetables are drained, reserve the water for use in soups, sauces and stocks. When thinning out vegetable plants in the garden, use the immature produce for garnishing dishes, or add it to casseroles and soups.
4. To boil vegetables: put root vegetables into cold salted water and bring it to the boil; put other vegetables into ready-boiling salted water.
5. Use only a little water for boiling vegetables and do not boil rapidly.
6. Do not add bicarbonate of soda to vegetables when boiling them. This is an old habit which dies hard and which destroys the nutritional value of foods.

7. Do not overcook vegetables.
8. Never leave boiled vegetables in their hot water as they will soon overcook and become mushy.
9. Drain all boiled vegetables thoroughly. This can best be achieved by using a colander, returning the drained vegetables to their saucepan with a knob of butter and heating gently for one or two minutes to dry completely.

Introduction to the chart on vegetable cooking times and methods

The following chart is intended to be an easy reference table showing the various methods by which vegetables may be cooked and the relevant cooking times.

It must be remembered that these cooking times are average figures only. You must take into account such factors as the size and age of the vegetables you are preparing. For example, young carrots take less time to cook than old, and the smaller ones require less cooking time than the larger ones.

Where we have ticked the column entitled 'Soup' you will find the relevant recipe in the chapter featuring that vegetable.

We have not included a column of cooking times for the pressure cooker because of the different times given by each manufacturer. If you wish to pressure cook your vegetables, follow the times given in the manufacturer's recipe leaflet.

Chart of Vegetable Cooking Times and Methods

Vegetable	Boil	Steam	Braise	Sauté	Deep Fry	Grill, Bake, Roast	Soup
Beetroot	1½–2 hrs.	2 hrs.	—	—	—	Bake, 1–1½ hrs.	√
Broad Beans	10–20 mins.	10–25 mins.	In stock, oil, lemon and herbs, 10–15 mins.	—	—	—	√
Broccoli	10–20 mins.	15–25 mins.	—	—	Parboil, 7–8 mins.; fry in batter, 4–5 mins.	—	√
Brussels Sprouts	10 mins.	15 mins.	In stock, 15 mins.	—	Parboil, 5 mins.; fry in batter, 4–5 mins.	—	√
Cabbage	7–10 mins.	10–20 mins.	Red cabbage 1½ hrs.	—	Parboil, 5 mins.; fry in flour, 4–5 mins.	Parboil, 5 mins.; bake, 45 mins.	√
Carrots	10–25 mins.	15–40 mins.	In stock, 15–25 mins.	Parboil, 10 mins.; in butter, 10 mins.	Parboil, 10 mins.; fry in flour, 4–5 mins.	—	√
Cauliflower	10–20 mins.	15–25 mins.	Florets: in stock, 20 mins.	Parboil, 7 mins.; in egg and breadcrumbs, 3 mins.	Parboil, 7 mins.; fry in batter, 4–5 mins.	Parboil, 5 mins.; bake, 30 mins.	√
Celery	15–25 mins.	20–30 mins.	In stock, 30 mins.	In herbs, butter and lemon, 20 mins.	Parboil, 15–20 mins.; fry in batter, 4–5 mins.	—	—
Courgettes	10–15 mins.	10–20 mins.	—	In butter, 10–15 mins.	Fry in egg and crumbs, 3 mins.	Bake, 40–45 mins.	—
Cucumbers	10 mins.	10–20 mins.	—	In herbs and butter, 10–15 mins.	—	Parboil, 5 mins.; bake, 15 mins.	√

Chart of Vegetable Cooking Times and Methods, cont.

Vegetable	Boil	Steam	Braise	Sauté	Deep Fry	Grill, Bake, Roast	Soup
French Beans	10–15 mins.	10–15 mins.	In stock, oil, lemon and herbs, 12–15 mins.	—	—	—	—
Leeks	10–20 mins.	15–25 mins.	In stock, oil, lemon and herbs, 10–12 mins.	In butter, 15–20 mins.	Parboil, 5 mins.; fry in batter, 4–5 mins.	—	√
Lettuce	7–10 mins.	12–15 mins.	10–15 mins.	—	—	—	√
Marrows	5–10 mins.	15–20 mins.	With onion and tomatoes, 10–15 mins.	In butter and herbs, 7–10 mins.	—	Stuffed, 2 hrs.	—
Mushrooms	—	20 mins.	—	In butter and lemon, 6–8 mins.	Button mushrooms: fry in batter, 5 mins.	Grill, 6–8 mins. Bake, 20–25 mins.	√
Onions	20–40 mins.	30–45 mins.	40 mins. to 1 hr.	In butter or fat, 5–10 mins.	Fry in flour or batter, 3–5 mins.	Bake or roast, 1–1½ hrs.	√
Parsnips	15–25 mins.	30–40 mins.	In stock, 30–40 mins.	Parboil, 10 mins.; in butter, 5–10 mins.	Slivers, plain or in flour, 5–10 mins. Or parboil, 10 mins.; fry in batter, 4–5 mins.	Parboil, 2 mins.; bake, 20 mins., or roast, 45 mins.	√
Peas	10–20 mins.	15–25 mins.	15–20 mins.	—	—	—	√
Potatoes	15–20 mins.	30–35 mins.	With onion, dripping and water, 1–1½ hrs.	Parboil, 10 mins.; in lard, 6–8 mins.	Chips: 1st frying, 4 mins.; 2nd frying, 2–3 mins.	Parboil, 5 mins.; roast, 45 mins.– 1 hr. Bake, 1–1½ hrs.	√
Runner Beans	15 mins.	20 mins.	With onion and tomatoes, 20–25 mins.	—	—	—	—

Vegetable	Boil	Steam	Braise	Sauté	Deep Fry	Grill, Bake, Roast	Soup
Spinach	10–15 mins.	20–25 mins.	In stock, 10–15 mins.	Shredded, in butter, 7–10 mins.	—	—	√
Swedes	15–20 mins.	25–30 mins.	—	Parboil, 10–15 mins.; in butter, 5 mins.	Parboil, 10–15 mins.; in batter, 4–5 mins.	—	√
Tomatoes	—	—	—	In butter or fat, 5–6 mins.	—	Grill, 5 mins. Bake, 25–30 mins.	√
Turnips	15–25 mins.	20–30 mins.	In stock, butter and spices: sauté 10 mins., braise 10 mins.	In butter or margarine, 15–20 mins. (also with herbs or onion and bacon)	—	Parboil, 5 mins.; roast, 45–60 mins.	√

1 Beetroot

Introduction

Beetroot has a distinctive purple, bulbous root and, like other root vegetables, it is easily stored during the winter in boxes with sand or peat. But it differs from other root crops in that it is regarded mainly as a salad vegetable normally served cold. However, beetroot does make tasty hot vegetable dishes. After lifting from the ground in October to store, the leaves should be twisted off to within 3 cm (1 inch) of the crown, taking care not to damage the root in any way.

Beetroot is easily grown, but a cold, wet spring can mean that the spring crop fails to form roots and the tops go to seed. A new crop can be sown in early summer for winter harvesting. The season lasts from July to October.

Preparation and cooking

Handle the beetroot carefully, to prevent it 'bleeding'. The leaves are cut off to within 3 cm (1 inch) of the beet but the thin tail root is left intact. Beetroot takes a long time to cook whether boiled, steamed or baked. To test for readiness, gently press the skin and if it slides off easily the beet is completely cooked.

To boil: Choose beetroots of an even size and wash very thoroughly. Place in a pan of cold salted water, bring to the boil, cover and simmer gently for 1½ to 2 hours, depending on size. Drain, leave to cool slightly, then rub off the skins and trim off the top and thin root.

To steam: Place the prepared roots in a steamer over a pan of boiling water, cover and cook for 2 hours. Skin as above.

To bake: Wrap the prepared roots in greased greaseproof paper or foil and bake in a moderate oven (180°C, 350°F, gas mark 4) for 1 to 1½ hours depending on size.

How to deal with a glut

1. Freezing: Beetroots can only be frozen when completely cooked. Choose small young beetroots, cook as above for the full time, leave to cool slightly, then remove the skins. Chill and, leaving roots whole, pack into wax or foil containers, seal, label and freeze. Storage time: 6 months.

The Russian soup, borsch, made with beetroots, can also be stored in the home freezer (see below).

2. Preserving: Beets are preserved in spiced vinegar (p. 328), or made into chutney (p. 26) or jam (p. 26).

3. Storing: Store in boxes layered with sand or peat and keep in a cool dry shed, or outdoors in a heap or 'clamp'.

Borsch

Serves 6–8

500 g	uncooked beetroots	1 lb
1½ litres	good stock	2½ pints
1	small carrot	1
1	medium onion	1
175 g	cabbage	6 oz
1	*bouquet garni*	1
	salt and pepper	
½	lemon, juice only	½
6–8 tbsps	sour cream	6–8 tbsps

Wash the beetroots carefully and place in a large saucepan with the stock.

Peel and dice the carrot and onion. Wash and finely shred the cabbage. Add all vegetables to the saucepan with the *bouquet garni* and the salt and pepper. Cover the pan, bring to the boil and simmer gently for 2 hours until the beetroots are cooked. Remove them from the soup and discard the *bouquet garni*. Leave the beetroots to cool slightly, then remove the tops and roots and peel off the skins. Dice the flesh and add three quarters of it to the soup. Press the soup through a sieve or purée in a liquidizer. Add the lemon juice and the remaining diced beetroot to the purée, bring back to the boil and serve hot with a tablespoon of sour cream in the centre of each bowl.

* Suitable for freezing before adding the sour cream.

Hot Stuffed Beetroots

Serves 4

500 g	cooked beetroots (4) (see p. 22)	1 lb

For the stuffing

1	small onion	1
50 g	bacon	2 oz
25 g	butter or margarine	1 oz
25 g	fresh breadcrumbs	1 oz
	freshly ground pepper	

While the beetroots are cooking, prepare the stuffing. Peel and chop the onion. Remove any rind and bone from the bacon and dice it. Heat the butter or margarine in a saucepan and add the onions and bacon. Sauté gently until the onions are soft and the bacon is becoming crisp. Add the breadcrumbs and cook a further 2 to 3 minutes until the crumbs are becoming crisp. Season the mixture with pepper. (Salt may not be needed with the bacon.)

When the beetroots are cooked, drain them and leave to cool slightly. Remove the roots and the tops, peel off the skins and, using a small knife, hollow out the centre, including the base, leaving the sides 2 cm (¾ inch) thick. Place the hollowed beetroots on a warm serving dish and press the hot stuffing mixture into the centres. If necessary, place under a medium hot grill to heat through and serve as a starter or a vegetable accompaniment.

Note: Dice the beetroot taken from the centres and use in a salad.

Beetroot in Yoghurt Sauce

Serves 3–4

500 g	cooked beetroots (see p. 22)	1 lb
1	small onion	1
1 level tbsp	margarine	1 level tbsp
2 level tbsps	plain flour	2 level tbsps
150 ml	natural yoghurt	¼ pint

	salt	
	freshly ground pepper	
	pinch of caster sugar	
1 level tsp	horseradish sauce	1 level tsp
	chopped parsley	

Leave the beetroots to cool, skin and chop them finely. Peel and finely chop the onion, heat the margarine in a saucepan and fry the onion until tender. Stir in the flour and cook for a minute then remove from the heat. Gradually add the yoghurt and stir until smooth. Season with a little salt and pepper and a pinch of sugar then stir in the horse-radish sauce. Return to the heat, bring to the boil and cook for 1 minute. Stir in the chopped beetroot and cook for a further minute.

Turn into a warm serving dish and garnish with a little chopped parsley sprinkled over the top.

Beetroot Napoli

Serves 4–6

250 g	cooked beetroots (see p. 22)	8 oz
one 140-g tin	sardines in oil	one 4¾-oz tin
1	red-skinned apple	1
3–4 tbsps	mayonnaise (p. 342)	3–4 tbsps
1	lettuce	1

Drain and peel the cooked beetroots and, when cold, mash them.

In a bowl, place the sardines with their oil and mash them with a fork. Stir in the mashed beetroots. Leave the apple unpeeled and then grate it into the beetroot mixture. Add the mayonnaise and stir to mix all the ingredients together well. Check to see if any seasoning is necessary – a little salt may be needed.

Wash the lettuce and arrange the leaves around the sides of a shallow bowl or serving dish, spoon the beetroot mixture into the centre and serve as an hors d'œuvre or as a salad dish.

Note: Frozen beetroots may be used in place of the fresh.

Beetroot Chutney

Makes about 3 kg (6 lb)

1 kg	cooked beetroots (see p. 22)	2 lb
1 kg	cooking apples	2 lb
500 g	onions	1 lb
250 g	sultanas	8 oz
2 level tsps	ground ginger	2 level tsps
2 level tsps	ground cinnamon	2 level tsps
1 tbsp	salt	1 tbsp
1 litre	vinegar	1½ pints
550 g	brown sugar	1 lb

a preserving pan or large saucepan

Drain the cooked beetroots and leave to cool slightly. Remove the skins and dice the flesh finely so that the pieces are bite-sized.

Peel, core and chop the apples; peel and finely chop the onions and place these ingredients in the pan with the sultanas, ground ginger, cinnamon, salt and vinegar.

Bring the contents to the boil and cook until the apples are soft – about 15 minutes. Add the brown sugar, cook gently to dissolve it completely, then bring to the boil and boil rapidly until the mixture is becoming thick – about another 15 minutes.

Finally, fold in the diced beetroot, remove the pan from the heat, and pour the chutney into warm, clean, dry jars, cover with wax discs and seal with thick polythene and lids if available. Store in a cool, dry place.

Note: Frozen beetroots and apples may be used.

This chutney will begin to lose its bright red colour inside 6 months but will keep for up to a year.

Beetroot Jam

Makes 2 kg (4 lb)

1 kg	cooked beetroots (see p. 22)	2 lb
500 g	cooking apples	1 lb

600 ml	water	1 pint
1	lemon, juice only	1
1½ kg	granulated or preserving sugar	3 lb
	a knob of butter	

a preserving pan or large saucepan

Drain the cooked beetroots, cool slightly and skin.

Peel, core and slice the apples and place in a preserving pan or large saucepan with the water and lemon juice. Cover and cook gently until the apples are tender and pulpy.

Mash the apples to a pulp, then coarsely grate the skinned beetroots into the pan. Return to the heat and cook for about 5 minutes.

Stir in the sugar and heat very gently until all the sugar is dissolved. Add a knob of butter to help prevent a scum forming and bring to a rapid boil for about 20 minutes until setting point is reached (see p. 311 for full jam-making instructions). Pour into clean, warm, dry jars, cover with wax discs and cellophane, label and store in a cool dry place. It keeps for at least a year.

Note: Frozen beetroots may be used to make this jam.

2 Broad Beans

Introduction

The broad bean is an easy vegetable to grow in even the most difficult of soils and is an excellent crop for the small garden as it takes up relatively little space considering the size of its pods.

Experts have discovered that the presence of the savory plant between rows of beans in the garden acts as a deterrent to the black fly. At the first sign of attack by black fly the plants should be sprayed with an insecticide like Derris.

Pick the pods when they are full, still green and about 15–20 cm (6–8 inches) long. When the bean pods start to develop black patches then the beans are passing their best. The larger the beans grow, the tougher their skins become and it is then necessary to discard the grey skins. The season lasts from mid June until the end of July, but there are a few winter varieties which can be sown in November to give a much earlier crop.

Preparation and cooking

Unlike the French and runner beans, the broad bean is removed from its pod. It is only necessary to discard the grey skins of the larger, tougher beans.

To boil: Bring a saucepan of salted water to the boil, add the prepared beans, cover and simmer for 10 to 20 minutes, depending on size. The addition of a sprig of savory to the pan during the cooking adds special flavour to the beans. Drain well.

To steam: Place the prepared beans in a steamer over a pan of boiling water, cover and steam for 10 to 25 minutes.

Serving suggestions: The cooked beans can be tossed in butter or coated with parsley, cream or hollandaise sauce (pp. 341, 341, 342). Served cold they make interesting salads, e.g. bean and cucumber salad (p. 32) and bean and mushroom salad (see p. 31).

How to deal with a glut

Freezing: Prepare the beans as above, blanch for 3 minutes, chill and drain well. Pack into polythene bags, wax or foil containers; seal, label and freeze. Storage time: 9 to 12 months.

Broad bean soup (below) can also be stored in the home freezer.

Broad Bean Soup

Serves 4–5

1½ kg	broad beans in their pods, to give 500 g (1 lb) beans when podded	3 lb
1¼ litres	chicken stock	2 pints
1 sprig	fresh savory	1 sprig
	or	
1 level tsp	dried, chopped savory	1 level tsp
	salt and pepper	

Pod the beans and remove their skins. Place the beans in a large saucepan with the stock, savory, salt and pepper, cover and simmer for 1 hour until the beans are soft enough to purée. When using dried savory it is better to put the soup through a fine sieve than to use a liquidizer as the dried savory tends to be tough and twiggy. The sprig of fresh savory is removed before the soup is puréed.

Check the soup for seasoning and serve sprinkled with a little chopped fresh savory.

Note: Frozen beans may be used in place of the fresh.

* Suitable for freezing.

Cornish Lamb Stew

Serves 4

¾ kg	broad beans in their pods, to give about 250 g (8 oz) beans when podded	1½ lb
1 kg	piece of top leg of lamb	2 lb

1 level tbsp	plain flour	1 level tbsp
1 level tsp	salt	1 level tsp
¼ level tsp	chilli powder	¼ level tsp
1 tbsp	cooking oil	1 tbsp
6–8	shallots	6–8
250 g	tomatoes	8 oz
½	small head of celery	½
300 ml	water	½ pint
1	bay leaf	1
1 level tsp	parsley, chopped	1 level tsp

a 2¼-litre (4-pint) flameproof casserole

Pod the beans.

Trim any excess fat from the meat, remove the bone and cut the lamb into 3-cm (1-inch) pieces. Mix together the flour, salt and chilli powder and toss the meat in it to coat well.

Heat the oil in the casserole or a large saucepan, then fry the meat quickly, turning frequently, to brown on all sides. Peel and chop the shallots, skin the tomatoes (see p. 172) and chop the flesh roughly, and add to the meat. Cook for 2 minutes.

Wash the celery, trim the ends and slice thinly. Add the celery and broad beans to the casserole, mix well then blend in the water. Add the bay leaf, bring to the boil, cover and simmer gently over a low heat for 1½ to 1¾ hours until the meat and vegetables are tender.

Just before serving sprinkle with the chopped parsley. Serve with new potatoes.

* Frozen broad beans may be used but add them 20 minutes before the end of the cooking time.

Broad Beans à la Grecque

Serves 2–3

500 g	broad beans in their pods, to give about 200 g (7 oz) beans when podded	1 lb
150 ml	light stock	¼ pint
1 tbsp	olive oil	1 tbsp
2 tsps	lemon juice	2 tsps

1	bay leaf	1
1	sprig of thyme	1
	a good pinch of salt	
	freshly ground pepper	

Pod the beans. Put the stock, olive oil, lemon juice, bay leaf, sprig of thyme, salt and pepper in a saucepan and bring to the boil. Add the beans and simmer uncovered for about 10 to 15 minutes until the beans are tender.

Remove the bay leaf and sprig of thyme, then turn the beans and their liquid into a warm serving dish and serve as a vegetable accompaniment or leave to get cold and serve as an hors d'œuvre.

Bean and Mushroom Salad

Serves 4

1 kg	small, young broad beans in their pods, to give about 350 g (10–12 oz) beans when podded	2 lb
100 g	mushrooms	4 oz
2 tbsps	French dressing (see p. 343)	2 tbsps
	salt and freshly ground pepper	

Pod the beans and steam or boil until tender. Drain well and leave them to cool.

Wipe the mushrooms and slice them thinly, leaving the stalks on. Place in a bowl and sprinkle the French dressing over them. Stir in the cold beans and leave them to marinate for at least 1 hour before serving. Sprinkle with salt and pepper to taste, then serve as a salad accompaniment.

Note: Older, larger beans can be used in this salad, but remember to remove the skins before cooking.

Bean and Cucumber Salad

Serves 3–4

500 g	small, young broad beans in their pods, to give about 200 g (7 oz) podded beans	1 lb
100 g	cucumber	4 oz
2 tbsps	mayonnaise	2 tbsps
1 tbsp	cream	1 tbsp
1 tbsp	lemon juice	1 tbsp
¼ level tsp	paprika pepper	¼ level tsp
	salt to taste	
½	lettuce	½

Pod the beans and steam or boil until tender. Drain thoroughly and leave to cool.

Wipe the cucumber and cut into small dice. For the dressing, place the mayonnaise, cream, lemon juice, paprika and salt in a bowl and mix together.

Put the cold beans and diced cucumber into the bowl of dressing and toss the vegetables gently to coat them in the sauce. Leave to marinate for at least 1 hour before serving.

Wash some lettuce and place in a glass serving dish. Spoon over the bean and cucumber salad and serve as an accompaniment.

Note: Small, young beans are best for this salad, but the larger ones can be used if their skins are removed before cooking.

3 Broccoli

Introduction

Broccoli is a delicious vegetable, easily grown in the garden. There are several well-known varieties – green and purple sprouting and the Italian green-sprouting variety, called calabrese, which is similar to cauliflower.

Broccoli and cauliflower are very similar and in certain places, like Cornwall, this can lead to a great deal of confusion as cauliflowers are advertised for sale there as 'broccoli'. Elsewhere, though, 'broccoli' is understood to mean the sprouting type of cauliflower and not the tight-headed cauliflowers.

Broccoli will produce more crops the more it is picked. Pick generously when the heads are fairly small (including about 5 cm (2 inches) of the stem and adjoining side leaves) to encourage further growth.

Birds, especially pigeons, are very fond of the Brassica family to which broccoli belongs and can strip the leaves to their veins. A net will protect your crops from these frustrating attacks.

Preparation and cooking

Trim the base of the stalks, leaving the small leaves and heads intact, and wash well.

To boil: Bring a pan of salted water to the boil, add the prepared broccoli, cover and cook for 10 to 20 minutes. Drain well.

To steam: Prepare as above and put the broccoli in a steamer over a pan of boiling water and cook for 15 to 25 minutes.

To deep fry: Prepare and parboil for 7 minutes, coat in batter (see p. 343) and fry for 5 minutes.

Serving suggestions: The steamed or boiled broccoli can be tossed in butter or coated with a cheese or hollandaise sauce (see pp. 340, 342). It can also be served with a bacon, egg and crumb topping as in broccoli Newport (p. 37).

How to deal with a glut

1. Freezing: Choose the larger heads for freezing, prepare as above but remove the small leaves. Blanch for 3 to 4 minutes, depending on the thickness of the stalks. Chill, drain, pack into wax or foil containers, seal, label and freeze. Storage time: 9 to 12 months.

Broccoli soup (below) freezes well.

2. Preserving: Larger heads can be pickled in spiced vinegar as for cauliflowers (see p. 328).

Broccoli and Pork Soup

Serves 4–5

500 g	broccoli	1 lb
300–350 g	belly of pork	10–12 oz
1	medium onion	1
1	large carrot	1
1½ litres	water or stock	2½ pints
	salt and freshly ground pepper	
	a sprig of fresh chervil	

Wash the broccoli, remove the larger leaves and thick stems and place them in a large saucepan. Reserve the broccoli heads to be added later.

Remove the excess fat, skin and any bone from the belly of pork and chop the meat into cubes. Add to the pan.

Peel and dice the onion and carrot and add to the pan with the water or stock, seasonings and sprig of chervil. Cover and simmer gently for 1 hour. Strain off the broccoli leaves and stalks (pressing gently to extract the juice) and the chervil. Remove the chunks of pork, cut up the meat finely and return to the soup.

Break the broccoli spears into small sprigs, add to the soup, cover and simmer for a further 10 minutes. Check for seasoning and serve hot. This is a warming 'chunky' soup.

Note: Frozen broccoli may be used in this soup.

* Suitable for freezing.

Broccoli Scallops

Serves 4

300 ml	béchamel sauce (p. 340)	½ pint
100 g	peeled prawns	4 oz
	salt and freshly ground pepper	
500 g	cooked potatoes	1 lb
	knob of butter	
1 tbsp	cream or top of the milk	1 tbsp
250 g	broccoli spears	8 oz
	grated Parmesan or Cheddar cheese	

4 scallop shells
a piping bag with no. 8 large star nozzle attached

Prepare the béchamel sauce then fold in the peeled prawns, season with salt and pepper and keep hot.

Drain the potatoes well, mash until very smooth, beat in the butter and cream or milk, and season to taste with salt and pepper. Leave to cool slightly.

Wash and trim the broccoli spears; boil or steam until tender but still whole. Drain well, place in the centres of the four scallop shells and pour over the hot prawn sauce. Put the creamed potato in the piping bag and pipe a decorative border of potato around the outside of the scallop shells. Sprinkle the tops with grated Parmesan or Cheddar cheese and put the scallops under a hot grill for 3 to 4 minutes to brown. Serve as an hors d'œuvre.

Note: Frozen broccoli may be used in this recipe.

Plaice Fillet Rolls

Serves 3–4

4	small plaice fillets	4
250 g	broccoli spears	8 oz
1 level tsp	lemon juice	1 level tsp
	freshly ground pepper	

| 300 ml | mornay sauce, coating consistency (p. 340) | ½ pint |
| 1 | medium tomato | 1 |

a 1½-litre (2½-pint) shallow ovenproof dish

Preheat the oven to 180°C, 350°F, gas mark 4.

Remove any black skin and any bones from the fish fillets. Trim the broccoli and wash well. Steam or boil until tender, drain well and cool slightly.

Lay the plaice fillets skin side uppermost on a board. Sprinkle with a little lemon juice and pepper. Divide the broccoli spears into four and lay one portion on the tail end of each of the fillets, stalks pointing inwards. Roll up the fish and lay in the dish.

Make the mornay sauce and pour over the rolls. Slice the tomato thinly and lay the slices round the edge of the dish. Bake on the centre shelf of the preheated oven for 25 to 30 minutes until the fish is cooked.

Note: Frozen broccoli may be used in place of the fresh vegetable.

* Suitable for freezing.

Broccoli and Chicken in Lemon Sauce

Serves 4

| 4 | chicken quarters | 4 |
| 500 g | broccoli | 1 lb |

For the sauce

300 ml	chicken stock	½ pint
2 level tbsps	sugar	2 level tbsps
1 heaped tbsp	cornflour	1 heaped tbsp
1	medium lemon, rind and juice	1
1	small onion	1
	oil or fat for frying	
	salt and pepper	

Place the chicken under a grill at low heat and cook, turning once or twice, for 35 to 45 minutes until tender and browned. Place in the centre of a large warmed serving plate.

Meanwhile, trim the broccoli and steam or boil until tender. Place the broccoli around the chicken quarters.

While the broccoli and chicken are cooking, prepare the lemon sauce. Put the stock, sugar, cornflour and lemon juice in a saucepan over heat and, stirring constantly, cook until thick. Peel and very thinly slice the onion. Sauté in fat or oil with the coarsely grated lemon rind until soft and golden. Add the onion and lemon to the thickened sauce, season with salt and pepper and pour evenly over the chicken and broccoli. Serve hot.

Note: Frozen broccoli may be used in this recipe.

* Suitable for freezing.

Broccoli Newport

Serves 3–4

500 g	broccoli	1 lb
50 g	streaky bacon	2 oz
50 g	butter	2 oz
50 g	fresh white breadcrumbs	2 oz
1	hard-boiled egg	1
	salt and pepper	

Trim the broccoli and steam or boil until tender – about 15 minutes. Drain well.

Meanwhile remove the rind and any bone from the bacon and chop finely. Heat the butter in a small saucepan and fry the bacon until lightly browned, then add the breadcrumbs and fry until golden brown. Remove from the heat.

Finely chop the hard-boiled egg and mix with the breadcrumbs and bacon mixture, season with salt and pepper, and sprinkle over the broccoli. Serve hot.

Note: This dish is delicious enough to serve as an unusual hors d'œuvre, or as a luncheon dish with buttered new potatoes. Frozen broccoli may be used in this recipe.

Try substituting broccoli for the main vegetable in the following recipes:

Baked pork and cauliflower (p. 63)
Celery *au gratin* (p. 68)
Italian cauliflower salad (p. 65)

4 Brussels Sprouts

Introduction

Brussels sprouts are one of Britain's most popular vegetables and an essential ingredient of a Christmas turkey dinner.

The best sprouts are those which are small and tight-budded and which have been exposed to a touch of frost. The larger loose-leafed sprouts cannot match these in flavour.

They thrive in a soil which has been well manured the previous autumn and grow much stronger if planted in a tightly packed soil so it is not necessary to dig over the soil after lifting the earlier crop.

The seedlings are planted out in early summer, often following early peas or lettuces. As the buds become ready for picking, start at the bottom of the bush, working upwards as the buds mature. Any yellow leaves towards the base of the plant can be removed at the start of the sprouts season, which lasts throughout autumn and winter.

Preparation and cooking

Remove the looser or damaged outer leaves and trim the stalks. Opinions vary about the usefulness of cutting a cross at the base of the stalk, but we believe it cuts down on cooking time by a couple of minutes, thus saving flavour and fuel.

To taste their best, sprouts should be green and a little crunchy. Too often they are served mushy and watery through being overcooked and not drained carefully enough.

To boil: Bring a pan of salted water to the boil, add the prepared vegetables, cover and simmer for 10 minutes. Drain well.

To steam: Place the prepared sprouts in a steamer over a pan of boiling water, cover and cook for 15 minutes.

To deep fry: Parboil the prepared sprouts for 5 minutes, drain well, then coat in fritter batter (see cauliflower fritters on p. 64) and deep fry for 4–5 minutes.

To braise: Prepare 500 g (1 lb) sprouts and add to a pan of 300 ml

($\frac{1}{2}$ pint) boiling stock; season, cover and cook for 15 minutes. Drain the sprouts and reduce the stock by rapid boiling to a thickish glaze which is then poured over the sprouts.

Serving suggestions: The steamed or boiled sprouts can be tossed in butter, or served *à la crème* (p. 43), *à la française* (p. 141) or with chestnuts.

To many people's great surprise sprouts make an excellent and delicately flavoured soup. Because of the strong taste of the vegetable only a small quantity is required for this recipe which makes an economical soup (see below).

How to deal with a glut

1. Freezing: Choose medium-sized tight-budded sprouts. Prepare, place in cold salted water for $\frac{1}{2}$ hour (3 teaspoons salt to 600 ml/1 pint water), drain and then blanch for 3 minutes. Chill, drain, pack into polythene bags or wax or foil containers, seal, label and freeze. Storage time: 9 to 12 months.

Brussels sprouts soup (below) can also be deep frozen.

Cream of Brussels Sprouts Soup

Serves 6

250 g	Brussels sprouts	8 oz
1$\frac{1}{2}$ litres	good stock	2$\frac{1}{4}$ pints
1	small onion	1
2	rashers of streaky bacon	2
25 g	butter or margarine	1 oz
	large pinch of powdered mace	
4–6 tbsps	cream or top of the milk	4–6 tbsps

Wash the sprouts and prepare as on p. 39. Place the stock in a large saucepan and bring to the boil. Blanch the sprouts for 5 minutes in the boiling stock and drain, reserving the stock.

Peel and finely chop the onion. Remove the rinds and any bone from the bacon and dice it. Heat the butter or margarine in a large saucepan and fry the onion and bacon until soft. Chop the sprouts roughly, add them to the pan and continue cooking for a further 5 minutes before adding the stock. Season the soup, add the mace, cover and cook gently for 1 hour.

Put the soup through a fine sieve or liquidize. Add the cream and reheat the soup, but do not boil. To serve put an extra teaspoon of cream into each bowl of soup.

Note: Frozen sprouts may also be used to make the soup.

* Suitable for freezing.

January Suet Pudding

Serves 4–5

200 g	self-raising flour	8 oz
	a pinch of salt	
75 g	shredded suet	3 oz
75 g	strong cheese, grated	3 oz
250 g	carrots	8 oz
250 g	swede	8 oz
250 g	Brussels sprouts	8 oz
2	small leeks	2
50 g	butter	2 oz
	salt and pepper	
¼ level tsp	ground nutmeg	¼ level tsp

a 1¼-litre (2-pint) greased pudding basin
a saucepan with steamer on top

Sift the flour and salt into a bowl. Stir in the suet and grated cheese, then add enough cold water to make a soft dough. Roll out two thirds of the pastry to line the greased pudding basin, overlapping the top edge. Do not trim. Roll out the remaining one third a little bigger than the top of the basin, and keep it on one side.

Prepare the vegetables: peel and finely dice the carrots and swede; wash the sprouts, keep them whole but remove any damaged outer leaves; wash the leeks well, trim the tops and bases and then cut into 1-cm (½-inch) slices.

Place all the vegetables in a pan of cold salted water, and bring to the boil. Boil for 2 minutes, drain, then layer the vegetables in the basin with little knobs of butter, salt, pepper and nutmeg. Damp the top edge of the pastry and put on the pastry lid. Fold the overlapping pastry over the lid and seal well.

Cover with foil with a pleat down the centre. Tie a double piece of string under the top edge of the basin to hold on the foil and make a handle with extra string to lift out the hot pudding basin. Place in the steamer over a pan of gently simmering water, put on the lid and steam for 2 hours, checking that the water does not boil dry during cooking. If necessary, replenish with boiling water.

Turn out on a shallow heated plate to serve.

Note: This makes a delicious and economical supper dish. Deep frozen vegetables may be used in place of the fresh vegetables.

Sprouts with Crispy Bacon Topping

Serves 4

500 g	Brussels sprouts	1 lb
2	rashers streaky bacon	2
1	small onion	1
25 g	butter	1 oz
25 g	fresh white breadcrumbs	1 oz
	freshly ground pepper	

Prepare the sprouts and boil or steam until cooked. Keep warm.

Meanwhile, remove any rind and bone from the bacon and chop very finely. Peel and chop the onion very finely. Heat the butter in a small frying pan and add the bacon and onion. Fry gently, turning frequently, until the onion is soft, then add the breadcrumbs, season with pepper, and continue frying, still turning frequently, for about 15 minutes until the crumbs are crisp.

Turn the sprouts into a warm serving dish and scatter over the crispy topping. Serve at once.

Note: Frozen sprouts may be used in this recipe.

Brussels Sprouts à la Crème

Serves 3–4

350 g	Brussels sprouts	12 oz
50 g	mushrooms	2 oz
25 g	butter or margarine	1 oz
	salt and freshly ground pepper	
	a pinch of ground nutmeg	
2 tbsps	soured cream	2 tbsps

Wash and trim the sprouts and make a cross at the base of each stalk. Wipe and thinly slice the mushrooms.

Heat the butter or margarine in a saucepan and sauté the mushrooms very gently for 2 minutes, then add the sprouts, salt, pepper and nutmeg. Cover and cook gently, stirring occasionally, for about 12 minutes until tender but not breaking up.

Remove from the heat and stir in the soured cream and serve at once as a vegetable accompaniment.

Note: Frozen sprouts may be used in place of the fresh.

Brussels Sprouts with Almonds

Serves 4

500 g	Brussels sprouts	1 lb
25 g	butter	1 oz
¼ level tsp	chopped mixed herbs	¼ level tsp
	a knob of butter	
25 g	almonds, flaked	1 oz

Prepare the sprouts and boil or steam for 8 or 13 minutes respectively. Drain well.

Heat the butter in a pan, add the herbs and the partly cooked sprouts, cover and cook gently for 2 to 3 minutes until tender. Turn into a warm serving dish.

Melt the knob of butter in the pan, add the flaked almonds and, turning frequently, cook for 1 minute until the nuts are beginning to brown. Scatter over the sprouts and serve hot as a vegetable accompaniment.

Try substituting Brussels sprouts for the main vegetable in the following recipes:

Pois à la française (p. 141)
Celery *au gratin* (p. 68)

5 Cabbage

Introduction

Cabbages are the most useful of all garden produce. There are so many different varieties of cabbage for all the seasons of the year, that it is possible to have a succession of crops all year round. For example, there are spring, summer and winter cabbages, the red cabbage and the savoy with its distinctive crinkly leaves. Spring greens are only immature cabbages without a heart.

Most cabbages are cut when required for use, but the variety Dutch winter white can be stored in a shed or even in an outdoor heap protected from frost by a covering of straw. These cabbages should be cut for storage before the arrival of severe frosts – i.e. in early November.

The seedlings should be planted out in soil which has been manured for a previous crop and require frequent hoeing during the summer. The plants are prone to several pests, such as cabbage caterpillars and flies, cabbage root fly, etc., but these can be counteracted with insecticides and Bromphos powder.

Preparation and cooking

Cabbages are far more versatile than most people imagine, but too often they evoke bad memories of soggy, watery dishes with a pungent smell, usually associated with school lunches. Cabbage should be firm and crisp. The longer you cook it the more you destroy the texture, food value and flavour.

To prepare, peel off any damaged outer leaves, then either cut the vegetable into four wedges and remove the hard white centre, or shred the leaves. Then wash the cabbage and, if it is not thoroughly drained, the shredded and still moistened cabbage can now be cooked in a pan with salt, pepper, a knob of butter and no extra water. Cover the pan and cook for about 20 minutes, tossing occasionally.

To boil: Bring a pan of salted water to the boil, add the prepared cabbage, cover and cook for 7 to 10 minutes. Drain well.

To steam: Place the prepared vegetable in a steamer over a pan of boiling water, cover and cook for 10 to 20 minutes.

To braise: See braised red cabbage (p. 50).

To bake: See baked cabbage and tomato (p. 49) and cabbage savoury (p. 48).

To deep fry: Shred the cabbage leaves as above, parboil for 5 minutes, drain well, then toss in flour and deep fry in hot fat for 4–5 minutes.

Serving suggestions: The steamed or boiled cabbage can now be tossed in butter and sprinkled with ground nutmeg.

How to deal with a glut

1. Freezing: Prepare as above and place in a bowl of salted water for ½ hour (3 teaspoons of salt to 600 ml/1 pint water).

Drain, then blanch for 2 minutes, chill and drain well before packing into polythene bags or wax or foil containers. Seal, label and freeze. Storage time: 6 months. Cabbage soup (below) can also be deep frozen.

2. Preserving: Pickled red cabbage in spiced vinegar (p. 328).

3. Storing: Dutch winter whites can be stored as explained earlier. Another suggestion for storing winter cabbages is to leave the roots and stems attached to the cabbages and hang them upside down in bundles of six in a cool shed. As the cabbages are required, cut them from the stems.

Cabbage and Bacon Soup

Serves 4–6

1	small onion	1
100 g	bacon pieces	4 oz
	knob of butter or margarine	
1	medium potato	1
500 g	cabbage	1 lb
1¼ litres	chicken or turkey stock	2 pints
	salt and pepper	
	a few tablespoons of single	
	cream or top of the milk	

Peel and dice the onion. Remove the rinds and any bone from the bacon and dice. Melt the butter or margarine in a large saucepan and add the onion and bacon. Fry gently until the onion is soft and the bacon is becoming crisp.

Remove any damaged outer leaves from the cabbage and any of the hard centre core. Shred the cabbage and add to the pan. Fry for a few minutes longer without browning.

Peel and dice the potato and add to the pan. Pour on the stock and add the seasoning, remembering that the bacon will make the soup fairly salty, so less salt than usual is required.

Cover the saucepan and cook for about 1 hour until the cabbage is tender. The bacon and cabbage will still be fairly firm and therefore not easy to put through a sieve. The best way to purée the soup is in a liquidizer or through a Mouli vegetable mill. After puréeing, serve hot with a tablespoon of cream swirled in the centre of each bowl.

* Suitable for freezing.

Stuffed Cabbage Leaves

Serves 4–6

1	green cabbage	1
125 g	pork fillet, minced	4 oz
250 g	long grain rice, cooked	8 oz
1 level tsp	fresh marjoram, chopped	1 level tsp
½ level tsp	salt	½ level tsp
	freshly ground pepper	
4 tbsps	hot stock	4 tbsps

For the sauce

25 g	margarine	1 oz
25 g	plain flour	1 oz
300 ml	chicken stock	½ pint
2	large eggs	2
1	lemon, juice only	1
2 tbsps	cold water	2 tbsps

a 1½-litre (2½-pint) ovenproof casserole dish

Preheat the oven to 190°C, 375°F, gas mark 5.

Peel off the larger leaves of the cabbage (about 10 to 12), trim off the hard stalk at the base. Wash them and lay in a large saucepan. Cover with boiling salted water and cook for 7 minutes until tender but not breaking up. Drain well.

In a bowl, mix together the minced pork, cooked rice, chopped marjoram, salt and pepper.

Lay a cabbage leaf out on a chopping board and place a little filling in the centre of the stem, then fold over the stem end, fold up the sides and roll into a small parcel about 6 cm (2½ inches) wide.

Lay the stuffed cabbage leaf in the ovenproof dish and repeat the process with the other leaves, filling and packing them closely into the dish.

Pour the hot stock over them, cover and bake on the centre shelf of the preheated oven for 35 minutes; strain off juices to add to sauce.

Keep warm while preparing the sauce. Heat the margarine in a saucepan, stir in the flour and cook for 1 minute. Remove from the heat and stir in the hot stock a little at a time until smooth; keep hot.

Beat the eggs together in a bowl until light and frothy then beat in the lemon juice and then the cold water. Gradually add the hot sauce to the eggs a little at a time, then return to the pan and heat gently, but do not boil or the eggs will curdle.

Remove the stuffed cabbage leaves from the dish and lay on a warm serving plate, then pour the egg and lemon sauce over them and serve at once.

Note: This makes a good supper dish served with French bread or an unusual first course for a dinner party.

* Suitable for freezing.

Cabbage Savoury

Serves 4

1	medium-sized white cabbage	1
1	large egg	1
25 g	butter	1 oz
	a good pinch of ground nutmeg	
50 g	fresh white breadcrumbs	2 oz
25 g	cheese, grated	1 oz
	salt and pepper	

a 1½-litre (2½-pint) ovenproof dish

Preheat the oven to 190°C, 375°F, gas mark 5.

Wash the cabbage, remove the hard white centre core, and chop the leaves roughly. Cook in boiling salted water for about 10 minutes until tender. Drain well and then mix in the lightly beaten egg, half of the butter, and the ground nutmeg. Put the mixture in a lightly buttered ovenproof dish.

Mix together the fresh breadcrumbs and grated cheese, and sprinkle over the top of the cabbage. Season with salt and pepper, and dot with the remaining butter.

Bake on the shelf above centre of the preheated oven for 15 to 20 minutes until the top is beginning to brown.

Note: This vegetable dish goes very well with baked gammon or a stew. Frozen cabbage may also be used to make this recipe.

Baked Cabbage and Tomato

Serves 4–6

500 g	cabbage	1 lb
350 g	tomatoes	12 oz
1	medium onion	1
	knob of butter or margarine	
	salt and pepper	
25 g	cheese, grated	1 oz
150 ml	white wine	¼ pint

a 1¼-litre (2-pint) ovenproof casserole

Preheat the oven to 180°C, 350°F, gas mark 4.

Remove any damaged outer leaves from the cabbage and any hard centre core. Shred the cabbage fairly finely. Bring some salted water to the boil and add the cabbage. Cook for 5 minutes and drain thoroughly.

Put the tomatoes in a basin of boiling water for ½ minute, drain and then peel off the skins. Peel and slice the onion into rings. Melt the butter or margarine in a pan and fry the onions until soft and golden.

Lay half the cabbage in the base of the greased casserole dish, add half the onion and half the sliced tomatoes, season with salt and pepper, and finally add the rest of the cabbage, onion and tomatoes. Season well, then sprinkle with the grated cheese and pour the wine over the top.

Cover and cook on the centre shelf of the preheated oven for 45 minutes.

Note: We used home-made apple wine in this dish, but you could use a good stock or any dry white wine instead.

Braised Red Cabbage

Serves 3–4

350 g	red cabbage	12 oz
	knob of butter	
1 tbsp	cider vinegar	1 tbsp
3 tbsps	water	3 tbsps
300 g	cooking apples (2 medium)	10 oz
	salt and pepper	

Wash and finely shred the cabbage. Heat the butter in a heavy saucepan, add the cabbage, vinegar and water, cover and cook over a very low heat for 45 minutes. Stir occasionally to prevent the cabbage from sticking to the pan and browning.

Meanwhile, peel, core and dice the apples and after the 45 minutes' cooking time, add to the pan. Season with salt and pepper, cover the pan and cook gently for a further 30 minutes until the apples and cabbage are tender. Serve hot.

Coleslaw

500 g	white cabbage	1 lb
	salt and freshly ground pepper	
	mayonnaise, mustard dressing, or any other salad dressing	

Extra ingredients

2	medium carrots	2
1	red-skinned apple	1
3 sticks	celery	3 sticks
a bunch	spring onions	a bunch

½	cucumber	½
1	medium leek	1
1	green pepper	1
25 g	sultanas	1 oz

Remove any damaged outer leaves and any hard centre core from the cabbage and shred the leaves very finely.

Choose a selection of extra ingredients for your coleslaw and prepare as follows: peel and grate the carrots; grate the apple, including the red skin to add colour to the salad; wash and thinly slice the celery; remove any damaged parts from the spring onions and slice fairly thinly; dice the cucumber (peeled or left with its skin on, according to preference); remove any damaged parts of the leek, cut off the root and the leaves to within 3 cm (1 inch) of the white part and finely slice the white flesh; halve the green pepper, remove the seeds and finely slice the flesh.

When you have a selection of your chosen vegetables prepared, place them in a large serving bowl with the shredded cabbage. Sprinkle with salt and pepper and finally add sufficient mayonnaise or dressing to make the coleslaw moist but not watery. Serve by itself as an hors d'œuvre or as a salad accompaniment to a main meal.

Sauerkraut

500 g	winter white or Dutch cabbage	1 lb
1 level tbsp	kitchen salt	1 level tbsp
¼ level tsp	caraway seeds	¼ level tsp

Note: It is extremely important that all utensils and storage containers are thoroughly sterilized with boiling water before being used otherwise the result will not be satisfactory and the cabbage will not keep.

Always use firm, fresh, winter white or Dutch cabbage for sauerkraut. Prepare the cabbage and shred it very finely into a large bowl. Stir in the salt and caraway seeds and mix together very thoroughly.

Have ready a large sterilized earthenware jar or a wooden tub and pack in the sauerkraut as full and as tightly as possible. Cover with a clean linen cloth and then a good fitting lid. Press the lid down with a heavy weight (e.g. large tins of fruit or a heavy stone) to exclude as much air as possible.

Leave the container in a warm place for a few days during which time a brine will have formed which will cover the lid of the container. The sauerkraut should be left in a warm place for 2 to 3 weeks to ferment. Every 3 days remove any scum from the surface and replace the cloth with a clean one. If the level of brine falls below the lid, then top up the container with brine (25 g/1 oz salt dissolved in 1¼ litres/2 pints water).

After 2 to 3 weeks, when fermentation has stopped, the sauerkraut is ready for use. It will keep for about another week but if it is to be stored for longer then it must be processed. To do this, drain the cabbage from its brine, pour the brine into a pan and bring to the boil. Add the cabbage, bring back to the boil, then put the cabbage and brine immediately into warm, sterilized preserving jars (e.g. Kilner). Put on the lids, seal and process in a pan of simmering water for about 25 minutes so that the water comes to within 3 cm (1 inch) of the tops. Remove the jars from the water, tighten the seals and leave to get cold.

Processed sauerkraut will keep for at least 1 year, but once the jars are opened it should be used within a week.

To cook sauerkraut, drain well, put in a pan with only a little water, cover, bring to the boil and simmer gently for about 10 minutes. Drain and serve with boiled pork or casseroles.

Sweetcorn Relish

Makes 2¼ kg (5 lb)

1 kg	sweetcorn kernels (corn off the cob)	2¼ lb
500 g	white cabbage	1 lb
½ head	celery	½ head
2	large green peppers	2
2	large red peppers	2
1	large onion	1
1 level tbsp	salt	1 level tbsp
1 level tbsp	mustard	1 level tbsp
900 ml	white or cider vinegar	1½ pints
1 kg	granulated sugar	2 lb

a preserving pan or large saucepan

Remove hard core from the cabbage, trim the celery, de-seed the peppers and peel the onion. Wash all the vegetables, then either put them through a coarse mincer or chop fairly finely with a large sharp knife.

Place the prepared vegetables in a large pan or preserving pan with the salt, mustard and vinegar and bring to the boil. Cook for 15 to 20 minutes.

Remove from the heat and stir in the sugar. Heat gently to dissolve all the sugar and then bring to the boil and boil for 5 minutes. Spoon into warm, dry, clean jars, cover with wax discs, and seal with polythene and preferably screw tops. Store in a cool, dry place for 1 month before using. It will keep for 6 to 8 months.

Note: Frozen sweetcorn, celery, peppers and onions may be used to make this relish.

The following recipes also include cabbage:

Borsch (p. 23)
Pickled cabbage (p. 328)

Try substituting white cabbage for the main vegetable in the following recipes:

Celery *à la provençale* (p. 69)
Parsnips *à la polonaise* (p. 132)

6 Carrots

Introduction

Carrots are the most versatile vegetable that a cook can grow in the garden. They can be eaten raw in salads, and cooked in soups, casseroles or stews, and they are rich in vitamins, especially vitamin A, and minerals, e.g. calcium and iron.

Another advantage of the carrot is its bright orange flesh which can contrast pleasantly with other ingredients.

Carrots require only a minimal amount of work once the seeds have been sown. The chief danger to the crop is the carrot fly, so, to avoid this pest, sow the seeds thinly and only thin the young carrots in the evening when the flies have disappeared. The baby carrots pulled during thinning are delicious raw in salads and can also be used to garnish dishes.

Carrots should never be grown in soils which have been freshly manured as the roots will become forked and misshapen. Crops left in the ground for storage should be lifted in October, the tops carefully twisted off and the earth shaken from the roots. The season lasts from July to October.

Preparation and cooking

New carrots should be washed and lightly scraped if necessary; old carrots should be peeled. The roots are then topped and tailed. Small carrots may be cooked whole or halved and larger ones cut into rings or diced.

To boil: Put the prepared carrots into a pan of cold salted water, bring to the boil, cover and simmer for 10 to 25 minutes depending on size. Drain well.

To steam: Place the prepared vegetables in a steamer over a pan of boiling water, cover and cook for.15 to 40 minutes, depending on size.

To braise: Put the prepared carrots (500 g/1 lb) in some good flavoured stock (300 ml/½ pint), bring to the boil, cover and simmer gently for

15 to 25 minutes. Drain the carrots and reduce the stock by rapid boiling to a thickish glaze which is then poured over the carrots.

To deep fry: Prepare the carrots as above, leaving the small ones whole and cutting the larger ones into quarters lengthwise, and parboil for 10 minutes. Drain well, then toss in flour and deep fry for 4 to 5 minutes.

To sauté: Prepare the carrots as above, parboil for 10 minutes, then sauté for 10 minutes in butter, turning often.

Serving suggestions: The boiled or steamed carrots may be tossed in butter and sprinkled with a little chopped fresh parsley. They may also be coated in a cheese or fresh parsley sauce (pp. 340, 341).

How to deal with a glut

1. Freezing: Choose small new carrots rather than large, old ones. Wash, scrape, top and tail, and leave whole or cut into strips, rings or dice. Blanch for 3 minutes – 5 minutes for larger carrots. Chill, drain and pack into polythene bags or wax or foil containers. Seal, label and freeze. Storage time: 9 to 12 months.

Carrot and lentil soup (below) freezes well.

2. Storing: Store in boxes layered with soil or sand or in an outdoor heap covered with soil to protect from frosts.

Carrot and Lentil Soup

Serves 10–12

300 g	lentils	10 oz
1¾ kg	carrots	4 lb
350 g	onions	12 oz
350 g	swede	12 oz
175 g	bacon scraps	6 oz
25 g	dripping	1 oz
2¼ litres	good white stock	4 pints
1 level tsp	salt	1 level tsp
	freshly ground pepper	
	bunch of fresh herbs:	
	thyme, rosemary, bay leaf	

Soak the lentils in cold water overnight.

Peel the carrots and cut into 3-cm (1-inch) pieces; peel and roughly chop the onions. Peel the swede and cut into 3-cm (1-inch) pieces. Remove any rind or bone from the bacon before dicing it.

Melt the dripping in a large saucepan and fry the prepared vegetables and bacon for about 10 minutes, turning frequently, but do not allow to brown.

Drain the water from the soaked lentils and add them to the pan. Fry for a further 2 to 3 minutes. Stir in the stock, season with salt and pepper and add the bunch of herbs. Bring to the boil, cover and simmer, stirring occasionally, for ¾ hour.

Cool the soup slightly, then pass through a fine sieve or liquidize. Test for seasoning before serving.

Note: This is a thick soup which can be thinned before serving with milk or stock. Do not add the milk if the soup is to be frozen. This soup is ideal for using up damaged or end-of-season carrots. Frozen vegetables may also be used in place of the fresh.

* Freezes well.

Autumn Stew

Serves 5–6

¾ kg	shin of beef	1½ lb
2	large onions	2
500 g	carrots	1 lb
½ head	celery	½ head
50 g	mushrooms	2 oz
2 tbsps	oil for frying	2 tbsps
1 heaped tbsp	flour	1 heaped tbsp
300 ml	stock made with herb or beef stock cube	½ pint
300 ml	dry cider	½ pint
1 level tsp	salt	1 level tsp
	freshly ground pepper	
250 g	parsnips	8 oz

a 3-litre (5-pint) flameproof casserole dish

Preheat the oven to 160°C, 325°F, gas mark 3.

Trim any excess fat from the meat and cut it into 3-cm (1-inch) cubes. Peel and slice the onions and carrots; wash and slice the celery; wipe and slice the mushrooms.

Heat the oil in the casserole and fry the meat quickly to brown lightly. Remove from the casserole and leave on a plate. Sauté the onions in the oil until soft and golden, but do not brown. Return the meat to the casserole and stir in the flour. Add the prepared vegetables to the casserole and cook for a minute. Stir in the stock, cider, salt and pepper, cover and cook in the centre of the preheated oven for 2 hours.

Peel and quarter the parsnips and add to the casserole. Continue to cook, covered, for a further 1 hour before serving.

Note: Frozen vegetables may be used in this stew.

* Suitable for freezing, but cook for 2¼ hours only.

Braised Beef

Serves 4–5

¾ kg	braising steak	1½ lb
2	medium onions	2
500 g	new baby carrots	1 lb
1	small head celery	1
1 tbsp	dripping	1 tbsp
1 level tsp	salt	1 level tsp
½ level tsp	chilli powder	½ level tsp
	freshly ground pepper	
1	tin of consommé (small)	1

a 1¾-litre (3-pint) ovenproof casserole

Preheat the oven to 180°C, 350°F, gas mark 4.

Trim any excess fat from the meat and cut it into thin slices about 8 cm (3 inches) square. Peel the onions and cut them into quarters; scrub the carrots and cut off the tops and roots, but leave them whole; trim the celery and wash it well, then cut it into 8-cm (3-inch) lengths.

Melt the dripping in a large frying pan and fry the meat slices quickly on both sides to brown. Place on a plate. Fry the onions for a few minutes to brown lightly then add to the meat on the plate. Add the carrots and celery to the frying pan and fry quickly to brown them. Add the salt, chilli powder and pepper and stir in the consommé. Bring to simmering point then return the onions and meat to the pan and cook for a minute. Place the mixture in the casserole, cover and cook on the centre shelf of the preheated oven for 1¾ hours until the meat is tender. Serve with jacket potatoes.

Note: Frozen carrots, celery and onions may be used.

* Suitable for freezing.

Honey-Glazed Carrots

Serves 4–6

500 g	carrots	1 lb
25 g	butter or margarine	1 oz
2 level tsps	honey	2 level tsps
	salt and freshly ground pepper	

Peel or scrape the carrots and slice according to preference – rings, matchsticks or strips. Boil or steam until just tender – about 10 to 15 minutes or 20 to 25 minutes, respectively.

Melt the butter or margarine and honey in a saucepan. Season with a little salt and pepper. Now add the carrots and toss gently to coat in the honey sauce, taking care not to break or spoil the carrots. Cook for a few minutes over a medium hot heat, tossing gently every now and then, until the carrots are nicely glazed. Serve hot with grilled gammon steaks.

Note: Frozen carrots may be used in this dish.

Carrot Salad

Serves 4–5

250 g	carrots	8 oz
1	small onion	1
½ level tsp	coarse French mustard	½ level tsp
2 tbsps	French dressing	2 tbsps
	salt and freshly ground pepper	

Peel and finely grate the carrots into a bowl. Peel the onion, slice it very thinly and break the slices into rings. Mix with the carrots.

Add the mustard (we used '*Moutarde de Meaux Pommery*') to the French dressing with a little salt and pepper, stir to combine well and then pour it over the carrot salad. Leave to stand for 10 minutes before serving as a salad accompaniment.

Carrot Tea Cake

Makes a 1-kg (2-lb) loaf

300 g	carrots	10 oz
50 g	currants	2 oz
50 g	chopped mixed peel or a mixture of chopped mixed peel and chopped nuts	2 oz
175 g	soft margarine	6 oz
175 g	light, soft brown sugar	6 oz
3	large eggs	3
300 g	plain flour	10 oz
3 level tsps	baking powder	3 level tsps
1 rounded tsp	ground cinnamon	1 rounded tsp
$\frac{1}{4}$ level tsp	salt	$\frac{1}{4}$ level tsp

a 1-kg (2-lb) loaf tin, greased and base-lined

Preheat the oven to 160°C, 325°F, gas mark 3.

Top, tail and peel the carrots and grate them into a bowl. Add the currants and mixed peel (or the mixture of mixed peel and chopped nuts).

Put in a large bowl the soft margarine, sugar and eggs and sift in the flour, baking powder, ground cinnamon and salt. Using a wooden spoon, beat the mixture until it is light and smooth. Stir in the carrots, currants and peel until well combined. Spoon the mixture into the greased loaf tin and level off the surface. Bake on the centre shelf of the preheated oven for 1½ hours until the loaf is fully cooked and the top browned. Remove from the tin onto a cooling rack and serve as a teatime treat in slices, with or without butter.

* Suitable for freezing.

The following recipes also include carrots:

Coleslaw (p. 50)
Stuffed marrow (p. 103)
Cucumber relish (p. 83)
January suet pudding (p. 41)
Mushrooms in sour cream (p. 113)
September lamb hotchpotch (p. 168)
Scotch broth (p. 167)
Rabbit and damson stew with dumplings (p. 258)

Try substituting carrots for the main vegetable in cream of Brussels sprouts soup (p. 40).

7 Cauliflower

Introduction

The cauliflower is easy to grow from seed, but often the end result can be most disappointing – a sprouting mass with a generous supply of caterpillars. And here speaks the voice of experience.

The two main requirements for a good crop are a richly manured soil and plenty of water especially during a very dry summer.

Garden pests cause a lot of problems to cauliflowers, but caterpillars can soon be dismissed with a dusting of Derris or some similar insecticide which will also guard against attacks from root flies, white flies and aphids.

To keep the cauliflower heads white it is a good idea to break a few of the larger leaves over the plants to protect them. The vegetables should be picked when the florets are still compact and before they start to open out. The season lasts from September until the end of the year.

Preparation and cooking

There can be nothing nicer than the crisp taste of a cauliflower with the addition of a good cheese sauce – and nothing worse than a disintegrated mush clogged with a thick, tasteless sauce. So always take care not to overcook the vegetables as they quickly break up.

To prepare, cut off the outer leaves and trim the stalk. If the cauliflower is to be cooked whole (this makes a more attractive dish for the dinner table), cut a criss-cross mark at the base of the stalk to shorten the cooking time.

Alternatively, break the cauliflower into florets. Wash in cold water (the addition of a little vinegar or salt to the water will help to draw out any unwanted bugs).

To boil: Bring a pan of salted water to the boil, add the prepared cauliflower, cover and cook for 10 to 12 minutes for florets and 15 to 20 minutes for whole cauliflowers. Drain well.

To steam: Place the prepared vegetable in a steamer over a pan of boiling water, cover and cook for 15 minutes for florets and 20 to 25 minutes for whole cauliflowers.

To bake: See baked pork and cauliflower (p. 63); parboil for 5 minutes and bake for 30 minutes.

To sauté: Parboil for 7 minutes, drain well, coat in beaten egg, then in dried breadcrumbs, and sauté for 3 minutes in butter, turning frequently.

To deep fry: Parboil for 7 minutes, drain well, then coat in batter and deep fry in hot fat for 4 to 5 minutes (see cauliflower fritters, p. 64).

Serving suggestions: Boiled or steamed cauliflower can now be seasoned and topped with grated cheese or coated with a white or cheese sauce (pp. 339, 340). To make a spicy cauliflower cheese, add 1 teaspoon of ready-made mustard to the cheese sauce. After coating the cauliflower with the sauce, slice 3 to 4 tomatoes over the top and place under a hot grill for 5 to 10 minutes until browned.

How to deal with a glut

1. Freezing: Prepare as above and break into florets. Blanch for 3 to 4 minutes, chill, drain and pack into polythene bags; seal, label and freeze. Storage time: 6 to 8 months.

Cauliflower vichyssoise (see below) and pre-cooked cauliflower cheese or spicy cauliflower cheese (see above) all freeze well.

2. Preserving: Pickle in spiced vinegar (p. 328) or in a mixed pickle (p. 330); use to make piccalilli (p. 88).

Cauliflower Vichyssoise

Serves 6–8

¾ kg	cauliflower	1½ lb
350 g	onions	12 oz
250 g	potatoes	8 oz
1¼ litres	water	2 pints
2	chicken stock cubes	2
1	bay leaf	1
1 level tsp	salt	1 level tsp
	freshly ground pepper	
150 ml	milk	¼ pint
150 ml	top of the milk or single cream	¼ pint
	a few chives	

Trim the cauliflower and cut it into florets. Wash well and place in a large saucepan. Peel the onions and chop them roughly. Peel and dice the potatoes and add them to the pan with the chopped onion. Add the water and the stock cubes, or 1¼ litres (2 pints) of home-made chicken stock, to the pan with the bay leaf, salt and pepper. Bring to the boil, then cover and simmer gently for 25 to 30 minutes until the vegetables are cooked.

Remove the bay leaf and pass the soup through a sieve twice, or purée in a liquidizer and then put through a sieve. This will give a smoother texture to the soup. Return the soup to the heat, bring back to the boil, then remove from the heat and stir in the milk and most of the cream. Leave the soup to get cold. Before serving, check for seasoning; serve cold garnished with a swirl of cream and a few chopped chives.

Note: This makes a delicious winter soup served hot with fried croûtons to garnish. Frozen cauliflower may be used in place of the fresh.

* Suitable for freezing before adding the milk and cream.

Baked Pork and Cauliflower

Serves 4

1 kg	belly of pork	2 lb
25 g	lard	1 oz
250 g	onions	8 oz
1	medium cauliflower	1
1 level tsp	fresh sage, chopped	1 level tsp
	salt and freshly ground pepper	
300 ml	tomato juice (see p. 175)	½ pint

Topping

50 g	fresh white breadcrumbs	2 oz
50 g	cheese, grated	2 oz
½ level tsp	paprika	½ level tsp

a shallow 1¾-litre (3-pint) casserole dish

Preheat the oven to 180°C, 350°F, gas mark 4.

Using a sharp knife, remove the skin, bones and any excess fat from the meat and cut it into 3-cm (1-inch) pieces.

In a pan, heat the lard and fry the meat for 5 minutes to brown lightly, then lay in the casserole.

Peel and thinly slice the onions and fry in the hot lard for a few minutes to soften but do not brown. Scatter the onions over the meat.

Meanwhile, cut the cauliflower into florets and blanch in boiling salted water for 5 minutes only. Drain well.

Sprinkle the meat and onions with the chopped sage, salt and pepper, then pour the tomato juice over. Lay the cauliflower florets on top and cover with a lid or foil.

Bake on the centre shelf of the preheated oven for 1 hour. Remove from the oven and prepare the topping ingredients. Mix the breadcrumbs with the grated cheese and paprika. Put the topping evenly over the cauliflower and return to the oven, uncovered, to cook for a further 30 minutes. The top should be brown and crisp. Serve with buttered new potatoes.

Note: Frozen cauliflower may be used in this dish.

* Suitable for the freezer.

Cauliflower Fritters

Serves 3–4

1	large cauliflower	1
150 ml	fritter batter (p. 343)	¼ pint
	fat or oil for deep frying	

Remove the outer leaves from the cauliflower and, keeping it whole, wash well. Bring a saucepan of salted water to the boil, add the cauliflower and parboil for 2 to 3 minutes. Drain thoroughly and leave to cool slightly.

Meanwhile prepare the fritter batter and just before use add the baking powder.

Break the cauliflower into florets and dip each piece carefully into the batter to coat it. If you feel there is going to be too much batter on the florets, leave them on a plate for a few minutes to drain off some of the excess batter.

Heat a large quantity of fat or oil in a chip pan or large saucepan. When the fat is hot enough to turn a cube of bread brown, put a few coated florets into it and fry them for 4 to 5 minutes until the batter is puffed and browned. Drain on kitchen paper and repeat the process until all the florets have been used. Serve immediately on a heated dish.

Note: Reheat the fat between each batch of fritters.

Italian Cauliflower Salad

Serves 4

1	cauliflower	1
one 45-g tin	anchovies	one 1¾-oz tin
8	green olives, stoned	8
1	small onion	1
3 tbsps	olive oil	3 tbsps
1 tbsp	wine vinegar	1 tbsp
	freshly ground pepper	
2	eggs, hard-boiled	2

Wash the cauliflower and cut it into florets. Place them in a saucepan of boiling salted water and cook for 7 minutes. Drain and leave to get cold.

Place the anchovy fillets in a saucer of milk and leave for 10 minutes to help remove some of the excess saltiness. Then cut the fillets in half lengthwise and place in a bowl.

Slice the stoned olives fairly thinly and add to the bowl. Peel and finely chop the onion and add to the bowl. Stir in the oil and vinegar and season with pepper.

Gently fold the cooled cauliflower sprigs into the mixture in the bowl and leave in a cool place to marinate for 1 hour.

To serve, pile the cauliflower salad in the centre of a dish. Cut the hard-boiled eggs into quarters and arrange them around the edge of the salad.

Note: This makes a delicious and unusual starter or salad. Frozen or pickled cauliflower may be used to make this salad.

The following recipes also include cauliflower:

Vegetable curry (p. 169)
Pickled cauliflower (p. 328)
Mixed pickle (p. 330)
Piccalilli (p. 88)

Try substituting cauliflower for the main vegetable in the following recipes:

Cream of Brussels sprouts soup (p. 40)
Celery *au gratin* (p. 68)
Spinach soufflé (p. 161)

8 Celery

Introduction

There are two types of celery which can be grown in the garden. The self-blanching type does not require a trench or an earthing-up process. But it is far more vulnerable to frosts and thus has a much shorter season. To ensure that it is not affected by frosts this celery should be lifted from the ground in late September.

The white stems of the self-blanching celery are achieved by planting the seedlings in blocks fairly close together to shade each other.

Trench celery, as the other variety is usually called, is planted out after a trench has been prepared with a spreading of manure over the bottom. When the plants are a foot high, they should be earthed up. The celery will be more compact and the stems whiter if the stalks are loosely tied together just below the leaves before the earth is piled up to the base of the leaves. The plants are pulled when required for use and as they can withstand frosts may remain in the ground during the winter.

Preparation and cooking

Celery is probably best known as a salad plant although it makes some interesting and tasty hot vegetable dishes. It is becoming increasingly popular in stews and soups where it adds an almost peppery flavour.

Served raw, it is a delicious ingredient in any salad and is always popular at buffets when served stuffed with cream cheese.

To prepare, remove the individual stalks from the head, trim off the leaves and base and wash well in cold water. If cooking, cut the celery into thin slices or 5- to 8-cm (2- to 3-inch) strips.

To boil: Bring a pan of salted water to the boil, add the prepared celery, cover and cook for 15 to 25 minutes, depending on the size of the pieces. Drain well.

To steam: Place the prepared vegetables in a steamer over a pan of boiling water, cover and cook for 20 to 30 minutes.

To braise: See celery *à la provençale* (p. 69) or cook 500 g (1 lb) prepared celery in 300 ml ($\frac{1}{2}$ pint) stock for 30 minutes, drain, then reduce the stock by rapid boiling to a thickish glaze and pour it over the celery.

Sauté in butter, lemon juice and herbs for 20 minutes (see sautéed lemon celery, p. 69).

To deep fry: Prepare the celery as above and cut into fairly thin strips (5 to 8 cm or 2 to 3 inches long), parboil for 20 minutes, drain well, then coat in batter (see p. 343) and deep fry for 4 to 5 minutes.

Serving suggestions: The boiled or steamed celery can be tossed in butter or coated in a cheese sauce (p. 340). See also celery *au gratin* (below).

How to deal with a glut

1. Freezing: Remove all the celery hearts to freeze separately. Prepare the stalks as above, cut into 1-cm ($\frac{1}{2}$-inch) slices, blanch for 3 minutes, chill and drain. Pack into polythene bags, or wax or foil containers, seal, label and freeze. Storage time: 9 to 12 months.

2. Storing: Trench celery in the ground until required.

Celery au Gratin

Serves 4

500 g	celery	1 lb
50 g	cheese, finely grated	2 oz
50 g	fresh breadcrumbs	2 oz
	salt	
	paprika	

Prepare the celery and steam or boil until tender. Drain well and place either in a gratin dish or a shallow ovenproof serving dish.

Mix together the grated cheese, breadcrumbs, salt and paprika and sprinkle over the celery. Place under a hot grill for 4 to 5 minutes until the top is golden brown. Serve hot as a vegetable accompaniment.

Note: Frozen celery may be used in this dish.

Celery à la Provençale

Serves 3

1	small onion	1
250 g	tomatoes	8 oz
250 g	celery (half head)	8 oz
1 clove	garlic	1 clove
	salt and pepper	
	knob of butter or margarine	

Peel and finely chop the onion. Place the tomatoes in a bowl of boiling water for ½ minute, drain and peel off the skins. Chop the tomato flesh. Break the celery into stalks and wash carefully. Chop the celery into 1-cm (½-inch) slices. Crush the garlic with a little salt.

Melt the butter or margarine in a saucepan and add the onion and crushed garlic. Fry gently until softened, then add the chopped tomatoes and finally the sliced celery and the seasonings.

Cover the pan with a lid and cook the celery over a gentle heat for 20 to 30 minutes until it is tender. If the tomato sauce starts to run dry, add a few tablespoons of stock. Serve hot as a vegetable dish or cold as an hors d'œuvre.

Note: Frozen tomatoes and celery may also be used in this dish.

* Suitable for freezing.

Sautéed Lemon Celery

Serves 4

350 g	celery	12 oz
75 g	butter or margarine	3 oz
½	lemon, juice only	½
a small bunch	fresh chives	a small bunch
	salt and pepper	

Wash and chop the celery but not too thickly. Heat the butter or margarine in a large saucepan or frying pan and add the celery. Sprinkle with the lemon juice, chopped chives, salt and pepper, cover the pan and sauté gently for about 15 minutes. Remove the cover from the pan and cook for a further 5 minutes until the celery is tender. Serve hot as a vegetable accompaniment.

Note: Frozen celery may be used in place of the fresh.

Waldorf Salad

Serves 6

500 g	crisp, red-skinned apples	1 lb
1	lemon, juice only	1
1 level tsp	caster sugar (optional)	1 level tsp
150 ml	mayonnaise	$\frac{1}{4}$ pint
1 head	celery (medium)	1 head
50 g	halved walnuts	2 oz
1	lettuce	1

Wipe the apples, quarter and core them. Slice one apple thinly and place in a small bowl with 1 teaspoon of lemon juice to prevent it discolouring. Dice the remaining apples and place in a bowl with the remaining lemon juice, sugar and 1 tablespoon mayonnaise. Mix well and leave to one side.

Trim the base and leaves from the celery and wash the stalks well. Slice the celery fairly thinly.

About $\frac{1}{2}$ hour before serving, add the sliced celery to the diced apple. Roughly chop most of the walnuts and add to the salad with the rest of the mayonnaise.

Wash the lettuce and lay in a serving bowl to line the base and sides. Spoon the mixture into the centre and decorate with the sliced apple and the remaining halved walnuts.

Celery Sauce

Makes 300 ml ($\frac{1}{2}$ pint)

3	sticks celery	3
25 g	butter or margarine	1 oz
3 level tbsps	plain flour	3 level tbsps
300 ml	milk	$\frac{1}{2}$ pint
	salt and pepper	

Wash the sticks of celery, trim both ends and, starting at the bases, grate the celery. Any thin strips left at the end can be finely chopped.

Heat the butter or margarine, add the celery and sauté gently for about 10 minutes until it is cooked but not browned. Add the flour and cook for a further 1 minute; remove from the heat and then gradually stir in the milk. Season with salt and pepper, return the pan to the heat and, stirring constantly, cook until the sauce is thick. Cook for a further 2 minutes, then serve, e.g. with Monday pancakes (p. 199).

* Suitable for freezing.

The following recipes also include celery:

Autumn stew (p. 56)
Braised beef (p. 57)
Cornish lamb stew (p. 29)
Red tomato relish (p. 182)
Sweetcorn relish (p. 52)
Pork and gooseberry casserole (p. 237)

Try substituting celery for the main vegetable in the following recipes:

French beans *à la grecque* (p. 87)
Leek soufflé (p. 92)

9 Courgettes

Introduction

Courgettes, or zucchini (as the Italians, Americans and Australians call them), are really baby marrows, though distinctly different in taste from the larger, less tasty marrow.

Although once considered a luxury vegetable they are astonishingly easy to grow, and once they have taken root they almost take over the garden. Three to four plants will suffice to produce a good crop of courgettes for the average family. Try one or two of the unusual yellow variety to make an interesting colour combination with the more common green kind. Pick young and fairly small, for the more you pick the more they grow.

Courgettes thrive on a well-manured soil or compost heap. A good tip for keeping the roots well watered is to sink a flower pot into the soil fairly close to the plant and then water through the pot.

The most successful varieties are those bred specifically for picking young and small. Planting marrows and picking them young does not have quite the same results when it comes to flavour.

Preparation and cooking

Courgettes are always cooked in their skins; these are tender and help to stop the vegetable from disintegrating. To prepare, wipe, top and tail, then either leave whole or cut into 1-cm (½-inch) slices. Boiling courgettes is not really very satisfactory, as they become too watery.

To boil: Prepare as above, bring a pan of salted water to the boil, add the courgettes and cook for 10 to 15 minutes. Drain well.

To steam: Place the prepared vegetables in a steamer over a pan of boiling water, cover and cook for 10 to 20 minutes depending on size.

Bake, stuffed (see p. 74), for 40 to 45 minutes.

Sauté, sliced in butter and mixed herbs, for 10 to 15 minutes.

To deep fry: See courgettes *à l'italienne* (p. 75); prepare and halve lengthwise, dip in egg and cheese crumbs, deep fry for 3 minutes.

Serving suggestions: The steamed courgettes can be tossed in butter and sprinkled with chopped fresh herbs, or coated in a tomato sauce (p. 185).

How to deal with a glut

1. *Freezing:* Prepare as above; cut in half or slice or leave whole. Blanch for 2 to 3 minutes, chill, drain and pack into polythene bags or wax or foil containers. Seal, label and freeze. Storage time: 9 to 12 months.
   Stuffed courgettes freeze well.
   2. *Preserving:* Pickle in spiced vinegar (p. 328) or use in mixed pickle (p. 330).
   Overgrown courgettes can also be used in late summer chutney (p. 106).

Lamb Casserole

Serves 4

1–1¼ kg	best end of neck of lamb	2–2½ lb
50 g	plain flour	1½ oz
1 level tsp	salt	1 level tsp
	freshly ground pepper	
350 g	courgettes	12 oz
250 g	leeks	8 oz
450 ml	good light stock	¾ pint
	a few drops of Worcester-	
	shire sauce	

a 2-litre (3½-pint) ovenproof casserole

Preheat the oven to 180°C, 350°F, gas mark 4.

Wipe the meat and cut into chops between the bones. Trim off most of the fat and remove the spinal cord. Mix the flour with the salt and plenty of pepper, coat the chops in the seasoned flour and lay half of them in the base of the casserole.

Wipe and trim the ends of the courgettes and slice them thinly. Wash the leeks well in cold water, trim the base and tops and slice thinly. Place half the leeks and courgettes on the meat, lay on the remaining chops and add the rest of the leeks and courgettes. Heat the stock with the Worcestershire sauce, pour over the casserole, cover and bake on the centre shelf of the preheated oven for 1¾ to 2 hours until the meat is tender.

* Suitable for freezing, but cook for only 1½ hours.

Baked Pork Chops with Courgettes

Serves 2

2	pork chops	2
250 g	courgettes	8 oz
	knob of butter	
1 tsp	lemon juice	1 tsp
½ level tsp	salt	½ level tsp
	pinch of thyme	
	freshly ground pepper	
2 tbsps	double cream	2 tbsps

Preheat oven to 190°C, 375°F, gas mark 5.

Have ready two squares of tin foil to wrap the chops in and lay a chop on each piece of foil. Slice the courgettes fairly thinly and scatter over the chops. Dot with butter, add the lemon juice, salt, thyme and pepper and 1 tablespoon of cream for each chop. Seal up the foil round the chops to make a parcel.

Bake on the centre shelf of preheated oven for 45 to 50 minutes, until the chops are tender and the courgettes are cooked. Serve with creamed or sautéed potatoes.

Note: Frozen sliced courgettes may be used in place of the fresh.

Stuffed Courgettes

Serves 4

500 g	courgettes, medium size (6)	1 lb
50 g	mushrooms	2 oz
2	tomatoes	2
25 g	fresh brown breadcrumbs	1 oz
	sprig of fresh marjoram	

a few drops of tabasco
salt

a large shallow ovenproof dish, buttered

Preheat the oven to 180°C, 350°F, gas mark 4.

Top and tail the courgettes, wipe them and cut in half lengthwise.

Using a teaspoon scoop out the centres and finely chop them, then place in a mixing bowl. Wipe the mushrooms and finely chop them. Peel the tomatoes by putting them in boiling water for ½ minute, draining them and then removing the skins. Chop the tomato flesh very finely, then add to the bowl with the mushrooms, breadcrumbs, chopped marjoram, tabasco and salt, and mix well together.

Lay the courgette halves in the buttered dish and spoon the filling down the centre of each half. Cover the dish with foil and bake on the shelf above the centre of the preheated oven for 40 to 45 minutes until the vegetables are tender but still whole. Serve as a vegetable accompaniment.

Note: Frozen halved courgettes may be used in this recipe.

* Suitable for freezing.

Courgettes à l' Italienne

Serves 4

500 g	small courgettes	1 lb
50 g	dried breadcrumbs	2 oz
50 g	cheese, finely grated	2 oz
	Parmesan or Cheddar	
½ level tsp	salt	½ level tsp
	freshly ground pepper	
1 level tsp	fresh oregano, chopped	1 level tsp
	or	
½ level tsp	dried oregano	½ level tsp
1	large egg	1
	oil for frying	

a deep-fat frying pan

Wipe the courgettes, trim the ends, and cut in half lengthwise. Cut each half into two long strips.

In a bowl, mix together the breadcrumbs, cheese, salt, pepper and finely chopped oregano. Break the egg into another bowl and beat lightly with a fork.

Heat the oil in the pan for deep frying the courgettes. Now dip the quartered courgettes into the egg, then coat in the breadcrumb and cheese mixture. Drop them into the hot fat and cook for about 3 minutes until golden brown and tender. (*Note:* It is best to cook them in batches, a few at a time.)

Drain on kitchen paper and place on a warm serving dish. Serve immediately as a vegetable accompaniment.

Baked Courgettes and Tomatoes

Serves 4

250 g	courgettes	8 oz
25 g	butter or margarine	1 oz
	a sprinkling of mixed herbs	
	salt and pepper	
250 g	tomatoes	8 oz
50 g	cheese, grated	2 oz
50 g	fresh breadcrumbs	2 oz

a 1¼- to 1¾-litre (2- to 3-pint) ovenproof casserole

Preheat the oven to 190°C, 375°F, gas mark 5.

Wash the courgettes, top and tail them and cut into ½-cm (¼-inch) slices. Heat the butter or margarine in a saucepan and add the mixed herbs and sliced courgettes. Sauté gently, stirring frequently, for 5 minutes. Remove from the heat and season with salt and pepper. Lay half the courgettes in the bottom of the casserole dish.

Peel the tomatoes by putting them in boiling water for ½ minute, draining them and then removing the skins. Slice the tomatoes and lay half of them over the courgettes in the casserole. Add the remaining courgettes and top with the rest of the tomatoes.

Mix the grated cheese and breadcrumbs together and sprinkle over the top of the casserole. Bake on the centre shelf of the preheated oven for 30 to 40 minutes until the top is brown and crispy.

Serve hot with roasted joints or grilled chops or steaks.

Note: Frozen courgettes and tomatoes may be used in this dish.

* Suitable for freezing.

Courgettes with Almonds

Serves 4

500 g	courgettes	1 lb
25 g	butter	1 oz
¼ tsp	chopped mixed herbs	¼ tsp
	knob of butter	
25 g	almonds, flaked	1 oz

Wipe, top and tail, and slice the courgettes thinly. Heat the butter in a pan, add the herbs and sliced courgettes. Cover and cook gently for 10 to 15 minutes until the vegetables are tender. Place in a warm serving dish.

Melt the knob of butter in the pan, add the flaked almonds and, turning frequently, cook for 1 minute until the nuts are beginning to brown. Scatter over the courgettes and serve hot as a vegetable accompaniment.

Note: Frozen courgettes may be used in place of the fresh.

The following recipes also include courgettes:

Mixed pickle (p. 330)
Pickled courgettes (p. 328)
Late summer chutney (p. 106)

Try substituting courgettes for the main vegetable in French beans *à la grecque* (p. 87).

10 Cucumbers

Introduction

Cucumbers come in two main varieties – those that require the shelter of a greenhouse and the outdoor or ridge cucumber. Now there are even outdoor varieties which can be grown up against netting or trained up sticks.

All cucumbers do best in a soil rich in organic matter (e.g. manure, compost and well-rotted straw), and all require frequent watering. None of the varieties has any resistance to frosts and so they should never be planted in the open until late May or early June, unless under the protection of a cold frame or cloches.

The vegetables should be picked young to encourage further crops and the tops of the plants should be pinched off after the first five or six leaves have formed to help develop the side shoots where most of the cucumbers will be borne.

The season lasts from July until October.

Preparation and cooking

Although cucumbers are primarily a salad vegetable, there are a few hot dishes which make a delicious change, e.g. stuffed or herbed cucumbers.

They can cause digestive problems, but to our great amusement we have even seen varieties billed as 'burpless'. They can be eaten with or without their skins and are usually thinly sliced for salad dishes.

To prepare, wipe, trim the ends, skin if desired and slice or dice.

To boil: Prepare as above, then place the vegetables in a saucepan of boiling salted water, cover and cook for 10 minutes. Drain well.

To steam: Place the prepared cucumber in a steamer over a pan of boiling water, cover and cook for 10 to 20 minutes.

To bake: See stuffed cucumbers (p. 81); parboil for 5 minutes, drain, stuff and bake for 15 minutes.

Sauté in butter and herbs for 10 to 15 minutes (see herbed cucumber, p. 82).

Serving suggestions: The boiled or steamed cucumbers can be tossed in butter and, if desired, sprinkled with chopped fresh herbs; or they can be coated in a cheese sauce (see p. 340).

How to deal with a glut

1. Freezing: Cucumbers have too high a water content to freeze successfully; however, cucumber soup can be frozen.

2. Preserving: Cucumbers can be made into cucumber relish (p. 83), piccalilli (p. 88) or mixed pickle (p. 330), or they can be pickled in spiced vinegar (see p. 328).

3. Storing: Cucumbers will keep for about 3 weeks in the salad compartment of the fridge if they are left uncut.

Cucumber Soup

Serves 4–5

2–3	spring onions	2–3
500 g	cucumber	1 lb
1 litre	strong chicken stock	1½ pints
	salt and pepper	
1	sprig of mint	1
25 g	cornflour	1 oz
150 ml	milk	¼ pint
	croûtons	
	chopped spring onions	
	or	
	cream and chopped fresh mint	

Wash the spring onions, remove the roots and slice thinly. Peel the cucumber and dice the flesh. Put the onions and cucumber into a large saucepan with the stock, salt, pepper and the washed sprig of mint. Bring to the boil and simmer for 20 minutes.

Remove from the heat and take out the mint. Purée the soup in a liquidizer or put through a sieve. Blend the cornflour with a little of the milk, add the rest of the milk and stir it into the soup. Return to the heat, cook gently, stirring constantly, until the soup has thickened.

Note: This soup is traditionally served chilled. To garnish, serve with bowls of croûtons and chopped spring onions. The soup is also delicious served hot with a spoonful of cream in the centre of each bowl and a sprinkling of chopped fresh mint to garnish.

* Suitable for freezing before adding the cornflour, milk and cream.

Cucumber and Prawn Hors d' Œuvre

Serves 4

½	medium cucumber	½
25 g	butter or margarine	1 oz
300 ml	milk infused with 1 small carrot and 1 small onion, 6 peppercorns, 1 bay leaf, 1 blade of mace	½ pint
25 g	plain flour	1 oz
	salt and freshly ground pepper	
½ tsp	anchovy essence	½ tsp
125 g	peeled prawns	4 oz
4	large slices of bread	4
	oil for frying	

Peel the cucumber and cut into dice. Heat the butter or margarine in a saucepan, add the diced cucumber and cook gently for about 10 minutes, turning occasionally, without browning. When the cucumber is cooked but still firm, remove from the pan using a draining spoon. Leave on a plate and keep warm.

Meanwhile, infuse the milk with the herbs and vegetables. Add the flour to the butter in the saucepan, cook for 1 minute and then remove from the heat. Strain the infused milk and gradually add it to the roux in the pan. Return to the heat and, stirring constantly, cook until thick. Add the salt, pepper and anchovy essence and cook for a further 2 minutes.

Carefully fold the cooked cucumber and peeled prawns into the béchamel sauce, heat gently for a further 2 minutes, then remove from the heat.

While the sauce is cooking, cut out four large circles from the bread slices, using an 8- to 10-cm (3- to 4-inch) round cutter or soup bowl. Make breadcrumbs for the topping from the trimmings.

Heat the oil in a frying pan and fry the rounds of bread on both sides until golden brown. Drain on kitchen paper and place one piece of fried bread on each serving plate. Spoon the cucumber and prawn mixture evenly over the rounds of bread. Finally, sprinkle the breadcrumbs on top and place under a hot grill for a few minutes until they are beginning to brown. Serve hot as a first course.

Cucumber and Apple Salad

Serves 3–4

½	medium cucumber	½
2	crisp eating apples	2
1 level tbsp	walnuts, chopped	1 level tbsp
3 tbsps	sour cream	3 tbsps
	salt	
	lettuce leaves	
	paprika	

Wipe the cucumber and dice it. (Skin only if necessary, as the green skin adds colour to the dish.) Peel, core and dice the apples and put in a small bowl with the cucumber and chopped walnuts. Stir in the sour cream and season with salt. Chill before serving. Spoon the mixture onto lettuce leaves – in individual glass dishes for an hors d'œuvre, served with brown bread and butter, or in a large serving dish for a salad. Sprinkle the top with paprika.

Stuffed Cucumber

Serves 2–4

500 g	cucumber (1 medium)	1 lb
50 g	long-grain rice	2 oz
100 g	cooked lamb, e.g. left-over Sunday roast	4 oz
3–4	fresh mint leaves	3–4

H.G.C. – 5

1	apple	1
	salt and freshly ground pepper	
300 ml	cheese sauce (see p. 340) (optional)	½ pint

Preheat the oven to 190°C, 375°F, gas mark 5.

Wipe the cucumber and cut it in half, then slice the two halves lengthwise, giving four long pieces. Carefully scoop out the seeds and some of the cucumber flesh with a teaspoon, leaving the centres hollow for the stuffing. Parboil the cucumber cases in boiling salted water for 5 minutes and drain thoroughly.

Meanwhile, place the rice in a saucepan of boiling salted water and cook for 12 minutes, drain and put in a bowl.

Chop the cooked lamb finely and add to the bowl with the finely chopped mint leaves. Peel the apple and grate into the bowl, add the salt and pepper and mix the stuffing well.

Pack the stuffing generously into the cucumber hollows and lay the stuffed vegetables on a greased baking tray. Bake on the shelf above the centre of the preheated oven for about 15 minutes.

Serve hot with a gravy boat of cheese sauce to pour over the cucumber, if desired.

Note: An alternative stuffing for this dish may be found in mushroom risotto (see p. 113). The scooped-out cucumber flesh can be diced and served in a salad.

Herbed Cucumber

Serves 2–3

250 g	cucumber (half)	8 oz
25 g	butter	1 oz
	a sprig of parsley	
	a small bunch of chives	
	salt and freshly ground pepper	

Wipe the cucumber, top and tail (peel only if desired) and cut into large dice. Heat the butter in a large saucepan or frying pan, add the diced cucumber and the finely chopped parsley and chives, cover and sauté gently for 10 to 15 minutes until the cucumber is tender.

Remove from the heat, season to taste with salt and pepper and serve as a vegetable accompaniment.

Cucumber Relish

Makes 1–1¼ kg (2–2½ lb)

500 g	cucumber	1 lb
500 g	cooking apples	1 lb
400 g	onions	12 oz
1	medium carrot	1
300 ml	white vinegar	½ pint
2 level tsps	salt	2 level tsps
¼ tsp	dried tarragon	¼ tsp
	or	
	a few fresh tarragon leaves	
¼ tsp	cayenne pepper	¼ tsp
250 g	granulated sugar	8 oz
¼ tsp	green colouring (optional)	¼ tsp

a preserving pan or large saucepan

Wipe and finely dice the cucumber, but do not peel it. Peel, core and finely dice the apples. Peel and finely chop the onions. Scrape the carrot and coarsely grate it.

Place all the prepared vegetables and fruit in the preserving pan, add the vinegar, salt, finely chopped fresh or dried tarragon and cayenne pepper. Bring to the boil, cover and simmer for 30 to 35 minutes. Remove from the heat, add the sugar, return to the heat and bring back to the boil. Boil rapidly, uncovered, for 10 minutes by which time the relish should be fairly thick. Remove from the heat and stir in a little green colouring, if desired.

Pour into clean, warm, dry jars. Cover with thick polythene and lids if available. Seal, label and store in a cool, dry place.

Note: This is a fairly sweet chutney which is ideal as an accompaniment to curries. Pickled cucumbers may be used in this relish.

The following recipes also include cucumbers:

Gazpacho (p. 173)
Greek stuffed tomatoes (p. 177)
Bean and cucumber salad (p. 32)
Coleslaw (p. 50)
Piccalilli (p. 88)
Mixed pickle (p. 330)
Pickled cucumbers (p. 328)

11 French Beans

Introduction

The French bean is a thinner, tastier version of the runner bean. There are many dwarf varieties on the market which do not usually require poles for support in growing. The plants are very prolific, providing you pick the beans frequently when they are small.

If left too long the beans can become tough and stringy, but some of the over-grown beans can still be used if thinly sliced like runner beans. If the bean snaps cleanly without leaving a frayed edge, then it should not be stringy.

French beans benefit from deep digging and the addition of manure to the soil before planting. During their growing season, the surrounding ground should be regularly hoed. Some support may be required by the heavier plants which might be flattened in a rain storm.

At the first sign of pests, such as black fly or caterpillars, the plants should be sprayed with insecticide before the beans have formed. The season lasts from May to September.

Preparation and cooking

French beans are eaten whole. To prepare: top, tail and wash them (it is unnecessary to string the beans).

To boil: Bring a pan of salted water to the boil, add the prepared beans, cover and simmer for 10 to 15 minutes.

To steam: Place the prepared beans in a steamer over a pan of boiling water, cover and cook for 10 to 15 minutes.

To braise: Bring a pan of 300 ml ($\frac{1}{2}$ pint) stock to the boil, add 500 g (1 lb) prepared beans, cover and simmer for 12 to 15 minutes. Drain the beans and reduce the stock by rapid boiling to a thickish glaze which is then poured over the beans.

Serving suggestions: The steamed or boiled beans can be tossed in butter or coated with a hollandaise sauce (p. 342). The beans are also delicious served cold, tossed in French dressing (p. 343) or cooked *à la grecque* (p. 87), as a salad or an hors d'œuvre.

How to deal with a glut

1. Freezing: Prepare as above, blanch for 3 minutes, chill and drain. Pack into polythene bags or wax or foil containers. Seal, label and freeze. Storage time: 9 to 12 months.

   2. Preserving: French beans can be salted (see p. 155), pickled as part of a mixed pickle (see p. 330) or used to make piccalilli (see p. 88).

Minestrone Soup

Serves 4–6

50 g	haricot beans	2 oz
1¾ litres	stock made from bones cooked with sprigs of parsley, thyme, a bay leaf and 6 peppercorns	3 pints
2	rashers of streaky bacon	2
1	small onion	1
1 clove	garlic, peeled	1 clove
1	small carrot	1
2	sticks celery	2
1	large leek	1
25 g	cabbage	1 oz
175 g	French beans or runner beans	6 oz
100 g	tomatoes	4 oz
	handful of spaghetti or noodles	
2	medium potatoes	2
	grated Parmesan cheese	

Soak the haricot beans overnight in cold water.

   Prepare the stock, simmering the bones with the herbs in 1¾ litres (3 pints) water for about 1½ hours. Strain and reserve the stock.

   Remove the rind and any bone from the bacon and fry the rinds with the bacon, cut into dice, in a large saucepan until crisp. Remove the rinds and discard them. Peel and chop the onion and add to the bacon; crush the garlic with a little salt and add to the pan. Fry for a few minutes until soft and golden.

Peel the carrot and dice it; slice the washed celery and leek; shred the washed cabbage leaves; top and tail the green beans and slice thinly into short strips. Add all these vegetables to the pan and fry for a few minutes.

Peel the tomatoes (see p. 172), chop the flesh roughly and add to the pan with the strained stock, the drained haricot beans and the spaghetti, broken into 5-cm (2-inch) pieces, or the noodles. Peel and dice the potatoes and add to the soup.

Cover the pan and simmer gently for at least 1 hour. Check for seasoning and serve hot with a sprinkling of grated cheese in each bowl.

Note: This Italian peasant soup is a meal in itself and sets a record for using the greatest number of garden vegetables in any recipe. You may use frozen vegetables in place of the fresh ones in the recipe.

* Suitable for freezing.

French Beans à la Grecque

Serves 3–4

500 g	French beans	1 lb
300 ml	light stock	½ pint
2 tbsps	olive oil	2 tbsps
½	a lemon, juice only	½
¼ level tsp	salt	¼ level tsp
	freshly ground pepper	
1	bay leaf	1
1	sprig of thyme	1

Wash the beans, top and tail them and cut in half. Place the stock, olive oil, lemon juice, salt, pepper, bay leaf and sprig of thyme in a saucepan and bring to the boil. Plunge in the prepared beans and simmer for 12 to 15 minutes, uncovered, until the beans are tender.

Remove the bay leaf and sprig of thyme, then turn the beans and their liquid into a warm serving dish and serve as a vegetable accompaniment, or leave to get cold and serve as an hors d'œuvre.

Note: Frozen beans can be used with only 150 ml (¼ pint) stock; or salted beans used without the ¼ level teaspoon salt.

Worcestershire Beans

Serves 4–5

500 g	French beans	1 lb
500 g	tomatoes	1 lb
200 g	onions	6 oz
	knob of butter	
1 tbsp	Worcestershire sauce	1 tbsp
	salt	

Wash, then top and tail the beans. Skin the tomatoes by putting them in boiling water for $\frac{1}{2}$ minute, draining them and then removing the skins; chop the tomato flesh roughly. Peel and finely chop the onions.

Heat the knob of butter in a saucepan, add the onions and sauté gently until the onions are soft but not browned. Add the tomatoes, beans, Worcestershire sauce and salt, cover and cook over a low heat for about 20 minutes until the beans are cooked. Stir the contents of the pan occasionally to prevent the vegetables from sticking to the pan.

Place the beans in a warm serving dish with the tomato sauce spooned over them and serve hot.

Note: Frozen beans may be used instead of the fresh; salted beans may be used but without the addition of extra salt.

Piccalilli

Makes about $2\frac{3}{4}$ kg (6 lb)

1	large cauliflower	1
1	large cucumber	1
500 g	onions	1 lb
1	medium marrow	1
500 g	French beans, topped and tailed	1 lb
4 level tbsps	salt	4 level tbsps
2 level tsps	ground ginger	2 level tsps
1 level tsp	curry powder	1 level tsp
1 level tbsp	ground turmeric	1 level tbsp
50 g	dried mustard	2 oz
100 g	granulated sugar	4 oz

1¼ litres	white vinegar	2 pints
2 level tbsps	cornflour	2 level tbsps

a preserving pan or large saucepan

Wash all the vegetables. Break the cauliflower into florets; dice the cucumber; peel and dice the onions and the marrow; and cut the French beans into 1-cm (½-inch) pieces. Place all these vegetables in a large bowl and sprinkle the salt over. Cover and leave overnight.

Next day, drain and wash the vegetables well. Put the ground ginger, curry powder, ground turmeric and dried mustard into the preserving pan or large saucepan with the sugar and vinegar. Bring to the boil, add the vegetables and simmer for 20 minutes.

Blend the cornflour with a little cold vinegar and stir into the mixture. Still stirring, boil the mixture for 5 minutes then pour into clean, warm, dry jars, cover with wax discs and polythene covers and lids if available. Label and store in a cool, dry place. It will keep for about 9 months.

Note: Frozen vegetables may be used instead of the fresh.

The following recipes also include French beans:

Vegetable curry (p. 169)
Mixed pickle (p. 330)

Try substituting French beans for peas in Spanish chicken and rice (p. 138), and for runner beans in salted runner beans (p. 155).

12 Leeks

Introduction

Leeks belong to the onion family but are more easily digested than onions. The tastiest part is the characteristic white stem. To achieve this, drop the 15-cm (6-inch) tall seedlings into a hole (made with a dibber) that is almost as deep as the plants themselves. Do not fill in with soil but water the plants and as they grow they will expand into the hole.

Leeks are the hardiest of plants – they can be left in the ground throughout the winter and are seldom troubled by pests and diseases. They are a valuable crop for improving the condition of the soil.

Before lifting, water the soil well to help ease the roots from the hardened ground.

Preparation and cooking

The main difficulty in preparing leeks is ensuring that all the grains of earth which accumulate inside the leaves are removed. For this, careful washing is essential. One method to help remove the dirt is to cut a slit down the green top of the leek to help the water into the centre leaves.

The roots should be cut off and the green tops trimmed to within 5 cm (2 inches) of the white stem. They can be left whole or sliced.

The main problem when cooking leeks, especially when boiling them, is that the vegetable can become very watery and difficult to drain. This is why leeks are better steamed or sautéed. Uncooked, they make a delicious addition to a salad, e.g. coleslaw (see p. 50).

To boil: Prepare as above. Bring a pan of salted water to the boil, add the leeks, cover and cook for 10 to 20 minutes depending on size. Place in a sieve, cover with a lid and leave in a warm place to drain for a few minutes.

To steam: Place the prepared vegetables in a steamer over a pan of boiling water, cover and cook for 15 to 25 minutes.

To sauté: Prepare as above and slice the leeks, then sauté in butter for 15 to 20 minutes over a gentle heat.

To deep fry: Choose small whole leeks, wash well, parboil for 5 minutes, then drain very well. Coat in fritter batter (see p. 343) and deep fry for 5 minutes.

Serving suggestions: The boiled or steamed leeks can be tossed in butter and, if desired, fresh chopped herbs; or they can be coated with a white, cheese or tomato sauce (see pp. 339, 340, 185).

How to deal with a glut

1. Freezing: Prepare as above; leave whole or slice. Blanch for 2 to 4 minutes, depending on size, then chill, drain very well and pack into polythene bags or wax or foil containers. Seal, label and freeze. Storage time: 6 months. Leek and potato soup freezes well (see below).

2. Storing: Store in the ground until ready for use.

Leek and Potato Soup (Vichyssoise)

Serves 6

¾ kg	leeks	1½ lb
75 g	butter or margarine	3 oz
250 g	potatoes	8 oz
1	small onion	1
900 ml	chicken stock	1½ pints
	salt and freshly ground pepper	
300 ml	milk	½ pint
	a little single cream	
	fresh chives, chopped	

Wash the leeks in cold water, trim the base and top and slice them thinly. Melt the butter or margarine in a large saucepan, add the leeks and sauté gently for about 10 minutes, stirring occasionally and taking care that they do not brown.

Meanwhile, peel the potatoes and cut them into 1-cm (½-inch) dice; peel and thinly slice the onion; add these vegetables to the pan and cook for a further 5 minutes. Stir in the stock with the salt and pepper, bring to the boil, cover and simmer gently for about 25 to 30 minutes until all the vegetables are soft.

Put the soup through a fine sieve or liquidize. Return to the pan with the milk and bring back to the boil.

Note: The traditional vichyssoise is always served chilled. Garnish with a little cream swirled in the centre of each bowl and a sprinkling of fresh, finely chopped chives. It also makes a delicious hot winter soup.

Frozen leeks may be used instead of the fresh.

* Suitable for freezing before adding the milk or cream.

Baby Leeks Vinaigrette

Serves 4

500 g	baby leeks	1 lb
	French dressing (p. 343)	
1	large egg, hard-boiled	1
	paprika	

Trim the leeks and wash well. Leaving them whole, place in a pan of boiling salted water and cook for about 7 minutes until just tender. Drain very well, taking care not to break up the leeks. Leave to get cold.

Place the French dressing in a bowl and add the leeks, tossing them gently in the dressing. Leave for 1 hour before serving.

To serve, divide the leeks with their dressing between four individual small plates. Separate the white and yolk of the egg and first grate the white and divide over the four plates. Grate the yolk and sprinkle over the centre of the egg white. Finally top with a dusting of paprika. Serve as an hors d'œuvre with Melba toast.

Note: This is an ideal recipe to use up the very small leeks which fail to thicken out.

Leek Soufflé

Serves 4

500 g	leeks	1 lb
25 g	margarine	1 oz
25 g	plain flour	1 oz

150 ml	milk	¼ pint
3	large eggs	3
50 g	cheese, grated	2 oz
1 level tsp	salt	1 level tsp
¼ level tsp	cayenne pepper	¼ level tsp

a 1¼-litre (2-pint) soufflé dish, buttered

Preheat the oven to 190°C, 375°F, gas mark 5.

Wash the leeks very well then slice them thinly. Steam or boil until tender and drain very well.

Meanwhile melt the margarine in a large saucepan, add the flour and cook for 1 minute. Remove from the heat and gradually stir in the milk. Return to the heat and bring to the boil, stirring constantly, until the sauce thickens. Cool slightly, then separate the eggs and beat the yolks into the sauce.

Stir in the grated cheese and the cooked leeks and mix well. Season with salt and cayenne pepper.

Whisk the egg whites until stiff and dry and, using a metal spoon, fold a little of the beaten egg white into the leek mixture. Fold the rest in very carefully.

Spoon the soufflé mixture into a lightly buttered dish and cook on the centre shelf of the preheated oven for 30 to 35 minutes until the top is golden brown but the centre is still soft.

Serve the soufflé immediately otherwise it will start to sink after a few minutes.

Note: This recipe makes an ideal supper dish or an unusual first course for a dinner party. Frozen leeks may be used to make this soufflé.

New Zealand Casserole

Serves 4–5

¾ kg	lamb chops (4–6)	1½ lb
2 tbsps	cooking oil	2 tbsps
	a knob of butter or margarine	
500 g	leeks	1 lb
500 g	potatoes	1 lb
one 439-g	tin of baked beans	one 15½-oz

| 1 level tsp | salt | 1 level tsp |
| | freshly ground pepper | |

a 1¾-litre (3-pint) shallow ovenproof dish

Preheat the oven to 190°C, 375°F, gas mark 5.

Wipe the lamb chops and remove the spinal cord. Heat the oil and butter or margarine in a frying pan, fry the chops for 2 minutes on both sides to brown lightly and remove from the pan onto a plate.

Wash, trim and slice the leeks. Peel and cut the potatoes into dice the size of walnuts. Sauté the vegetables in the hot fat, turning frequently, for about 10 minutes, but do not brown. Lay in the ovenproof dish and stir in the baked beans, salt and pepper. Lay the chops on top, cover and bake on the centre shelf of the preheated oven for about 1 hour until cooked. Serve as a complete meal.

Note: Frozen sliced leeks may be used instead of the fresh.

Chicken and Leek Pie

Serves 4–6

100 g	shortcrust pastry (p. 334)	4 oz
75 g	cheese, grated	3 oz
1–1¼ kg	whole cooked chicken	2½ lb
350 g	leeks	12 oz
40 g	butter or margarine	1½ oz
50 g	button mushrooms	2 oz
25 g	plain flour	1 oz
300 ml	milk	½ pint
150 ml	chicken stock	¼ pint
1 level tsp	salt	1 level tsp
	freshly ground pepper	
1 level tsp	freshly chopped parsley	1 level tsp

a 1½-litre (2½-pint) pie dish

Preheat the oven to 190°C, 375°F, gas mark 5.

Before adding the water to the pastry, mix in the grated cheese. Make up the pastry and leave to stand for 20 minutes.

Remove all the meat from the cooked chicken and cut into large pieces. Trim and wash the leeks very thoroughly then slice them fairly thinly. Melt half the butter or margarine in a saucepan, add the leeks and sauté gently for 5 minutes. Wipe the mushrooms, slice thinly and add to the pan. Sauté for a further 5 minutes, turning frequently until soft. Remove the leeks and mushrooms on to a plate.

Add the remaining butter or margarine to the pan, then stir in the flour and cook for 1 minute. Remove from the heat and gradually stir in the milk and chicken stock, a little at a time. Season with salt and pepper and add the chopped parsley.

Return the saucepan to the heat and bring the sauce to the boil, stirring constantly, until thick. Cook for 2 minutes, remove from the heat, and stir in the cooked chicken, leeks and mushrooms. Pour the mixture into the pie dish.

Roll out the pastry on a lightly floured surface, making it large enough to fit the top of the pie dish. Damp the edges and cover the pie with the pastry. Trim the edges, roll the trimmings again and cut out pastry leaves to decorate the top of the pie.

Cook on the centre shelf of the preheated oven for 40 minutes until the pastry is golden brown. Serve with creamed potatoes and baked tomatoes.

* Suitable for freezing.

Lamb and Leek Curry

Serves 3–4

1 kg	middle neck of lamb	2 lb
	seasoned flour	
25–50 g	margarine	1–2 oz
200 g	leeks	6 oz
100 g	onions	4 oz
2 cloves	garlic	2 cloves
300 ml	good stock	½ pint
	salt and pepper	

For the home-made curry powder

1–2 level tsps	ground chillis	
	ground turmeric	
	ground cumin	
1 level tsp	ground coriander	
each	ground mace	
	fenugreek	
	cardamom seed	

$\frac{1}{2}$ level tsp
each
$\left\{\begin{array}{l}\text{ground ginger}\\\text{ground cloves}\\\text{mustard seed}\\\text{poppy seed}\end{array}\right.$

Or
1–2 level tbsps ready-made curry powder

Remove the fat and bone from the lamb, cut into cubes and toss in the seasoned flour. Heat the margarine in a large frying pan, add the lamb and brown on all sides, turning frequently. Remove onto a plate.

Wash the leeks and slice into 1-cm ($\frac{1}{2}$-inch) rings; peel and slice the onions into rings; peel the garlic and crush with a little salt. Add these vegetables to the pan and sauté until soft and golden.

Put all the curry powder ingredients into a small bowl and mix together. Add the powder (or the ready-made curry powder) to the pan, fry gently for a further 2 minutes then stir in the stock. Return the lamb to the pan, season with salt and pepper, cover and cook over a very low heat for $1\frac{1}{2}$ to 2 hours. Serve with boiled rice, sweet chutneys (e.g. mock mango chutney, p. 264, cucumber relish, p. 83, rhubarb chutney, p. 289) and popadums.

Note: The flavour of the curry will improve greatly if left for 24 hours before eating – this gives time for the meat to marinate in the spices and absorb them.

The amount of chilli powder and pepper used will determine how hot the curry is. You may also use whole spices instead of ground and crush them in a pestle and mortar.

* Freezes well.

The following recipes also include leeks:

Lamb casserole (p. 73)
Green tomato casserole (p. 180)
January suet pudding (p. 41)

Try substituting leeks for beans in French beans *à la grecque* (p. 87).

13 Lettuce

Introduction

Lettuce is one garden vegetable which can easily provide a glut of plants which cannot be dealt with in the usual way – freezing, preserving or storing.

Limper lettuces and those on the verge of going to seed are best used in cooked dishes and the crisper, fresher lettuce reserved for salads.

All the varieties – the soft-leaved cabbage lettuce, the round-shaped, curly-leaved Webb's Wonderful varieties and the more pointed cos lettuces – are easily grown in the garden, in pots or in boxes on windowsills. Plant a few seedlings at two-weekly intervals throughout the summer for a continuous crop, water well in dry spells and guard against slug attacks by putting down slug pellets.

It is even possible to grow lettuces during the winter as there are now available special winter varieties for harvesting in the spring.

Preparation and cooking

For those who have not discovered how tasty cooked lettuce dishes can be it is worth while trying to overcome an initial aversion to the idea. Lettuce braised with mushrooms and tomatoes is a particularly good vegetable dish.

To prepare, remove the loose, damaged outer leaves. (Any undamaged outer leaves can be used in the cooked lettuce recipes or in soups or stocks.) The other leaves are carefully peeled off and washed in cold water. The leaves must be thoroughly drained, preferably in a salad shaker, to remove the excess moisture. For cooked dishes the leaves should then be shredded. Lettuce, like spinach, shrinks considerably when cooked.

To boil: Bring a pan of salted water to the boil, add the shredded lettuce, cover and cook for 7 to 10 minutes. Drain well.

To steam: Place the prepared lettuce in a steamer over a pan of boiling water, cover and cook for 12 to 15 minutes.

To braise: See the recipe for lettuce with mushrooms and tomatoes (p. 99); braise for 10 to 15 minutes.

Serving suggestions: The boiled or steamed lettuce can be topped with a cheese sauce (p. 340) or just sprinkled with grated cheese.

How to deal with a glut

It is not a good idea to freeze lettuce because of its high water content. However, lettuce soup does freeze very well and is the best way of preserving a glut crop.

There are no recipes for lettuce preserves.

As the seeds are inexpensive, bolted lettuces should be pulled up and put on the compost heap where they will rot down to provide good humus.

Lettuce Soup

Serves 3–4

1	lettuce	1
1	small onion	1
175 g	potatoes	6 oz
900 ml	stock	1½ pints
	a sprig of parsley, chopped	
	salt and pepper	

Wash the lettuce and shred the leaves; peel and chop the onion; peel and dice the potatoes. Place all these vegetables in a large saucepan with the stock, chopped parsley, salt and pepper. Cover the pan, bring to the boil and simmer gently for about 30 minutes.

Purée the soup in a liquidizer or through a Mouli vegetable mill, check for seasoning and serve hot. A spoonful of cream in the centre of each bowl is a tasty addition.

* Suitable for freezing.

Lettuce Mornay

Serves 4

500 g	lettuce (e.g. 1 large cos)	1 lb
25 g	butter or margarine	1 oz
300 ml	cheese or mornay sauce (p. 340)	½ pint
	salt and pepper	
	a little grated cheese	

Wash and shred the lettuce finely. Heat the butter or margarine in a saucepan and add the lettuce. Cover the pan and simmer over a low heat for 7 to 10 minutes, by which time the lettuce will have greatly reduced in bulk and will be cooked but still a little crisp to taste.

Meanwhile prepare the cheese or mornay sauce. Place the lettuce in a warm dish, sprinkle with salt and pepper and spoon the hot cheese or mornay sauce over it. To serve, sprinkle the top with a little grated cheese and place under a hot grill for a few minutes until the top is beginning to brown. Serve hot as a vegetable accompaniment.

Lettuce with Mushrooms and Tomatoes

Serves 2–3

250 g	lettuce	8 oz
50 g	mushrooms	2 oz
2	tomatoes	2
	knob of butter or margarine	
	salt and pepper	

Wash and shred the lettuce very finely. Wipe and slice the mushrooms, including the stalks. Peel the tomatoes (see p. 172) and chop the flesh roughly.

Heat the butter or margarine in a large saucepan, add the mushrooms and sauté gently for 2 minutes. Add the chopped tomatoes and cook for a further 2 minutes. Finally add the shredded lettuce and seasonings and simmer gently, uncovered, for 10 to 15 minutes.

Place the lettuce and the tomato sauce in a warm serving dish. This recipe is delicious with roasts, chops and steaks.

The following recipes also include lettuce:

Greek stuffed tomatoes (p. 177)
Bean and cucumber salad (p. 32)
Pois à la française (p. 141)
Beetroot napoli (p. 25)
Waldorf salad (p. 70)

14 Marrow

Introduction

Large marrows have lost a lot in popularity as courgettes have gained (see Chapter 9). They lack the delicate flavour of courgettes and a greater variety of dishes that can be made from the smaller vegetable. However, they are still useful and easy plants to grow, making good jams and pickles and storing well.

Marrows like to grow on a rich, well-composted and manured site, but are not frost-hardy and are therefore not planted out until late May/early June. In the smaller garden they can be trained up poles to economize on space, but need to be strongly supported to hold the weight of the fully grown marrows.

When the first flowers are in bloom in early summer, the marrows can be encouraged to set by cross-pollinating the male and female flowers. During their growing time the marrows should be kept well watered. Some of the marrows should be cut fairly small to encourage the others to grow to their full size for storage.

Preparation and cooking

Cut off the stalk and top and peel, unless the marrow is very young and the skin tender. To remove the seeds, either cut in half and scoop out the seeds, or cut into rings and press the seeds out with the thumbs. The marrow can be halved, cut into rings or diced.

To boil: Prepare the vegetables as above. Bring a pan of salted water to the boil, add the marrow, cover and cook for 5 to 10 minutes, depending on size. Drain well.

To steam: Place the prepared marrow in a steamer over a pan of boiling water, cover and cook for 15 to 20 minutes, depending on size.

Braise in tomato and onion juices for 10 to 15 minutes.

To bake: See stuffed marrow (p. 103); bake for 2 hours.

To sauté: Cut into small strips or dice and fry in butter with fresh herbs for 7 to 10 minutes.

Serving suggestions: the boiled or steamed marrow can be coated in a cheese or tomato sauce (pp. 340, 185).

How to deal with a glut

Marrows are too watery to freeze successfully.

1. *Preserving:* late summer chutney (p. 106), marrow and ginger jam (p. 107), piccalilli (p. 88), mixed pickle (p. 330), pickled marrow (p. 329).
2. *Storing:* Hang large ones in a dry shed. A good tip is to hang them inside an old pair of stockings or tights. They will store for a short time, until Christmas at the latest.

Piquant Marrow Hors d'Oeuvre

Serves 4

¾ kg	marrow (1 small)	1½ lb
350 g	tomatoes	12 oz
1	medium onion	1
½ level tsp	salt	½ level tsp
½ level tsp	paprika	½ level tsp
1 clove	garlic, peeled	1 clove
	a few drops of tabasco sauce	
1 level tbsp	fresh parsley, chopped	1 level tbsp

Peel the marrow, trim off the ends, slice into very thin rings, ½ cm (¼ inch) thick, remove the centre pips and put in a saucepan of boiling, well-salted water. Cook for 5 minutes, drain very well through a sieve, leave to cool and then put the rings in the refrigerator to chill.

Meanwhile, make the sauce: Skin the tomatoes (see p. 172) and chop the flesh roughly; peel and chop the onion and put in a saucepan with the tomatoes, salt and paprika. Crush the clove of garlic with a little salt and add to the pan. Bring the contents to the boil, cover and simmer gently. Allow to cool, then stir in the tabasco to give a piquant, peppery flavour. Pour the cold sauce over the marrow rings and leave to marinate for 1 hour.

To serve, lay the marrow rings on a flat dish, neatly overlapping each other, and pour any extra sauce over them. Sprinkle the chopped parsley on top and serve as an hors d'œuvre with slices of wholemeal bread and butter.

Note: Frozen or bottled tomatoes may be used to make the sauce.

Stuffed Marrow

Serves 4–5

1¼ kg	marrow (1 medium-size)	2½ lb
25 g	cooking fat	1 oz
1	medium onion	1
500 g	minced beef	1 lb
2	medium carrots	2
250 g	potatoes	8 oz
1 level tbsp	tomato purée	1 level tbsp
	salt and pepper	
1 level tsp	fresh mixed herbs – chopped bay leaf, marjoram, thyme, oregano	1 level tsp
	or	
½ level tsp	dried mixed herbs	½ level tsp

Preheat the oven to 180°C, 350°F; gas mark 4.

It is not necessary to peel the marrow, but this can be done if preferred. To make the lid of the marrow, cut a wedge 8 cm (3 inches) wide and 20 to 25 cm (8 to 10 inches) long out of one side of the marrow, to within 5 cm (2 inches) of each end. Scoop out the seeds from the marrow and the underside of the lid.

To make the filling, heat the fat in a pan, peel and finely chop the onion and fry in the fat until soft, but not browned – about 7 minutes. Add the minced beef and cook for a further 5 minutes, stirring frequently. Peel the carrots and potatoes and grate into the mince mixture. Remove from the heat and stir in the tomato purée, salt, pepper, and the finely chopped herbs; fill the inside of the marrow with the stuffing.

Put the marrow on a piece of cooking foil, place the lid on the top, then seal the foil around the marrow. Bake on the centre shelf of the preheated oven for about 2 hours, until the marrow is tender.

Note: If you have peeled the marrow, it will only take 1¾ hours to bake.

Stuffed Marrow Rings

Serves 2

¾ kg	marrow (1 small)	1½ lb
300 ml	mornay or cheese sauce (see p. 340)	½ pint
For the stuffing		
100 g	cooked ham	4 oz
½	large onion	½
50 g	fresh bread	2 oz
	a bunch of fresh marjoram, thyme and parsley	
1	small egg	1
	salt and freshly ground pepper	

a 1¼-litre (2-pint) shallow ovenproof dish, buttered

Preheat the oven to 190°C, 375°F, gas mark 5.

Peel the marrow, trim off the ends and cut it into four 5-cm (2-inch) rings. Remove the centre pips.

Butter the ovenproof dish and lay the four slices in the dish. Put the ham, the peeled and quartered onion, the bread and bunch of herbs through a fairly fine mincer. Add the egg to the minced ingredients and mix well together. Season with salt and pepper, then divide the stuffing between the four marrow slices, pressing firmly into the centres.

Make the mornay or cheese sauce and pour over the marrow rings. Bake on the centre shelf of the preheated oven for about 35 to 40 minutes until the marrow is tender. Serve with a tossed salad and new potatoes.

Note: If a larger marrow is used, cut the rings from the centre of the marrow. The remaining marrow, if wrapped in foil or cling film, will keep for several days in the refrigerator.

Marrow Casserole

Serves 4

¾ kg	marrow	1½ lb
350 g	tomatoes	12 oz
	salt and pepper	
	sprinkling of chopped	
	mixed herbs	
75 g	cheese, grated	3 oz
4 heaped tbsps	fresh breadcrumbs	4 heaped tbsps

a 1¼-litre (2-pint) ovenproof casserole

Preheat the oven to 180°C, 350°F, gas mark 4.

Peel the marrow and cut into rings; remove the centre seeds then cut the marrow rings into quarters. Place in a bowl, sprinkle well with salt and leave for at least an hour to extract some of the water from the vegetable. Wipe dry with kitchen paper.

Skin the tomatoes (see p. 172) and slice them.

Grease the ovenproof dish and lay half the marrow in the base. Sprinkle with salt and pepper and some mixed herbs. Cover the marrow with half the sliced tomatoes, season them and cover with half the grated cheese.

Repeat the layers of marrow, tomatoes and seasonings and finally mix the rest of the cheese with the breadcrumbs, and sprinkle over the top of the dish. Cover the casserole and cook on the centre shelf of the preheated oven for 45 minutes. Then remove the cover of the casserole, return to the oven and bake for a further 15 minutes until the top is nicely browned.

Serve the casserole hot as a vegetable accompaniment to grilled chops, steaks or gammon.

Note: There is no need to add any liquid to the casserole as the marrow produces enough of its own.

Marrow Salad

Serves 3–4

500 g	marrow	1 lb
1 tbsp	mint sauce	1 tbsp
	salt and freshly ground	
	pepper	

Peel the marrow, halve it and scoop out the seeds. Cut each half again lengthwise, then slice the quarters into fairly thin strips, 8 to 10 cm (3 to 4 inches), and boil or steam until tender. Drain thoroughly.

When drained, place the marrow in a bowl and sprinkle over it the mint sauce, salt and pepper. Toss very gently to coat all the marrow, then leave in a cool place to marinate and chill for at least 1 hour before serving.

Note: This simple dish makes a refreshingly different salad or part of a mixed hors d'œuvre.

Late Summer Chutney

Makes about 1½–1¾ kg (3½ lb)

1 kg	marrow (or courgettes)	2 lb
25 g	salt	1 oz
500 g	cooking apples	1 lb
500 g	pears	1 lb
600 ml	malt vinegar	1 pint
1 level tsp	ground ginger	1 level tsp
½ level tsp	dry mustard	½ level tsp
¼ level tsp each	ground cloves, ground cinnamon and cayenne pepper	¼ level tsp each
1 level tsp	salt	1 level tsp
400 g	granulated sugar	12 oz

a preserving pan or large saucepan

Peel the marrow, cut it into slices and remove the seeds. Cut the slices into cubes, place in a bowl and sprinkle with the 25 g (1 oz) salt. Cover and leave to stand overnight. (*Note:* Although this recipe uses marrow, overgrown or excess courgettes can be used instead. To prepare them, wipe the vegetables, then top, tail and thinly slice them. There is no need to remove the seeds. Proceed as for the marrow.)

Next day drain the liquid from the marrow (or courgettes). Peel, quarter and core the apples and pears and put them and the marrow through a coarse mincer. Place in a bowl and add the vinegar, spices and seasonings, but not the sugar. Leave to stand for 1 hour.

Pour into a preserving pan or large saucepan, bring to the boil and simmer for about 30 minutes or until the fruits are soft and the mixture is quite thick.

Add the sugar, bring back to the boil and cook briskly until the chutney is thick, about 15 minutes. Pour into clean, warm, dry jars, cover with polythene and lids if available, label and store for 1 month in a cool, dry place before using.

Note: Frozen apples or pears may be used in this chutney.

Marrow and Ginger Jam

Makes about 2½ kg (5 lb)

2	marrows, to give about 1½ kg (3 lb) when prepared	2
25 g	root ginger	1 oz
2	lemons, juice only	2
¼ level tsp	ground ginger	¼ level tsp
1½ kg	granulated or preserving sugar	3 lb

a preserving pan or large saucepan

Peel the marrows, cut them into 3-cm (1-inch) slices and remove the pips. Cut the slices into cubes and place them in the top of a steamer. Crush the root ginger between two pieces of paper, using a rolling pin, tie in a piece of muslin and place it in the steamer with the marrow. Put the steamer over a pan of simmering water, cover and steam for about 20 minutes until the marrow is tender.

Mash the marrow and place it and the muslin bag of ginger in the preserving pan. Add the lemon juice and ground ginger, bring to the boil, then add the sugar and reduce the heat to low. Allow the sugar to dissolve slowly without boiling. When it has all dissolved, bring the jam to a rapid boil until setting point is reached – about 10 minutes (see p. 311 for full jam-making instructions).

Remove the muslin bag before pouring the jam into warm, clean, dry jars. Cover, label and store in a cool, dry place. The flavour of this jam improves if kept for at least 3 weeks before using.

The following recipes also include marrow:

Mixed pickle (p. 330)
Piccalilli (p. 88)
Pickled marrow (p. 329)

15 Mushrooms

Introduction

Home-grown mushrooms are a delight and in these days of the special home 'grow kits' everybody can produce their own crop without even having to own a garden or allotment. We kept our box in a corner of the kitchen and watched amazed at the beautiful white mushrooms that sprang up almost unaided.

The kits provide the grower with the two necessary requirements for cultivating mushrooms, the spawn (seed) and the special mushroom compost – a peaty mixture with small pieces of chalk in it. Without these and a sheltered environment, growing your own mushrooms can prove to be a tricky task.

The tight-capped white cultivated mushrooms are best picked before they start to open up and become soft. The other variety of mushroom available in this country is the field mushroom – a larger, flat-capped variety. Unless you are an expert on mushrooms we would not advise picking and eating wild mushrooms as many varieties are poisonous.

Preparation and cooking

Remember that mushrooms shrink a lot in cooking so allow for this when calculating how much will be needed for each portion. Mushrooms only require a short cooking time and make tasty additions to stews, soups, sauces and other dishes.

To prepare, gently wipe to remove any growing compost. There is certainly no need to peel off the skins, even of the field mushrooms, as the layer immediately below the skin is full of flavour. There is also no need to remove the stalks, simply trim the base. Either leave the mushrooms whole or slice them.

To steam: Place the prepared mushrooms in a steamer over a pan of boiling water, cover and steam for 20 minutes.

Grill by themselves or with lemon juice or fresh lime juice (1 teaspoon for every 50 g/2 oz mushrooms), turning occasionally, for 6 to 8 minutes.

Bake, stuffed, for 20 minutes.

Sauté in butter with lemon juice (optional); sauté the sliced mushrooms for 6 to 8 minutes and season to taste.

Deep fry in fritter batter for 4 to 5 minutes (see mushroom fritters, p. 114).

Serving suggestions: The steamed mushrooms can be tossed in butter and chopped fresh parsley or coated in a cream sauce (p. 341). Button mushrooms, sliced and marinated in French dressing (p. 343), can be served uncooked as a salad.

How to deal with a glut

1. Freezing: Wipe and trim stalks; leave whole or slice. Dip in lemon water (3 teaspoons lemon juice to 600 ml/1 pint water) to prevent discoloration.

Drain the mushrooms, then blanch for 2 to 4 minutes, depending on size. Chill, drain and pack into polythene bags or wax or foil containers. Seal, label and freeze. Storage time: 9 to 12 months. Also freeze mushroom soup (below).

2. Preserving: Pickle in spiced vinegar (p. 329) or make into mushroom ketchup (p. 115).

Fresh Mushroom Soup

Serves 3

250 g	mushrooms	8 oz
25–50 g	butter or margarine	1–2 oz
2 level tbsps	flour	2 level tbsps
300 ml	milk	½ pint
300 ml	chicken stock	½ pint
1	bay leaf	1
3 tbsps	fresh cream	3 tbsps
	chopped parsley	

Wipe the mushrooms carefully to remove any compost; trim and chop the stalks and slice the caps. Melt the butter or margarine in a frying pan and gently sauté the mushrooms for a few minutes until tender. Add the flour and cook for 1 minute. Remove from the heat and gradually add the milk; bring to the boil, stirring constantly, and cook for 1 minute. Slowly stir in the chicken stock; add the bay leaf and cook gently for about 10 minutes. Test for seasoning.

Serve hot with a spoonful of cream in each bowl and a sprinkling of chopped fresh parsley to garnish.

* Suitable for freezing before adding the cream.

Chicken in Orange and Mushroom Sauce

Serves 4–6

1½ kg	chicken or 4–6 chicken quarters	3–3½ lb
2 tbsps	flour seasoned with salt and pepper	2 tbsps
2 tbsps	oil for frying	2 tbsps
1	large orange	1
1 clove	garlic	1 clove
250 g	onions	8 oz
250 g	mushrooms	8 oz
	a sprig each of parsley and thyme	
	a bay leaf	
	salt and pepper	
150 ml	white wine	¼ pint
150 ml	chicken stock	¼ pint
1 heaped tbsp	cornflour	1 heaped tbsp

a 2¼-litre (4-pint) ovenproof casserole

Preheat the oven to 180°C, 350°F, gas mark 4.

Joint the whole chicken into eight or nine serving pieces; put the seasoned flour onto a plate and coat the pieces in it. Heat the oil in a frying pan and fry the chicken pieces until the meat is lightly browned. Remove the pieces from the pan and place in the casserole dish.

Grate a little orange rind over the chicken, then squeeze the juice from the orange and add it to the casserole.

Peel and crush the garlic with a little salt, and peel and finely chop the onions. Add both to the frying pan, cook gently until soft and golden and add to the casserole.

Wipe the mushrooms and slice them. Add to the casserole along with the parsley, thyme, bay leaf and seasoning. Pour the white wine and the chicken stock into the casserole, cover and cook in the centre of the preheated oven for 1 hour.

Before serving, remove the chicken pieces to a hot serving plate. To thicken the mushroom sauce, blend a little cold water with the cornflour, stir it into the juices in the casserole and, stirring, cook to thicken. Alternatively, reduce the sauce by boiling for a few minutes. Pour the sauce over the chicken pieces and serve with roast or jacket potatoes.

Note: Frozen sliced mushrooms may be used in this recipe.

* Suitable for freezing.

Minted Lamb Kebabs

Serves 4

¾ kg	lean lamb	1½ lb
4 tbsps	olive oil	4 tbsps
4 tbsps	mint sauce or fresh mint finely chopped and mixed with vinegar	4 tbsps
	salt and pepper	
10	button mushrooms	10
10	button onions	10
10	red baby tomatoes	10

4 long or 8 short kebab sticks

Trim any excess fat from the lamb and cut it into small cubes. Place the olive oil, mint sauce and seasonings in a bowl and add the lamb; toss the meat to coat it in the mint marinade and leave for at least 4 hours or overnight.

Wipe the mushrooms and peel the onions; wash the tomatoes. Thread the lamb cubes and vegetables onto the kebab sticks, alternating vegetables with lamb. Place the kebabs under a medium grill (or over a barbecue) and cook for about 20 minutes, turning several times until the meat is brown and tender. Serve with jacket potatoes and a green salad.

Note: Frozen mushrooms may be used in place of the fresh.

Mushroom Risotto

Serves 3–4

250 g	mushrooms	8 oz
75 g	butter or margarine	3 oz
1	small onion	1
150 g	long-grain rice	5 oz
300 ml	chicken stock	½ pint
	fresh or dried marjoram	

Wipe the mushrooms carefully to remove any compost; trim and chop the stalks and slice the caps. Melt half the butter or margarine in a saucepan and gently fry the mushrooms for a few minutes, then remove them to a plate.

Peel and finely chop the onion. Melt the other half of the butter in the saucepan, add the onion and fry until soft and golden. Add the rice and fry for a few minutes before adding the chicken stock and the chopped fresh marjoram or a sprinkling of dried marjoram. Simmer, uncovered, for 15 minutes until the rice is completely cooked and the stock evaporated. Add the buttered mushrooms and cook a further few minutes.

Note: This dish can be served hot with kebabs or chops, for example, or cold with salads. It can also be used to stuff large mushrooms or other vegetables, such as courgettes, marrow, cabbage leaves or tomatoes.

Frozen sliced mushrooms may be used to make this risotto.

Mushrooms in Sour Cream

Serves 2–3

250 g	mushrooms	8 oz
50 g	butter or margarine	2 oz
1	large carrot	1
4 tbsps	sour cream (or fresh cream)	4 tbsps
	salt and freshly ground	
	pepper	

Wipe the mushrooms and slice them, stalks as well as caps. Heat the butter or margarine in a saucepan and add the sliced mushrooms. Peel the carrot and grate it into the pan, cover and simmer gently for 5 minutes, tossing occasionally.

Remove from the heat and stir in the sour cream. Season to taste with salt and pepper and serve hot as a vegetable accompaniment.

Note: To sour cream, add lemon juice or vinegar to fresh cream. Frozen sliced mushrooms may be used instead of the fresh.

Mushroom Fritters

Serves 4

250 g	mushrooms (button)	8 oz
150 ml	fritter batter (p. 343)	¼ pint
	fat or oil for deep frying	

a deep-fat frying pan

Choose small button mushrooms, wipe them and leave them whole.

Prepare the fritter batter, then heat the fat or oil until a cube of bread turns golden brown almost immediately when dropped in the pan.

Dip the mushrooms in the batter to coat evenly, then fry in the fat, a few at a time, until golden brown on all sides. Serve immediately as a vegetable accompaniment or as an unusual hors d'œuvre, with tartare sauce.

Mushroom Stuffing

For a 6-kg (12-lb) turkey or capon

500 g	sausage-meat	1 lb
2	medium onions	2
100 g	mushrooms	4 oz
25–50 g	butter or margarine	1–2 oz
75 g	fresh breadcrumbs	3 oz
1 level tsp	fresh thyme, chopped	1 level tsp
	salt and pepper	
6 tbsps	white wine	6 tbsps
	or	
1	egg	1

Rinse out the inside of the bird and wipe with kitchen paper.

Place the sausage-meat in a large bowl. Peel and finely chop the onions, and wipe and slice the mushrooms. Heat the butter or margarine in a frying pan and first gently sauté the onions until they are soft and golden, then add the sliced mushrooms and cook for 1 minute longer. Add the contents of the pan to the sausage-meat along with the bread-crumbs, thyme, seasonings and the wine or egg to bind the mixture.

Using clean hands or a large fork, mix all the ingredients thoroughly until everything is evenly distributed. Put the stuffing inside the turkey or capon, then truss the bird before roasting. Calculate the cooking time according to the weight of the stuffed bird. Use half the above quantities to stuff a chicken.

Note: Frozen sliced mushrooms may be used in place of the fresh.

* Suitable for freezing.

Mushroom Ketchup

Makes about 1 litre (1½–1¾ pints)

1½ kg	mushrooms	3½ lb
75 g	salt	3 oz
1 rounded tsp	pickling spice	1 rounded tsp
¼ level tsp	ground cinnamon	¼ level tsp
¼ level tsp	ground cloves	¼ level tsp
¼ level tsp	ground mace	¼ level tsp
½ level tsp	dry mustard	½ level tsp
300 ml	malt vinegar	½ pint

Wipe the mushrooms and trim the base of the stalks. Chop them roughly into a bowl and sprinkle with the salt. Cover and leave to stand overnight.

Next day, rinse the mushrooms in cold water, then put them into a large saucepan and mash them. Add all the spices and vinegar, cover and simmer for about 30 minutes.

Strain through a sieve, pressing out as much juice as possible. Pour the hot sauce into warm, clean bottles – preferably small bottles with screw tops, e.g. small tonic or ketchup bottles. Seal tightly immediately, then stand them on a trivet or wad of newspaper in a pan of simmering water so that the water covers the sauce in the bottles.

Heat the water to 80°C (170°F) and simmer very gently for 30 minutes. Remove the bottles and leave to cool. Label, then store in a cool, dry place. The ketchup will keep for 6 to 9 months.

Note: Frozen mushrooms may be used in place of the fresh.

The following recipes also include mushrooms:

Fillet of lamb *en croûte* (p. 119)
Kidneys turbigo (p. 121)
Veal and onion pie (p. 123)
Stuffed courgettes (p. 74)
Lettuce with mushrooms and tomatoes (p. 99)
Spinach with mushrooms in cream (p. 163)
Brussels sprouts *à la crème* (p. 43)
Bean and mushroom salad (p. 31)
Pickled mushrooms (p. 329)

Try substituting mushrooms for cucumber in cucumber and prawn hors d'œuvre (p. 80).

16 Onions

Introduction

The onion is one of the tastiest vegetables for enhancing the flavour of most dishes – provided that you are not one of those unfortunate people who find it too indigestible.

There are many types of onion – the small pickling onion, shallots, spring onions, the ordinary onion and the larger, milder Spanish onion.

Onions can be grown from seeds or more easily from onion sets – specially produced small onion bulbs – and after they are established require virtually no looking after other than the usual weeding.

In late summer, when the stems become hollow, bend the leaves over to concentrate goodness into the bulbs. If any of the plants start to flower, pick off the heads at once.

By autumn the onions should be large enough to lift for storing, but first lay them out to dry thoroughly for about three weeks before storage.

Preparation and cooking

The smell of the onion is instantly recognizable, as are the tears of the cook preparing it. If the onion is too strong it may be peeled under cold water to prevent the unpleasant eye-stinging but this will also wash away some of its flavour.

To prepare, cut off the top and the root and peel off the brown outer skin (these onion skins can be used in the preparation of stocks or soups). Alternatively, leave the root intact as this can help reduce the onion vapour. The easiest way to slice onion is to cut it in half lengthwise and then lay each half inside down and slice it widthwise. The whole onion may also be sliced to produce rings.

To boil: Keep the onions whole, remove the outer skin and place in a pan of boiling salted water; cover and cook for 20 to 40 minutes, depending on size. Drain well.

To steam: Place the prepared onions in a steamer over a pan of boiling water, cover and cook for 30 to 45 minutes.

Braise in stock for 40 minutes to 1 hour.

To roast: Peel and put in a roasting pan with dripping or fat (or put around a roast joint) and bake for 1 to 1¼ hours, basting occasionally. See also stuffed onions (p. 124).

To sauté: Peel and slice the onions thinly into dice or rings, then sauté in dripping or butter for 5 to 10 minutes.

To deep fry: (French fried onions): Peel and slice the onions thinly, separate into rings; dip the rings in milk then coat in seasoned flour; deep fry in hot fat for 3 to 5 minutes. Drain well. The rings can also be coated in fritter batter (p. 343) and then deep fried.

Serving suggestions: The boiled or steamed onions may be coated with melted butter and sprinkled with fresh chopped parsley or served in a cheese or cream sauce (pp. 340, 341).

How to deal with a glut

1. Freezing: Frozen onions are best used in soups or casseroles, as they lose their crispness. Leave pickling onions whole; peel the onions and slice the larger ones; blanch for 2 minutes, chill, drain and pack into two polythene bags to prevent the smell passing on to other foods. Storage time: 2 to 3 months. French onion soup (below) and bacon and onion cheese flan (p. 124) both freeze well.

2. Preserving: Pickle small onions in spiced vinegar (p. 329); or make mixed pickle (p. 330) or onion and apple pickle (p. 330). Almost all chutney and relish recipes in the book have a good quantity of onions in them (see index at the back for a full list).

3. Storing: Store on trays or tied in bundles and hung in a cool shed or larder (see p. 117). Try our tip of hanging the onions inside old stockings or tights with a knot tied between each one to keep them separate.

French Onion Soup

Serves 4

500 g	onions	1 lb
25 g	butter or margarine	1 oz
1 tbsp	olive oil	1 tbsp

1 level tsp	salt	1 level tsp
1 level tbsp	flour	1 level tbsp
1¼ litres	good beef stock	2 pints
1	bay leaf	1
	freshly ground pepper	
4	thick slices of French bread	4
100 g	Gruyère cheese	4 oz

Peel and slice the onions thinly. Heat the butter or margarine and the oil in a large saucepan, then add the onions and salt and fry over a high heat, stirring frequently, until they are golden brown and tender – the onions should be well coloured but not burnt. Stir in the flour, then remove from the heat and slowly stir in the stock. Add the bay leaf and pepper, bring back to the boil, stirring constantly, cover and simmer gently for about 30 minutes. Test for seasoning.

Toast the slices of French bread on one side only and then remove from the grill. Slice the Gruyère cheese and lay the slices on the untoasted side and return to the grill until the cheese is bubbling and lightly browned. Place a slice of cheesy bread on the base of each soup bowl and pour the hot soup over it. Serve immediately.

Note: Frozen sliced onions may be used in this soup.

Fillet of Lamb en Croûte

Serves 4–5

200 g	puff pastry (p. 336)	8 oz
½–¾ kg	lamb fillets (2)	1¼–1½ lb
25 g	margarine or butter	1 oz
1 clove	garlic	1 clove
250 g	onions	8 oz
100 g	mushrooms	4 oz
	salt and pepper	
1 level tsp	mixed fresh herbs, e.g. thyme, rosemary, marjoram	1 level tsp
150 g	tomatoes	6 oz
	egg glaze	

a 23- by 35-cm (9- by 13-inch) swiss roll tin, greased

Preheat the oven to 220°C, 425°F, gas mark 7.

Make the pastry and leave to rest. Trim any excess fat from the fillets and wipe them. Heat the margarine or butter in a pan. Peel and crush the garlic with a little salt; peel and thinly slice the onions; wipe and slice the mushrooms. Add all these vegetables to the pan and sauté for a few minutes until the onions are tender. Remove from the heat and season with salt and pepper and the finely chopped mixed herbs. Allow to cool slightly.

Roll out the pastry on a floured surface to a rectangle 23 by 35 cm (9 by 13 inches). Slice the tomatoes and lay them down the centre of the pastry to within 5 cm (2 inches) of each end. Lay the lamb fillets on top, end to end, to give one long roll. Scatter the sautéed vegetables over the fillets. Damp the edges of the pastry and fold the sides over, sealing well to form a roll.

Fold up both ends, sealing well, and lay the roll on the greased tin, placing all the pastry joins underneath.

Brush the top and sides with egg glaze and very lightly mark a criss-cross pattern over the surface, using the point of a knife. Leave to rest for 10 minutes before baking on the shelf above the centre of the pre-heated oven for 15 minutes, then reduce the heat to 190°C, 375°F, gas mark 5, for a further 30 to 35 minutes. The lamb should be tender but still slightly pink in the centre when served.

Note: Egg glaze is made by lightly beating an egg with a little water and salt, to give a good colour and appearance to the pastry.

* Suitable for the freezer.

Chicken in Cider

Serves 4

4	large chicken quarters	4
1 tbsp	oil for frying	1 tbsp
25 g	butter or margarine	1 oz
250 g	onions	8 oz
2 cloves	garlic, peeled	2 cloves
50 g	button mushrooms	2 oz
250 g	aubergine (1 medium)	8 oz
1	small green pepper	1
175 g	tomatoes	6 oz

150 ml	chicken stock	¼ pint
150 ml	dry cider	¼ pint
25 g	flour	1 oz
	salt and freshly ground pepper	

a 1¾- to 2¼-litre (3- to 4-pint) ovenproof casserole

Preheat the oven to 180°C, 350°F, gas mark 4.

Cut the chicken pieces in half. Heat the oil and butter or margarine in a large frying pan and then quickly fry the chicken joints to brown the outside. Remove the joints and keep on a plate.

Peel and slice the onions, crush the garlic with a little salt, and fry both until soft and golden. Wipe and slice the mushrooms; wipe and cut the aubergine into pieces about the size of a walnut. Add to the pan and fry gently for a few minutes. Remove the seeds and white pith from the pepper, slice the flesh and add to the pan for 1 minute.

Spread the vegetable mixture on the base of the casserole, lay the sliced tomatoes on top and place the chicken joints over the vegetables. Mix together the stock and cider, add the flour to the pan and stir in the liquid. Bring to the boil, stirring to thicken, season to taste and pour over the casserole.

Cover the dish and bake on the centre shelf of the preheated oven for 1 hour until the chicken and vegetables are tender. Serve with creamed potatoes.

Note: Frozen onions, mushrooms and peppers may be used in this casserole.

* Suitable for freezing.

Kidneys Turbigo

Serves 3

500 g	lamb's kidneys	1 lb
100 g	chipolata sausages	4 oz
50 g	bacon	2 oz
25 g	butter or margarine	1 oz
100 g	baby onions	4 oz
200 ml	boiling water	⅓ pint
	half a stock cube	
50 g	button mushrooms	2 oz

100 g	baby tomatoes	4 oz
1 tbsp	flour	1 tbsp
2 tbsps	sherry	2 tbsps
1	bay leaf	1
	bunch of chopped parsley	
	or	
½ level tsp	dried parsley	½ level tsp
	salt and pepper	

a large frying pan

Using a pair of scissors, remove the skins from the kidneys, cut in half and carefully cut out the hard, white centre. Prick the sausages. Remove the rind and any bone from the bacon and chop it into cubes. Melt the butter or margarine in the frying pan and add the sausages and bacon; sauté until brown, then remove from the frying pan onto a warm plate.

Remove the roots and shoots of the baby onions, wash and drop them into the boiling water for 1 minute. Remove the onions from the water and peel off their brown skins. Now add the half stock cube to the onion water.

Add the button mushrooms, onions and whole baby tomatoes to the frying pan and fry gently until tender. Remove from the pan and lay on a warm plate.

Finally sauté the kidneys until they are almost cooked through. Remove from the pan and add the flour to the pan juices, cook until thick and then stir in the stock and the sherry. When the sauce has thickened, add the bay leaf, parsley and seasoning and return the kidneys and other ingredients to the pan. Stir gently, cover the pan and simmer over a low heat for about 15 minutes.

Serve with buttered new potatoes or mashed potatoes to soak up the beautiful thick gravy.

Note: Frozen onions and mushrooms may be used in place of the fresh.

* Suitable for freezing.

Veal and Onion Pie

Serves 4–5

100 g	puff pastry (p. 336)	4 oz
½–¾ kg	pie veal	1½ lb
25 g	plain flour	1 oz
1 level tsp	salt	1 level tsp
	freshly ground pepper	
250 g	onions	8 oz
100 g	button mushrooms	4 oz
300 ml	chicken stock	½ pint
	egg glaze	

a 1½-litre (2½-pint) pie dish

Preheat the oven to 220°C, 425°F, gas mark 7.

Make the pastry and leave to rest. Trim the meat, cutting off any excess fat, and then cut it into 3-cm (1-inch) cubes. Place in a bowl with the flour, salt and pepper and toss together to coat the meat.

Lay half the meat in the base of the pie dish and place a pie funnel or blackbird in the centre. Peel the onions, slice very thinly and scatter them over the meat. Wipe and slice the mushrooms very thinly, add to the dish, cover with the remaining meat and pour the stock over the top.

Roll out the pastry on a floured surface 3 cm (1 inch) bigger than the top of the pie dish. Cut off a 3-cm (1-inch) border, damp the edge of the dish and lay the 3-cm (1-inch) strip of pastry on the edge. Damp the pastry border, lay the pastry lid on top, seal the edges well and knock up and flute them.

Any pastry scraps can be rolled out and cut to make pastry leaves to decorate the top. Make an airhole in the centre of the pastry if you haven't used a pie funnel and brush the top with the egg glaze. Leave to rest for 15 minutes before baking on the centre shelf of the preheated oven for 20 minutes. Reduce the heat to 150°C, 300°F, gas mark 2, and bake for a further 1 hour 40 minutes. If the pastry is getting too brown during cooking, cover it lightly with a piece of foil.

Note: Frozen sliced onions and mushrooms may be used in this pie.

* Suitable for freezing.

Bacon and Onion Cheese Flan

Serves 4–5

100 g	shortcrust pastry (p. 334)	4 oz
175 g	onions	6 oz
100 g	bacon scraps	4 oz
	knob of margarine	
175 g	Cheddar cheese	6 oz
2	large eggs	2
300 ml	milk	½ pint
	salt and pepper	

a 20-cm (8-inch) plain flan ring on a baking sheet

Preheat the oven to 190°C, 375°F, gas mark 5.

Make the shortcrust pastry, roll it out on a lightly floured surface and line the flan ring. Trim the top edge.

Peel and slice the onions; remove the rind and any bone from the bacon and cut it into 3-cm (1-inch) pieces. Melt the margarine in a pan and fry the onion slices and bacon for a few minutes until soft and lightly browned. Leave to cool a little before spreading over the base of the flan.

Grate the cheese into the flan case. Break the eggs into a measuring jug, add the milk to make up to 450 ml (¾ pint), beat well and season with salt and pepper. Pour into the flan, then bake on the shelf above the centre of the preheated oven for 35 to 40 minutes. Serve either hot or cold.

Note: Frozen sliced onions may be used in this flan.

* Suitable for freezing.

Stuffed Onions

Serves 4

4	medium onions – each weighing about 175 g (6 oz)	4
125 g	liver	4 oz

25 g	fresh breadcrumbs	1 oz
1	large egg	1
1 level tsp	fresh sage, finely chopped	1 level tsp
	salt and freshly ground	
	pepper	
25 g	butter or margarine	1 oz
300 ml	tomato sauce (p. 185)	½ pint

a shallow ovenproof dish

Preheat the oven to 180°C, 350°F, gas mark 4.

Peel the onions and leave them whole. Steam them for ¾ to 1 hour until tender but still whole. Cool slightly then cut off the tops and, using a spoon, scoop out the centres leaving a shell of about 1 cm (½ inch) thick. Lay the onions on an ovenproof dish.

Chop up half the onion which has been scooped out of the centres and put in a bowl (use the remaining onion for the tomato sauce). Chop up the liver, and stir into the chopped onion with the breadcrumbs, egg, chopped sage, salt and pepper. Mix well, then divide between the four onions, filling them as full as possible. Put a knob of butter on top of each, cover the dish with foil and bake on the shelf above centre of the preheated oven for about 50 minutes to 1 hour, depending on the size of the onions.

Make the tomato sauce whilst the onions are baking. Serve the cooked onions with a little tomato sauce poured over each and accompany with a potato dish.

* Suitable for freezing – cooked and with the sauce poured over.

Sage and Onion Stuffing

500 g	onions	1 lb
150 ml	water	¼ pint
8	fresh sage leaves	8
175 g	fresh white breadcrumbs	6 oz
25 g	shredded suet	1 oz
½ level tsp	salt	½ level tsp
	freshly ground pepper	

Peel and quarter the onions and put in a saucepan with the water. Bring to the boil and simmer for about 10 minutes. Drain, reserving the onion water, and allow the onions to cool slightly before chopping them finely with the sage leaves. Put in a bowl and mix in the breadcrumbs, suet, salt and pepper. Use a little of the onion water to bind the ingredients together.

Use to stuff a goose or piece of pork, or cook the stuffing on its own in an ovenproof dish alongside the poultry or joint.

Note: Frozen onions may be used in this recipe.

* Poultry or meat already filled with sage and onion stuffing may be deep frozen.

The following recipes also include onions:

Carrot and lentil soup (p. 55)
Cauliflower vichyssoise (p. 62)
Tomato soup (p. 174)
Piquant marrow hors d'œuvre (p. 102)
French provincial tart (p. 176)
Autumn stew (p. 56)
Braised beef (p. 57)
Baked pork and cauliflower (p. 63)
Chicken in orange and mushroom sauce (p. 111)
Minted lamb kebabs (p. 112)
Spanish chicken and rice (p. 138)
Baked lamb chops (p. 145)
Vegetable curry (p. 169)
Country lamb and tomato (p. 177)
Gardener's pizzas (p. 178)
Pork and gooseberry casserole (p. 237)
Baked parsnips and onions (p. 132)
Worcestershire beans (p. 88)
Pois à la française (p. 141)
Peas with bacon and onion (p. 141)
Rabbit and damson stew with dumplings (p. 258)
Stovies (p. 147)
Coleslaw (p. 50)
Mushroom stuffing (p. 114)
Beetroot chutney (p. 26)
Runner bean chutney (p. 154)
Cucumber relish (p. 83)
Piccalilli (p. 88)
Red tomato relish (p. 182)

Green tomato chutney (p. 183)
Apple and date chutney (p. 208)
Bramble chutney (p. 217)
Gooseberry chutney (p. 244)
Pear chutney (p. 255)
Rhubarb chutney (p. 289)
Pickled onions (p. 329)
Mixed pickle (p. 330)
Onion and apple pickle (p. 330)

Try substituting onions for leeks in chicken and leek pie (p. 94).

17 Parsnips

Introduction

Parsnips provide one of the most useful crops as they remain in the soil throughout the winter and are only pulled when required for use.

Everyone agrees that parsnips benefit from being exposed to frost, so try to leave the crop until after a good frost before sampling them.

Parsnips require a deeply dug soil to accommodate their long roots, but some soils, for instance heavy clay, make this difficult. To overcome this problem, use a dibber to make deep holes, fill with a fine soil, then sow three seeds about 3 cm (1 inch) deep in each hole and cover with more fine soil. Prick out the two weakest seedlings, leaving the strongest to survive. It is very important not to manure the soil directly before you plant your parsnips as this will cause the roots to become forked.

Preparation and cooking

There was a time when parsnips had lost favour in this country, though we have heard that they were used in many different ways during the war, even disguised as mashed bananas. Recently parsnips have come back into fashion again – they are particularly delicious roasted around the Sunday joint.

To prepare, top and tail, then peel off the skins. Leave whole or halve lengthwise or cut into rings or dice.

To boil: Prepare as above, place in a pan of cold salted water, bring to the boil and cook for 15 to 25 minutes, depending on size. Drain well.

To steam: Place the prepared parsnips in a steamer over a pan of boiling water, cover and cook for 30 to 40 minutes, depending on size.

Braise in stock for 30 to 40 minutes (300 ml/½ pint stock for every 500 g/1 lb parsnips). Drain, then reduce the stock by rapid boiling and pour over the parsnips.

To bake: See baked parsnips and onions (p. 132). Thinly slice, parboil for 2 minutes, then bake for 20 minutes.

To roast: Prepare as above, leave whole and parboil 2 to 3 minutes. Drain, then roast in fat or around the Sunday joint for 45 minutes.

To sauté: Parboil the prepared parsnips for 10 minutes, drain and sauté in butter for 5 to 10 minutes.

To deep fry: Cut the prepared parsnips into thin slivers, leave plain or coat in flour, and deep fry for 5 to 10 minutes. Alternatively, parboil 10 minutes, coat in fritter batter (p. 343), then deep fry 4 to 5 minutes.

Serving suggestions: The boiled or steamed parsnips can be tossed in butter and fresh chopped parsley, mashed with butter and seasoned well with freshly ground pepper, or coated in a cheese sauce (p. 340).

How to deal with a glut

1. Freezing: Prepare as above and slice or dice. Blanch for 3 minutes, chill, drain and pack into polythene bags or wax or foil containers. Seal, label and freeze. Storage time: 9 to 12 months.

2. Storing: Store in the ground during the winter, but lift in March or earlier if severe weather is predicted. Cut off the tops and store in a cool shed.

There are no parsnip preserves, but they do make a good wine.

Eastern Parsnip Soup

Serves 6

1 kg	parsnips	2 lb
125 g	onion	4 oz
25 g	butter or margarine	1 oz
1 rounded tsp	curry paste	1 rounded tsp
250 g	tomatoes	8 oz
1¼ litres	chicken stock	2 pints
1	bay leaf	1
1 level tsp	salt	1 level tsp
	single cream or top of the milk	
	parsley	
	fried croûtons	

Peel and dice the parsnips, then peel and slice the onion, and fry them in the melted butter or margarine in a large saucepan for about 5 minutes until beginning to soften but not brown. Stir in the curry paste and cook for a minute.

Peel the tomatoes (see p. 172) and chop roughly. Add them to the pan with the stock, bay leaf and salt, bring to the boil, cover and simmer for 20 minutes.

Put the soup through a sieve, or liquidize in an electric blender and then put through a sieve. Return to the pan and heat through.

To serve, garnish with a swirl of cream and chopped parsley and serve with fried croûtons of bread.

Bacon and Parsnip Mornay

Serves 4

500 g	parsnips	1 lb
300 ml	milk infused with a small onion, a small carrot, bay leaf, 4 peppercorns, a sprig each of parsley and thyme, a pinch of powdered mace	½ pint
1 level tbsp	butter or margarine	1 level tbsp
2 level tbsps	flour	2 level tbsps
50 g	cheese, grated	2 oz
	salt and pepper	
4	rashers of streaky bacon	4

4 individual ramekins or serving dishes, ovenproof

Peel and dice the parsnips, place in a saucepan of cold salted water and bring to the boil. Cook for 15 minutes until tender and then drain, reserving some of the parsnip water for the sauce.

While the parsnips are cooking, infuse the milk with the vegetables and herbs. Bring it slowly almost to the boil, remove from the heat and leave to infuse.

Melt the butter or margarine in a saucepan, add the flour and cook for 1 minute. Remove from the heat, strain the milk from the vegetables and herbs and slowly add to the roux, stirring constantly. Return the pan to the heat and, still stirring, bring to the boil.

Cook for 2 minutes, then add the grated cheese and the seasonings.

If the sauce is too thick, add some of the parsnip water, although the sauce should be fairly thick.

Put the cooked parsnips through a sieve and mix into the mornay sauce. Divide the mixture among the four individual serving dishes.

Remove the rinds and any bone from the bacon and grill until almost cooked. Dice 1 slice of bacon onto the top of each dish and place under the grill to brown. Serve hot as an hors d'œuvre.

Notes: This is a surprising dish which usually has everyone guessing as to its contents. It is also a very economical starter.

Frozen diced parsnips may be used in place of the fresh.

* Suitable for freezing.

Parsnip and Apple Rolls

Serves 5–6

350 g	parsnips	12 oz
1	small onion	1
300 g	cooking apples	10 oz
25 g	butter	1 oz
	salt and pepper	
300 ml	cheese sauce (p. 340)	½ pint
5–6 slices	cooked ham	5–6 slices
	sprigs of fresh parsley	

a 1¼-litre (2-pint) ovenproof casserole or serving dish

Peel and dice the parsnips and the onion; peel, core and quarter the apples and cut into dice. Melt the butter in a saucepan and add the onion; sauté until soft and lightly golden. Add the diced parsnips and apples and the seasonings, cover and sauté gently for 15 minutes, stirring occasionally, then remove from the heat.

Meanwhile prepare the cheese sauce. Lay out a slice of ham for each person and divide the parsnip and apple stuffing amongst the slices. Roll up the ham tightly and lay each stuffed roll in the casserole dish. Finally, pour the cheese sauce over the top and sprinkle with extra grated cheese. Place the dish under a hot grill and leave until the top is nicely browned. Serve hot, decorated with sprigs of parsley.

Note: Frozen diced parsnips and frozen chopped onions may be used to make these rolls.

* Suitable for freezing.

Baked Parsnips and Onions

Serves 4

500 g	parsnips	1 lb
250 g	onions	8 oz
25 g	butter or margarine	1 oz
25–50 g	cheese, grated	1–2 oz

a 1-litre (1½- to 2-pint) ovenproof dish

Preheat the oven to 190°C, 375°F, gas mark 5.

Top and tail the parsnips, then peel and thinly slice them. Place in a saucepan of cold salted water, bring to the boil, cook for 2 minutes and drain well.

Peel and thinly slice the onions. Heat the butter or margarine in a saucepan and fry the onions until they are soft and golden – about 8 minutes.

Layer the parsnips and onions in the greased dish and sprinkle the top with grated cheese. Bake on the centre shelf of the preheated oven for about 20 minutes until the top is nicely browned.

Serve as a vegetable accompaniment, e.g. with roast chicken or lamb.

Note: Frozen sliced parsnips and onions may be used in this dish.

Parsnips à la Polonaise

Serves 4

500 g	parsnips	1 lb
1	large egg, hard-boiled	1
1 level dsp	chopped fresh parsley	1 level dsp
25 g	butter	1 oz
25 g	fresh white breadcrumbs	1 oz
	salt and freshly ground pepper	

Prepare the parsnips, cut into strips 5 cm by 3 cm (2 inches by 1 inch) and steam or boil until tender. Keep warm.

Meanwhile, separate the hard-boiled egg yolk and white and put them separately through a sieve. Mix the sieved egg yolk with the chopped parsley.

In a small frying pan, heat the butter and fry the breadcrumbs until browned and crisp. Remove from the heat and stir in the sieved egg white and season well with salt and pepper.

To serve, gently mix the egg yolk mixture with the cooked parsnips and turn into a warm serving dish. Scatter the egg white and bread-crumb mixture over the top and serve at once as a vegetable accom-paniment.

Note: Frozen parsnips cut into strips may be used in this recipe.

Parsnips au Gratin

Serves 4

500 g	parsnips	1 lb
50 g	cheese, finely grated	2 oz
50 g	fresh breadcrumbs	2 oz
	salt	
	paprika	

Prepare the parsnips and cut into 1-cm (½-inch) wide strips about 10 cm (4 inches) long. Steam or boil for 20 or 10 minutes, respectively, until tender, drain and place in a shallow ovenproof dish.

Mix together the grated cheese, breadcrumbs, salt and paprika and sprinkle over the parsnips. Place under a hot grill for 4 to 5 minutes until the top is golden brown. Serve hot as a vegetable accompaniment.

Note: Frozen parsnips may be used.

The recipe for autumn stew (p. 56) also includes parsnips.

18 Peas

Introduction

Fresh peas are a real luxury in an era dominated by frozen, dried and
tinned peas. None of these can compete with the sweet flavour of
freshly picked, home-grown peas.

All varieties – the round-seeded, wrinkle-seeded or marrowfat peas
and the mangetout, which is eaten whole, pod and all – thrive on a
well-manured soil.

Peas have very brittle stems which snap easily and even the dwarf
varieties, which are such a benefit to the smaller garden, require some
support – usually sticks, twigs or special pea netting. It is also wise to
protect seedlings from greedy birds with netting or twigs.

Pick the pods before they become taut with over-large peas, otherwise
you will have 'bullet' peas which are hard and unpleasant to eat, even
after cooking.

Preparation and cooking

Home-grown peas are simply delicious eaten raw. When cooked their
flavour is so good that, apart from the traditional addition of a few mint
leaves, they hardly need any further accompaniment.

Once removed from their pods, garden-grown peas do not need
washing unless you find any little worms inside the pods. Never soak
the peas in water for any length of time as they lose some of their
flavour and vitamins.

To boil: Bring a pan of salted water to the boil, add a sprig of mint
(optional) and the podded peas, cover and cook for 10 to 20 minutes.
Drain well and discard the mint.

To steam: Place the peas in a steamer over a pan of boiling water,
cover and cook for 15–25 minutes.

To braise: See *pois à la française* (p. 141); braise with butter, lettuce,
spring onions and mint leaves, for 15 to 20 minutes. See also peas with
bacon and onions (p. 141).

Serving suggestions: The boiled or steamed peas can be tossed in butter and sprinkled with a little fresh chopped mint (optional).

How to deal with a glut

1. Freezing: Pod the peas, blanch for 1½ minutes, chill, drain and pack into polythene bags or wax containers. Storage time: 9 to 12 months. Also freeze pea and ham soup (below), summer pea soup (p. 136) and pea tartlets (p. 139).

2. Storing: Dry in bunches and store in a cool airy place.

Pea and Ham Soup

Serves 4–6

1 kg	peas in their pods, to give 450–500g (1 lb) peas when podded	2¼ lb
1	medium onion	1
1¼ litres	stock (made with young pea pods)	2 pints
½–1 kg	knuckle or collar of gammon or bacon	1–2 lb
	pepper	
	a few mint leaves	
	a sprig of parsley	
1	bay leaf	1
	croûtons	

Pod the peas and wash them only if necessary. Place them in a large saucepan. Peel and chop the onion and add to the pan with the stock strained from the pea pods. (*Note:* Use only the young pods to make the stock.)

Remove any excess fat from the gammon or bacon joint and add it to the pan with the pepper, mint leaves, parsley and bay leaf. (Remember that no extra salt should be needed as the gammon or bacon makes the soup salty enough.) Cover the saucepan and simmer for 2 hours.

Remove the pan from the heat and take out of the soup the gammon or bacon joint, the bay and mint leaves and the sprig of parsley. Cut off 50 g (2 oz) of the meat from the joint and chop it finely. Reserve to add to the soup after it has been puréed. Keep the rest of the meat for sandwiches or for salads.

Purée the pea soup through a fine sieve or first blend it in a liquidizer and then pass it through a sieve – this gives a smoother, less grainy texture. Finally, stir in the chopped gammon or bacon, reheat and serve with a bowl of fried croûtons to garnish and, if desired, a tablespoon of cream in the centre of each bowl with a sprinkling of finely chopped fresh mint on top.

Note: Frozen peas may be used to make this soup.

* Suitable for freezing.

Summer Pea Soup

Serves 5

1 kg	peas in their pods, to give about 450–500 g (1 lb) peas when podded	2¼ lb
1	medium potato	1
½	large onion	½
25 g	butter or margarine	1 oz
1 bunch	watercress	1 bunch
750 ml	chicken stock	1¼ pints
1 level tsp	salt	1 level tsp
	freshly ground pepper	
300 ml	milk	½ pint
½	lemon, juice only	½
	top of the milk or single cream	
	a few sprigs of watercress	

Pod the peas and wash them only if necessary; peel and dice the potato; peel and roughly chop the onion.

Heat the butter or margarine in a large saucepan, then add the peas, diced potato and onion. Toss in the butter for 2 minutes, then wash the watercress, twist off and discard the stalks, before adding to the pan. Cook for a further 5 minutes. Pour on the stock, stir in the salt and pepper, cover the pan and bring to the boil. Simmer gently for about 25 minutes until the peas are tender.

Press the soup through a sieve twice or purée in a liquidizer and then put through a sieve. This will give a smoother texture to the soup. Stir in the milk and the lemon juice, check for seasoning and leave to chill.

This thick soup should be served well chilled with a swirl of top of the milk or single cream in the centre and a sprig of watercress.

Note: Frozen peas may be used to make this soup.

* Suitable for freezing.

Smoked Cod Gougère

Serves 5

1 quantity	choux pastry (p. 338)	1 quantity

For the filling

250 g	smoked cod	8 oz
300 ml	milk	½ pint
4	peppercorns	4
1	blade of mace	1
1	bay leaf	1
25 g	margarine	1 oz
25 g	plain flour	1 oz
500 g	peas in their pods, to give 175–250 g (6–8 oz) peas when podded	1 lb
250 g	tomatoes	8 oz
1	egg, hard-boiled	1

a greased baking sheet

Preheat the oven to 200°C, 400°F, gas mark 6.

Make the choux pastry and spoon the mixture onto the baking sheet in an 18-cm (7-inch) ring; spread a little mixture over the centre of the ring. Bake on the shelf above the centre of the preheated oven for 25 minutes. When cooked, lift the choux ring onto a warm, flat serving dish.

Meanwhile, place the fish in a saucepan with the milk, peppercorns, mace and bay leaf, cover and poach for 15 minutes until the fish is cooked. Strain off the liquid into a measuring jug and make up to 300 ml (½ pint) with water if necessary.

Remove any skin and bones from the fish and then flake it onto a plate. Heat the margarine in a medium-sized saucepan, add the flour and cook for 1 minute. Remove the pan from the heat, gradually stir in the strained milk, return to the heat and, stirring constantly, cook for 2 minutes. Stir in the flaked fish.

Pod the peas and boil or steam until tender; drain and stir into the sauce.

Chop the hard-boiled egg; reserve one tomato for decoration and roughly chop the rest. Lightly stir the chopped egg and tomato into the fish sauce mixture, check for seasoning and add salt and pepper if necessary.

Spoon the mixture into the centre of the warm choux ring. Cut the remaining tomato into eight wedges and place round the edge of the filling to decorate. Serve immediately with creamed potatoes.

Note: This dish can also be made with smoked haddock. Frozen peas may be used instead of fresh peas.

Spanish Chicken and Rice

Serves 5–6

1½ kg	boiling fowl	3–3½ lb
	a sprig each of parsley and thyme	
1	bay leaf	1
6	peppercorns	6
1 level tsp	salt	1 level tsp
250 g	onions	8 oz
250 g	tomatoes	8 oz
1	green pepper	1
¾ kg	peas in their pods, to give 300–350 g (10–12 oz) shelled peas	1½ lb
50 g	butter or margarine	2 oz
300 g	long-grain rice	10 oz
	salt and pepper	
175 g	peeled prawns	6 oz

a 1¾- to 2¼-litre (3- to 4-pint) ovenproof casserole or dish

Preheat the oven to 190°C, 375°F, gas mark 5.

Remove the giblets from the chicken, wash the carcass and put both in a large saucepan with the parsley, thyme, bay leaf, peppercorns and salt. Pour over enough cold water to cover the bird. Cover the pan, bring to the boil and simmer gently for about 1¼ to 1½ hours until the chicken is tender. Put the chicken onto a plate, leave to cool slightly and then remove all the meat from the bones, cutting it into bite-sized pieces. Strain the chicken stock and reserve.

Meanwhile prepare the vegetables: Peel and finely chop the onions; peel the tomatoes (see p. 172) and cut them into quarters; halve the green pepper, remove the seeds and white pith and slice the flesh into thin strips; pod the peas.

Heat the butter or margarine in a large frying pan, add the onions and sauté for a few minutes over a gentle heat until they are soft and golden. Add the quartered tomatoes, the strips of pepper, the peas and the long-grain rice and fry for a further 5 minutes, turning frequently.

Turn all the vegetables and rice into the casserole, add the chicken, salt and pepper, then pour over them 1 litre (1¾ pints) of the reserved chicken stock. Cover the casserole and cook on the centre shelf of the preheated oven for 30 minutes.

Remove the dish from the oven, gently stir in the peeled prawns and, if the casserole is becoming too dry, add a little more chicken stock. Return to the oven for a further 15 to 20 minutes by which time the rice should be cooked and the stock will have evaporated. Serve hot with French or runner beans.

Note: Frozen peas may be used in this recipe. Also, French or runner beans can be substituted for the peas.

* Suitable for freezing.

Pea Tartlets

Makes 12

For the pastry

100 g	plain flour	4 oz
	pinch of salt	
50 g	butter or margarine	2 oz
25 g	cheese, finely grated	1 oz

For the filling

100 g	cooked chicken	4 oz
500 g	peas in their pods, to give about 175 g (6 oz) peas when podded	1 lb
1	large egg milk salt and pepper	1

a tray of 12 patty cases

Preheat the oven to 200°C, 400°F, gas mark 6.

Sift the flour and salt into a bowl. Rub in the butter or margarine until the mixture resembles fine breadcrumbs. Stir in the finely grated cheese and add sufficient cold water to make a firm dough. Leave in a cool place for 20 minutes.

Roll out the pastry on a lightly floured surface. Using a round pastry cutter or the rim of a tumbler, cut out twelve rounds of pastry to line the patty cases.

Finely dice the cooked chicken and divide it evenly between the twelve patty cases.

Parboil the podded peas for 5 minutes in a saucepan of boiling salted water. Drain and divide the peas evenly between the patty cases.

Place the egg in a measuring jug and add sufficient milk to make the mixture up to 150 ml (¼ pint). Season with salt and pepper and pour the egg mixture into the tarts.

Bake on the centre shelf of the preheated oven for 10 minutes, then reduce the temperature to 180°C, 350°F, gas mark 4, and bake for a further 10 minutes, by which time the pastry will have become lightly browned and the egg mixture will have set. Serve hot with a green salad and minted new potatoes.

Note: Frozen peas may be used in this recipe.

* Suitable for freezing.

Pois à la Française

Serves 3–4

¾ kg	peas in their pods, to give about 300–350 g (10–12 oz) peas when podded	1½ lb
1	small lettuce	1
3	spring onions	3
25 g	butter	1 oz
4	mint leaves	4
	knob of butter	

Pod the peas; wash and finely shred the lettuce; trim and slice the spring onions thinly. Heat the 25 g (1 oz) butter in a saucepan and add the peas, lettuce and sliced onions. Finely chop the mint leaves and add to the pan, cover and simmer over a very low heat for 15 to 20 minutes until the peas are tender. Remove from the heat, add the knob of butter and stir gently to absorb it. Serve hot as a vegetable accompaniment.

Note: Frozen peas may be used in this recipe.

Peas with Bacon and Onions

Serves 3–4

1 kg	peas in their pods, to give 450–500 g (1 lb) peas when podded	2¼ lb
50 g	streaky bacon	2 oz
1	small onion or a few baby onions	1
	knob of butter	
	salt and pepper	

Pod the peas and only wash them if necessary. Remove any rind and bone from the bacon and dice it. Peel and finely chop the whole onion, or peel and top and tail the baby onions but leave them whole. Heat the butter in a saucepan and add the diced bacon and the onions. Cook over a medium heat for 2 to 3 minutes, then add the peas, cover the pan and reduce to a low heat. Simmer the peas in the bacon and butter juices for 15 to 20 minutes until they are tender, stirring occasionally to ensure they are not browning.

To serve, check for seasoning, remembering that the bacon will make the peas salty to taste. Spoon into a warm serving dish and serve as a vegetable accompaniment.

Note: Frozen peas and baby onions may be used in this recipe.

Pea and Rice Salad

Serves 6–8

¾ kg	peas in their pods, to give 300–350 g (10–12 oz) shelled peas	1½ lb
75 g	long-grain rice	3 oz
3	fresh mint leaves	3
1	small carrot	1
1	small onion	1
	knob of butter or margarine	
½ level tsp	curry powder	½ level tsp
	salt and pepper	

Pod the peas and only wash them if necessary. Place them in a saucepan of boiling salted water with the rice and the mint leaves. Cover the pan and cook for about 15 minutes until the peas and the rice are cooked. Drain thoroughly, removing the mint leaves.

Scrape the carrot and grate it. Peel and finely chop the onion. Heat the butter or margarine in a frying pan, add the curry powder, stir to mix and then add the onion and carrot. Sauté gently for 5 minutes, then add the drained rice and peas and stir well to combine the mixture. Sauté for a further 2 minutes, check for seasoning, then place in a serving bowl.

This dish can be served either hot or cold as a salad and can be decorated with four small mint leaves in the centre of the bowl.

Note: Frozen peas may be used in this dish.

19 Potatoes

Introduction

Potatoes are the staple diet of the British, yet they were largely taken for granted and often treated with little respect until the winter rains and summer drought of 1975/6 made everyone realize how dependent they were on the humble potato.

For the home gardener, the potato will help to clear the soil, especially newly cultivated ground, and will put back vital elements into the earth.

Buy your seed potatoes at the end of January or the beginning of February and place them in egg boxes on a bright windowsill to encourage green shoots to develop from the potato 'eyes'.

Plant out in March/April in fertilized trenches and, when the tops show through the soil, start to earth up around the plants to protect the leaves from frosts. This will also ensure that the potatoes below do not turn green with exposure to light and can help protect the crop from blight. After the flowers have died you may start to lift your crop.

For the smaller garden the 'early' crop is best as main-crop potatoes take up more space and take longer to mature.

Preparation and cooking

The potato must be the most versatile of all vegetables – there isn't much you cannot do with it – from soups and stews to pastry and scones. But it seems a shame not to take care in cooking potatoes, especially if you have gone to the trouble of growing them yourself – so follow these points:

1. Use a potato peeler for old potatoes as this saves potato and the valuable layer of vitamins under the skin – or, if possible, cook them in their skins and peel later. New potatoes should not be peeled, but scrubbed and cooked in their skins.

2. Use potatoes of even size or cut to an even size so that they are all cooked after the same length of time.

3. Do not boil potatoes over a high heat.

4. Drain carefully when cooked and return to the pan to dry thoroughly over a gentle heat.

To boil: Put the prepared potatoes in a saucepan of cold salted water, cover, bring to the boil and cook for 15 to 20 minutes. Drain well.

To steam: Place prepared potatoes in a steamer over a pan of boiling water, cover and cook for 30 to 35 minutes.

To braise: See stovies (p. 147); braise with onions, dripping and water over a low heat for 1 to 1½ hours.

To bake: Scrub the potatoes and make a cross on the skins or prick them with a fork to stop them bursting. Bake in their skins for 1 to 1½ hours. To make the jackets crispy, rub a little salt and flour into the skins. To keep the skins soft, wrap the potatoes individually in pieces of foil. Try serving the baked potatoes the Australian way with sour cream and chives mashed into the potato flesh. See also potato cheese dish (p. 146), fluffy baked potatoes (p. 149), *pommes Anna* (p. 148).

To roast: Parboil peeled potatoes for 5 minutes, drain well, then roast in a pan with fat or around the Sunday joint for 45 minutes to 1 hour.

To sauté: Peel the potatoes, parboil 10 minutes (or boil in their jackets for 10 minutes then remove the skins), cut into ½-cm (¼-inch) slices or dice, then sauté in lard or butter for 6 to 8 minutes until brown on all sides. Also sauté diced potatoes with fresh chopped parsley sprinkled over them. See also almond potato cakes (p. 149).

To deep fry: (chips or *pommes frites*): Peel the potatoes and cut into 5-cm (2-inch) strips, deep fry in hot fat for about 4 to 6 minutes. To produce the best chips, fry first in medium hot fat for 4 minutes, drain, then cook for a further 2 to 3 minutes in very hot fat. Game chips, wafer-thin, round slices of potato, are deep fried once for 2 to 3 minutes only. To make 'mock roast' potatoes, parboil small whole potatoes or halved larger potatoes for 10 minutes, drain and then deep fry in hot fat for 4 to 5 minutes until browned all over. Drain and serve hot.

Serving suggestions: Boiled potatoes may be mashed with butter, milk or cream or mixed with grated cheese when mashed. New potatoes can be tossed in butter and sprinkled with chopped fresh parsley or mint.

How to deal with a glut

1. *Freezing:* New potatoes do not freeze well, as they lose their distinctive texture. Old potatoes are best frozen as chips or roasted.

For chips, peel and cut into 5-cm (2-inch) strips, blanch in medium hot fat for 4 minutes, drain on kitchen paper and leave to get cold. Pack into polythene bags or plastic containers, e.g. old ice-cream containers. Storage time: 9 to 12 months. Also freeze leek and potato soup (vichyssoise) (p. 91), cheese and potato scones (p. 150).

2. *Storing:* Potatoes store well and easily – first in the ground until October/November, then lifted and stored in sacks, potato bags or boxes in a dark, cool place. If they are not stored in the dark the potatoes will start to turn green and be inedible.

Baked Lamb Chops

Serves 4

6–8	small lamb chops	6–8
1 dsp	lard	1 dsp
1	large onion	1
250 g	tomatoes	8 oz
	salt and pepper	
	a good pinch of thyme	
150 ml	stock	¼ pint
500 g	potatoes	1 lb
	a little melted butter	

a shallow 1¾- to 2¼-litre (3- to 4-pint) ovenproof casserole

Preheat the oven to 180°C, 350°F, gas mark 4.

Wipe the chops and remove any excess fat and bone. Place them in the base of the casserole dish.

Melt the lard in a frying pan. Peel and thinly slice the onion and fry in the fat for a few minutes until softened, but do not brown. Place the onion over the chops.

Peel (see p. 172) and slice the tomatoes, lay them over the onion, and season with salt, pepper and thyme. Pour the stock into the casserole.

Peel the potatoes, slice them very thinly and lay on top of the dish, overlapping at the edges. Brush the potatoes with melted butter and season with salt and pepper.

Bake on the shelf above the centre of the preheated oven for about 1½ hours until the chops are cooked and the potatoes are crispy on top.

Potato Cheese Dish

Serves 2–3

500 g	potatoes	1 lb
300 ml	milk infused with 1 bay leaf, 6 peppercorns, a pinch of mace, a sprig each of thyme and parsley	a good ½ pint (12 fl oz)
1	small onion	1
25 g	streaky bacon	1 oz
15g	butter or margarine	½ oz
2 level tbsps	flour	2 level tbsps
75 g	cheese, grated	3 oz
	salt and pepper	

a 1¼-litre (2-pint) ovenproof casserole or dish

Preheat the oven to 190°C, 375°F, gas mark 5.

Peel the potatoes, slice them very thinly and place in a bowl of cold water.

Put the milk in a saucepan with the bay leaf, peppercorns, mace, thyme and parsley, and bring very slowly to the boil. Remove from the heat and leave to infuse.

Drain the potatoes and dry them well on a clean tea towel. Peel and finely chop the onion. Remove the rind and any bone from the bacon and dice. Melt the butter or margarine in a saucepan, add the onion and diced bacon and cook for 2 to 3 minutes until the onion is softened, but not browned. Add the flour and cook for a further minute. Remove the pan from the heat.

Strain the milk and slowly pour into the saucepan with the onion and bacon mixture, stirring constantly. Still stirring, return to the heat, bring the sauce to the boil and add 50 g (2 oz) grated cheese and the seasonings. Add the sliced potatoes and gently stir them into the sauce to coat them.

Grease the casserole or ovenproof dish and pile in the potato mixture. Sprinkle the top with 25 g (1 oz) grated cheese. Bake, uncovered, on the centre shelf of the preheated oven for about 45 minutes until the potatoes are tender (test with a skewer) and the top nicely browned.

* Suitable for freezing.

New Potatoes in Mustard Dressing

Serves 4

¾ kg	new potatoes	1½ lb

For the dressing

2 level tbsps	plain flour	2 level tbsps
1 level tbsp	caster sugar	1 level tbsp
1 level tsp	salt	1 level tsp
1 level tbsp	made English mustard	1 level tbsp
	freshly ground pepper	
300 ml	milk	½ pint
1 dsp	olive oil	1 dsp
1	standard egg	1
4 tbsps	vinegar	4 tbsps

Scrub the potatoes and boil or steam for 15 to 30 minutes until tender.
Drain and keep hot.

Meanwhile, mix together the flour, sugar, salt, mustard and pepper
in a saucepan. Stir in the milk and then the oil. Lightly beat the egg and
mix it into the pan.

Place the pan over a gentle heat and, stirring constantly, bring slowly
to the boil. Cook for 2 to 3 minutes, stirring all the time. Remove from
the heat and gradually beat in the vinegar, a little at a time.

Put the potatoes in a dish, pour the mustard dressing over them and
serve with grilled or baked gammon.

Note: The mustard dressing is equally delicious served cold as a
salad dressing. To store, double the quantity of ingredients and, when
cooled, pour into clean, warm, dry jars. Cover, label and store for up to
1 month in the refrigerator.

Stovies

Serves 2–3

500 g	potatoes	1 lb
½	large onion	½
25 g	beef dripping	1 oz

| 150 ml | water | ¼ pint |
| | salt and pepper | |

Peel and slice the potatoes, but not too thinly; peel and slice the onion. Heat the dripping in a saucepan, add the onion and sauté gently until soft but not browned.

Add the potatoes to the pan with the water, salt and pepper; cover and cook over a very low heat for 1 to 1½ hours, by which time the potatoes should be cooked and the dish still moist.

During cooking, check to see that the potatoes have not stuck to the pan, but try to avoid stirring them around too much as they will start to break up.

Note: This is a traditional Scottish dish, always cooked on the top of the stove, hence the name.

Pommes Anna

Serves 4–6

¾ kg	large potatoes	1½ lb
50 g	butter	2 oz
	salt and pepper	

a 20-cm (8-inch) round cake tin or straight-sided ovenproof dish

Preheat the oven to 190°C, 375°F, gas mark 5.

Grease and base line the tin or dish. Peel the potatoes and either coarsely grate them or slice them very thinly into a bowl. Melt the butter in a pan and brush the lined base of the tin or dish. Place a layer of grated or sliced potato in the base of the dish, season with salt and pepper and pour over a little of the melted butter. Cover with another layer of potato, sprinkle with salt, pepper and a little melted butter. Continue until all the potato and butter is finished. Press down well and cover with a layer of greased paper. Bake on the centre shelf of the pre-heated oven for about 1¼ hours.

Turn out onto a warmed plate and serve cut into four or six portions.

Almond Potato Cakes

Makes 6

500 g	potatoes	1 lb
	knob of butter or margarine	
1–2 tbsps	milk or top of the milk	1–2 tbsps
	salt and pepper	
25 g	flaked almonds	1 oz
25 g	butter or margarine	1 oz

Peel the potatoes and place in a saucepan of cold salted water; cover and bring to the boil. Cook for about 15 to 20 minutes until the potatoes are soft. Drain thoroughly, return to the pan and add the butter and milk. Mash until smooth, season to taste and leave to cool slightly.

When cool enough to handle, divide the mixture into six equal portions and shape into round cakes. If the cakes are too sticky to handle, sprinkle over a little sifted flour.

Roughly chop the flaked almonds and roll the potato cakes in them to coat on both sides.

Heat the butter or margarine in a frying pan and, over a medium heat, sauté the cakes until both sides are golden brown. Serve hot with grilled chops, steak or chicken quarters and a side salad.

Note: Left-over mashed potatoes may be used in this recipe.

* Suitable for freezing.

Fluffy Baked Potatoes

Serves 4

4	large potatoes	4
	good knob of butter	
2 tbsps	cream or top of the milk	2 tbsps
	salt and pepper	
1	large egg, separated	1

Preheat the oven to 200°C, 400°F, gas mark 6,

Scrub the potatoes, mark with a cross and bake on the top shelf of the preheated oven for 1 to 1¼ hours, until tender.

Cut each potato in half lengthwise, carefully scoop out the flesh with a spoon into a warm bowl and reserve the potato jackets.

Add the butter and cream to the bowl and beat or mash until the potatoes are smooth and light. Season with salt and pepper. Beat in the egg yolk, then gently fold in the stiffly beaten egg white. Pile the potato mixture back into the jackets then return to the hot oven for a further 10 to 15 minutes until the potatoes are browned and fluffy on top. Serve immediately.

Cheese and Potato Scones

Makes about 12–14

400 g	potatoes	1 lb
25 g	margarine or butter	1 oz
	salt and pepper	
50 g	grated cheese	2 oz
100 g	self-raising flour	4 oz

a 7- to 8-cm (3-inch) plain cutter

Peel the potatoes and boil or steam until soft. Drain well, mash, add the butter or margarine and season to taste with salt and pepper. Leave to get cold.

When cold, stir in the grated cheese, then work in the flour to give a firm dough. Roll out the dough on a floured surface until it is fairly thin. Cut out 7- to 8-cm (3-inch) rounds, re-roll the trimmings and cut out more scones. Prick the scone surfaces with a fork.

Have ready a griddle or large frying pan which has been brushed with oil. Place over a medium heat and cook half the scones on it for about 3 minutes each side to lightly brown. Keep the first batch warm in a tea towel while the rest are cooking. Serve spread with butter, as a tea-time treat, or with a bacon and egg breakfast.

Note: Left-over mashed potatoes may be used to make the scones.

* Suitable for freezing.

Potato Pastry

Makes (225 g) 8 oz

150–175 g	potatoes	5–6 oz
100 g	plain flour	4 oz
½ level tsp	salt	½ level tsp
75 g	butter or margarine	3 oz
2 level tsps	baking powder	2 level tsps

Peel the potatoes and place in a saucepan of cold salted water; cover and cook for 15 minutes until soft. Drain thoroughly and then mash the potatoes until very smooth. Leave to get completely cold.

Sift the flour and salt into a bowl and, using the fingertips only, rub in the butter or margarine until the mixture resembles fine breadcrumbs. Stir in the baking powder.

Weigh 100 g (4 oz) of the cold mashed potato and mix this into the flour mixture. Add sufficient cold water to make a stiff dough, then leave to rest for 15 minutes before use.

Note: Left-over mashed potatoes may be used to make the pastry.

The following recipes also include potatoes:

Cauliflower vichyssoise (p. 62)
Leek and potato soup (p. 91)
Lettuce soup (p. 98)
Tomato soup (p. 174)
Turnip and chicken soup (p. 188)
Broccoli scallops (p. 35)
Stuffed marrow (p. 103)
New Zealand casserole (p. 93)
September lamb hotchpotch (p. 168)
Vegetable curry (p. 169)
Spinach croquettes (p. 162)
Swede patti-cakes (p. 170)

20 Runner Beans

Introduction

The runner bean is one of the most popular of garden-grown vegetables. As it grows to considerable height, it takes up relatively little space in the plot, but it does require the support of firm canes, sticks or netting which may be placed against a fence or wall.

The beans flourish on a well-manured soil and provide a good supply of vegetables from July until late autumn. A good tip to help the bean flowers to set into vegetables is to spray the flowers lightly with water when the sun is shining on them.

Once the plants have reached the top of the supports, the growing tips should be pinched off to restrict further growth and to encourage better development of the beans below.

Runner beans if left unpicked can grow to enormous lengths, but the longer and thicker they become the more likely they are to be tough and stringy.

The best test of readiness for eating is to snap the bean in two – it should be juicy and stringless.

Preparation and cooking

Runner beans should be topped, tailed, washed and then sliced into 5- to 7-cm (2- to 3-inch) lengths, about $\frac{1}{2}$ cm ($\frac{1}{4}$ inch) wide. The slices should be of similar length and thickness to ensure that all are cooked at the same time.

To boil: Bring a pan of salted water to the boil, add the prepared beans, cover and simmer for 15 minutes. Drain well.

To steam: Place the prepared beans in a steamer over a pan of boiling water, cover and cook for 20 minutes.

To braise: Cook the beans in tomato and onion juices (see p. 154) for 20 to 25 minutes.

Serving suggestions: The steamed or boiled beans can be tossed in butter or coated with a tomato sauce (p. 185). They can also be cooked *à la grecque* (p. 87) and served as a salad accompaniment or an hors d'œuvre.

How to deal with a glut

1. Freezing: Prepare as above, but cut the beans into thicker slices, about 1 cm (½ inch) wide and 5 to 7 cm (2 to 3 inches) long. Blanch for 3 minutes, chill, drain well and pack into polythene bags or wax or foil containers. Seal, label and freeze. Storage time: 9 to 12 months.

2. Preserving: Runner beans can be salted (p. 155) or made into a delicious spicy chutney (p. 154).

Country Bean Supper

Serves 4

500 g	runner beans	1 lb
1 rounded tsp	capers	1 rounded tsp
	salt and pepper	
4	large eggs, hard-boiled	4
300 ml	mornay sauce (coating consistency – see p. 340)	½ pint
	a little extra grated cheese	

a 1¼-litre (2-pint) shallow ovenproof dish

Top and tail the beans and cut them into 5-cm (2-inch) slices; steam or boil until tender. Drain well, stir in the capers and season with salt and pepper. Lay in the base of the dish. Slice the hard-boiled eggs and lay them over the beans.

Make the mornay sauce and pour it over the eggs and beans to cover them completely. Sprinkle over the top a little extra grated cheese and place under a medium hot grill for about 10 minutes to heat through and brown lightly.

Braised Runner Beans

Serves 3

250 g	runner beans	8 oz
250 g	tomatoes	8 oz
1	small onion	1
	knob of butter or margarine	

Wash, top, tail and thinly slice the beans. Skin the tomatoes (see p. 172) and roughly chop. Peel and chop the onion. Heat the butter or margarine in a saucepan, add the chopped onion and sauté until soft and golden. Add the tomatoes and cook for a further 2 minutes before adding the beans. Cover the pan and simmer gently for 20 to 25 minutes until the beans are tender. Serve as a vegetable accompaniment.

Note: Frozen or salted beans may be used for this recipe.

Runner Bean Chutney

Makes about 1½ kg (3–3½ lb)

1 kg	runner beans	2 lb
500 g	onions	1 lb
300 ml	water	½ pint
1 level tbsp	salt	1 level tbsp
1 level tbsp	mustard seed	1 level tbsp
75 g	sultanas	3 oz
1½ level tsps	ground ginger	1½ level tsps
1 level tsp	ground turmeric	1 level tsp
6	dried red chillies	6
600 ml	spiced vinegar (p. 326)	1 pint
500 g	demerara sugar	1 lb

a preserving pan or large saucepan

Wipe, top, tail and, if necessary, string the beans and cut them into small slices. Place in the pan with the peeled and finely chopped onions. Add the water, salt and mustard seed and simmer gently for about 20 to 25 minutes until the beans are just tender. Add the sultanas, ground ginger, ground turmeric, whole dried red chillies and spiced vinegar, bring back to the boil and simmer for a further 30 minutes or until the mixture is fairly thick.

Stir in the sugar, allow to dissolve, then boil steadily for about 20 minutes until the chutney is thick. Pour into warm, dry jars, cover with thick polythene and seal with a lid, if available. Label and store in a cool dry place for at least 3 months before using.

Note: If desired the hot chillies can be removed before potting. The chutney, which has a 'hot' spicy flavour, is delicious with cold meats. It will keep for at least 1 year.

Frozen beans can be used.

Salted Runner Beans

This is a good way of storing a glut of beans, especially if you are not a freezer owner, but always make sure that the beans to be salted are fresh, young and tender.

To prepare, wash the beans and dry them well; top and tail, string, if necessary, and slice into 5-cm (2-inch) lengths.

The best results are obtained using block kitchen salt, allowing 500 g (1 lb) salt to each $1\frac{1}{2}$ kg (3 lb) of beans. It is important to weigh the salt accurately, for if too little is used the beans will not keep and will become slimy. Ordinary table salt does not give satisfactory results.

Using clean glass or earthenware jars to pack the beans in, place a layer of salt in the base of the jars, add a layer of sliced beans and press them down firmly. Cover them with another layer of salt and then a further layer of beans. Continue in this way, pressing each layer of beans down firmly, until the jar is full, ending with a thick layer of salt. Cover the jar and leave it to stand for 48 hours, by which time the salt will have begun to dissolve, a brine will have formed and the beans will have shrunk sufficiently to allow more beans and salt to be packed into the jar.

Press the beans down firmly again, cover the jar with a cork or a thick layer of greaseproof paper and tie it down securely.

If the beans are not keeping well, it is either because too little salt was used or because the contents of the jar were not packed down firmly enough, thus leaving pockets of air which cause the beans to decompose.

To use salted beans, take out as many as you require, then re-cover the jar securely. Rinse the beans under running cold water, place in a bowl of warm water and leave to soak for 2 hours. Then cook by boiling or steaming, without any extra salt added, until they are tender.

Note: The longer the salted beans have been stored, the longer they will need to be soaked before being cooked. This preserving recipe can also be used for French beans; they should be topped and tailed and can either be left whole or cut in half.

The recipe for vegetable curry on p. 169 also includes runner beans.

Try substituting runner beans for French beans in French beans *à la grecque* (p. 87) and for peas in Spanish chicken and rice. (p. 138).

21 Spinach

Introduction

Spinach is a very valuable crop to cultivate in the garden as it is rich in iron and vitamins and grows very quickly. Using the three different varieties – summer, winter and perpetual or spinach beet – it is possible to have crops all the year round.

Summer spinach is lighter in colour and more delicate in taste than the other two varieties. When picking the leaves, pull off most of the spinach leaving a few stems in the centre to continue growth.

Winter spinach is sown first in August, in a sheltered position – a good tip to aid germination is to soak the seeds in cold water for 24 hours before planting. To protect the plants from hard frosts, cover them with straw or cloches in November. When harvested, only the larger outer leaves are picked.

Perpetual spinach is the hardiest of the three and so needs no protection from frosts. Otherwise, it crops like winter spinach. All varieties thrive best in well-manured, wet soil.

Preparation and cooking

Spinach needs careful washing in cold water. Because the leaves are watery, very little, if any, water is needed to cook it and often the spinach can be cooked in a saucepan with just the water clinging to its leaves after it has been rinsed. If it is to be cooked again as part of a dish, e.g. spinach flan (p. 161), it is necessary to drain the spinach very thoroughly or the dish will be too watery.

When allowing for portions, remember that spinach shrinks considerably during cooking and at least 1 kg (2 lb) is necessary for 4 people. Summer spinach takes less time to cook and all of it can be eaten. Winter and perpetual spinach need the tougher centre stems removed before cooking. The spinach leaves can be cooked whole or shredded.

To boil: Bring a pan of salted water to the boil, add the prepared spinach, cover and cook for 10 to 15 minutes. Alternatively, place the washed but not drained spinach in a pan with no extra water, cover and cook for 15 minutes until tender.

To steam: Place the prepared spinach in a steamer over a pan of boiling water, cover and cook for 20 to 25 minutes.

To sauté: Finely shred the washed spinach and sauté in 25 g (1 oz) butter or margarine for every 500 g (1 lb) spinach for 7 to 10 minutes. See also spinach and mushrooms in cream (p. 163) and spinach pancakes (p. 160).

Serving suggestions: The boiled or steamed spinach should be finely chopped and seasoned with freshly ground pepper and ground nutmeg or sprinkled with grated cheese and grilled to brown. Spinach can also be served raw, see spinach salad (p. 164).

How to deal with a glut

Freezing: Remove the coarse stems, if necessary, wash very well in cold salted water and blanch for 2 minutes. Chill, drain and pack into polythene bags or wax or foil containers. Seal, label and freeze. Storage time: 9 to 12 months.

Also freeze spinach soup (below), spinach pancakes (p. 160), spinach flan (p. 161) and spinach croquettes (p. 162).

There are no preserving recipes and, once picked, spinach does not store well.

Spinach Soup

Serves 4–5

1 kg	spinach	2 lb
25 g	margarine	1 oz
25 g	plain flour	1 oz
300 ml	milk	½ pint
600 ml	good light stock	1 pint
	salt and pepper	
	top of the milk or single cream	

Wash the spinach well in cold water and remove any thick centre stems. Cook the leaves in boiling salted water for about 12 minutes, until tender. Drain well in a sieve, reserving 150 ml (¼ pint) of the spinach water. Chop the vegetable finely.

Melt the margarine in a large saucepan, add the flour and cook for 1 minute; remove from the heat and gradually blend in the milk. Return to the heat and, stirring constantly, bring to the boil, then add the reserved spinach water, the chopped spinach and the stock. Season to taste with salt and pepper, bring to the boil, cover and simmer gently for 10 minutes.

Serve hot, garnished with a swirl of top of the milk or single cream in the centre of the bowl.

Note: Frozen spinach may be used to make this soup.

* Suitable for freezing.

Spinach and Sausage Pudding

Serves 4

¾ kg	spinach	1½ lb
175 g	streaky bacon rashers	6 oz
250 g	sausage-meat	8 oz
	salt and pepper	
	pinch of ground nutmeg	
300 ml	white sauce (binding consistency – see p. 339)	½ pint
2	large eggs, separated	2

a 1-kg (2-lb) pudding basin, greased

Wash the spinach well, remove any thick centre stems and boil for 10 to 15 minutes or steam for 20 to 25 minutes until tender. Drain very well, chop with a sharp knife and leave to drain further.

Cut off the rind and remove any bone from the bacon. Stretch the rashers slightly, using the back of a knife, and lay them up the inside of the pudding basin so that they overlap the top by about 3 cm (1 inch).

Stir the sausage-meat and seasonings into the drained spinach.

Prepare the white sauce and mix this into the spinach, together with the egg yolks. Whisk the egg whites until stiff and fold into the mixture, using a metal spoon.

Spoon the mixture into the lined pudding basin, smooth over the top and bring the overlapping ends of bacon over the filling. Cover with foil or a double layer of greaseproof paper with a pleat down the centre and secure with string. Place in a steamer over a pan of simmering water, cover and steam for 50 minutes.

Lift out the pudding, remove the foil or greaseproof paper and turn the pudding out onto a warm serving dish. Serve immediately, with potatoes, as a lunch or supper dish.

Note: Frozen spinach may be used in this recipe.

Spinach Pancakes

Serves 4

300 ml	pancake batter (p. 344)	½ pint
500 g	spinach	1 lb
25 g	butter or margarine	1 oz
600 ml	mornay or cheese sauce (p. 340)	1 pint
8 thin slices	cooked ham	8 thin slices
	salt and pepper	

Prepare the pancake batter and leave for 30 minutes before using. Then fry the pancakes in a medium-size saucepan and, when they are golden brown on both sides, place on a warm plate and cover with a cloth to keep warm.

Wash the spinach well and shred it finely. Heat the butter or margarine in a saucepan, add the spinach, cover and cook gently for 7 to 10 minutes until tender and cooked. Keep warm.

Meanwhile, prepare the mornay or cheese sauce and, while it is cooking for 2 minutes, assemble the pancakes. Lay them out flat and place a slice of ham on top of each one; divide the spinach equally between the pancakes and season well with salt and pepper. Starting at the end with the spinach, roll up the pancakes into a thin roll and lay them side by side in a warm heat-proof serving dish. Pour the sauce over them and sprinkle with extra grated cheese. Place under a hot grill until the top is nicely browned.

Note: Frozen spinach may be used in this recipe.

* Suitable for freezing.

Spinach Flan

Serves 4–5

100 g	shortcrust pastry (p. 334)	4 oz

For the filling

500 g	spinach	1 lb
175 g	Lancashire cheese	6 oz
300 ml	milk	½ pint
2	large eggs	2
½ level tsp	salt	½ level tsp
	freshly ground pepper	
	a good pinch of ground nutmeg	

a 20-cm (8-inch) plain flan ring on a baking sheet

Preheat the oven to 190°C, 375°F, gas mark 5.

Prepare the pastry, roll out on a floured surface and line the flan ring. Trim the top edges.

Wash the spinach and boil for 10 minutes or steam for 20 minutes until tender. Drain well, chop with a sharp knife, place in the base of the flan and crumble the cheese over it. Lightly beat together the milk, eggs and seasonings and pour into the flan case. Bake on the centre shelf of the preheated oven for 35 to 40 minutes until well risen and golden brown. Serve at once with a green salad.

Note: Frozen spinach may be used to make this flan.

* Suitable for freezing.

Spinach Soufflé

Serves 4

500 g	spinach	1 lb
25 g	margarine	1 oz
25 g	plain flour	1 oz
150 ml	milk	¼ pint
3	large eggs	3

50 g	cheese, grated	2 oz
1 level tsp	salt	1 level tsp
¼ level tsp	cayenne pepper	¼ level tsp
	pinch of ground nutmeg	

a 1¼-litre (2-pint) soufflé dish, buttered

Preheat the oven to 190°C, 375°F, gas mark 5.

Wash the spinach very well and steam or boil until tender; drain very well through a sieve and chop with a sharp knife.

Meanwhile, melt the margarine in a large saucepan, add the flour and cook for 1 minute. Remove from the heat and gradually stir in the milk. Return to the heat and bring to the boil, stirring constantly, until the sauce thickens. Cool slightly, then separate the eggs and beat the yolks into the sauce.

Stir in the grated cheese and chopped spinach. Season well with salt, cayenne and nutmeg.

Whisk the egg whites until stiff and dry; using a metal spoon, fold a little into the mixture and then carefully fold in the rest.

Spoon the soufflé mixture into the buttered dish and cook on the centre shelf of the preheated oven for 30 to 35 minutes until the top is golden brown but the centre is still soft.

Serve the soufflé immediately, otherwise it will start to sink after a few minutes.

Note: Frozen chopped spinach can be used.

Spinach Croquettes

Makes 18–20

500 g	spinach	1 lb
¾ kg	potatoes	1½ lb
	salt and freshly ground pepper	
	a good pinch of dry mustard	
1	egg	1
	dried breadcrumbs	

Prepare the spinach and boil or steam until tender. Drain well, chop finely and leave in the sieve to get cold.

Peel the potatoes and boil for 15 to 20 minutes until tender. Drain well, mash and leave to get cold.

Place the chopped spinach and mashed potato together in a bowl, add the salt, pepper and dry mustard and mix together well with the egg.

Put the dried breadcrumbs in a bowl, then form the spinach mixture into small croquettes and coat in the crumbs.

To cook, fry the croquettes in hot deep fat for 3 minutes or in shallow fat, turning occasionally, for 5 minutes. Serve as a vegetable accompaniment.

Note: 75–100 g (3–4 oz) grated cheese may be added to make it a more substantial supper dish. Frozen spinach and left-over potatoes may be used to make the croquettes.

* Suitable for freezing before frying.

Spinach and Mushrooms in Cream

Serves 2–3

350 g	spinach	12 oz
100 g	mushrooms	4 oz
25 g	butter or margarine	1 oz
2 tbsps	cream	2 tbsps
	salt and freshly ground pepper	

Wash the spinach thoroughly in cold water, remove any centre stalks and shred the leaves. Wipe the mushrooms and slice them thinly.

Heat the butter or margarine in a saucepan, add the spinach and mushrooms, cover the pan and sauté gently for about 10 minutes over a low heat until the vegetables are tender. Remove from the heat and stir in the cream. Season to taste with salt and pepper.

To serve, spoon the spinach and mushrooms into a warm serving dish and pour the cream sauce over them. Serve as a vegetable accompaniment.

Spinach Salad

Serves 3

50 g	spinach	2 oz
50 g	radishes	2 oz
1 tbsp	salad dressing, e.g. French dressing (p. 343), or thousand island dressing salt and pepper	1 tbsp

Wash the spinach thoroughly, remove any thicker centre stems and shred the leaves finely. Wash the radishes, remove the tops and roots and thinly slice into rings.

Place the spinach and three quarters of the radish rings in a glass serving dish, toss in the salad dressing and season to taste with salt and pepper. Decorate the top of the salad with the remaining radish rings and serve with other salad dishes as an alternative to lettuce.

Try substituting spinach for the main vegetable in the following recipes:

Brussels sprouts with almonds (p. 43)
Lettuce mornay (p. 99)

22 Swedes

Introduction

The swede is one of the hardiest winter root vegetables. It should be grown in a well-fertilized soil which benefits from the addition of a little lime to help prevent club root disease attacking the crops. The ground should not be manured, otherwise, like carrots and parsnips, the roots will become misshapen.

After sowing the seeds in May/June, the seedlings should be kept well watered to avoid attack by the flea beetle, which will eat little holes in the leaves.

In autumn the roots can be lifted for storage or left in the ground until the end of the year, provided that frosts are not too severe. The season lasts from September until May.

Preparation and cooking

Swedes belong to the same family as turnips and are prepared and cooked in the same way. On their own they are not very popular, but they are tasty ingredients in soups, stews and casseroles. They also make a delicious soup with fresh parsley.

To prepare, top, tail and remove the skin with a vegetable peeler, then dice.

To boil: Place the prepared swedes in a saucepan of cold salted water, bring to the boil, cover and cook for 15 to 20 minutes. Drain well.

To steam: Place the prepared vegetables in a steamer over a pan of boiling water, cover and cook for 25 to 30 minutes.

To sauté: Parboil for 10 to 15 minutes, then sauté in butter for 5 minutes.

To deep fry: Parboil strips of swede for 10 to 15 minutes, drain well, coat in fritter batter (p. 343) and deep fry in hot fat for 4 to 5 minutes. Drain and serve hot.

Serving suggestions: The boiled or steamed swedes are usually mashed with butter and pepper and, served this way, are an essential ingredient of a Scottish 'Burns' Supper' where 'mashed neeps, champit tatties' and haggis are the traditional fare presented with a blast of the bagpipes.

The swede may also be diced and, after cooking, coated in a parsley or mornay sauce (see pp. 341, 340).

How to deal with a glut

1. Freezing: Top, tail, and peel off the skin. Cut into 2- to 3-cm (1-inch) cubes, blanch for 3 minutes, chill, drain and pack into polythene bags or wax or foil containers. Seal, label and freeze. Storage time: 9 to 12 months.

Also freeze swede and parsley soup (below) and swede patti-cakes (p. 170).

2. Storing: Leave in the ground until the end of the year, then lift, twist off the tops and store in sacks or under straw in a dry shed.

Swede and Parsley Soup

Serves 4–6

½	large onion	½
500 g	swede	1 lb
1 litre	good stock	1½ pints
2 level tbsps	fresh parsley, chopped	2 level tbsps
	salt and pepper	
15 g	butter or margarine	½ oz
2 level tbsps	flour	2 level tbsps
300 ml	milk	½ pint
	a little extra parsley	

Peel and dice the onion and the swede. Place in a large saucepan with the stock, the chopped parsley (including any stalk) and the salt and pepper. Bring to the boil, cover and simmer gently for 40 minutes. Purée the soup in a liquidizer or put through a sieve.

While the soup is cooking, melt the butter in a small saucepan, add the flour and cook for 1 minute. Remove the pan from the heat, stir in the milk gradually, return to the heat and, stirring continuously, bring to the boil. Cook for a few minutes and then stir the white sauce into the puréed soup. Check the seasoning and serve hot, sprinkled with a little chopped parsley.

Note: This makes a very economical winter soup. Frozen swede may be used in place of the fresh.

* Suitable for freezing.

Scotch Broth

Serves 4–6

50 g	fresh peas or 25 g (1 oz) dried peas	2 oz
¾ kg	breast of lamb	1½ lb
1½ litres	water	2½ pints
½	large onion	½
175 g	carrots	6 oz
175 g	swede	6 oz
25 g	butter or margarine	1 oz
25 g	barley	1 oz
	salt and pepper	
50–75 g	cabbage, shredded	2–3 oz

Soak the dried peas overnight in cold water. If possible, prepare the stock the day before. Place the breast of lamb, roughly chopped, in a large saucepan with the water, cover, bring slowly to the boil and simmer for about 1 hour until the meat is falling away from the bone.

Strain the stock into a bowl and leave it to cool. Remove the skin and bone from the lamb, chop the meat and reserve it for the soup. When the stock is cold, skim off the layer of fat which will have formed on the surface.

The following day, peel and finely chop the onion, and peel and dice the carrots and swede. Melt the butter or margarine in a large saucepan, add the vegetables and fry them gently for about 10 minutes.

Now add the lamb stock, meat pieces, barley and seasonings. Cover the pan and simmer for about 40 minutes.

Finally add the shredded cabbage and simmer for a further 10 minutes. Test for seasoning before serving.

Note: Traditionally this Scottish soup is a meal in its own right and should be made with more expensive cuts of meat like flank, scrag end or middle neck. Breast of lamb, being the cheapest lamb cut on the market, serves just as well and the soup is still worthy of being served as a lunchtime dish.

 * Suitable for the freezer.

September Lamb Hotchpotch

Serves 4

¾ kg	stewing lamb	1½ lb
	fat or oil for frying	
1	medium onion	1
2–3	spring onions	2–3
½	green pepper	½
2–3	cooking apples	2–3
350 g	swede	12 oz
250 g	carrots	8 oz
	salt and pepper	
500 g	potatoes	1 lb
	fresh parsley, chopped	
300 ml	chicken stock	½ pint

a 1¾-litre (3-pint) ovenproof casserole dish

Preheat the oven to 160°C, 325°F, gas mark 3.

Trim any excess fat from the lamb. Heat the fat or oil in a frying pan, brown the lamb on both sides and place in the casserole dish.

Peel and chop the onion and spring onions; remove the seeds from the green pepper and dice the flesh. Fry the onions and pepper in the lamb juices for a few minutes and add them to the casserole.

Peel, core and quarter the apples and slice them into the casserole; peel and dice the swede and carrots and add to the dish. Sprinkle well with salt and pepper.

Peel the potatoes and slice them very thinly. Lay them across the top of the casserole and sprinkle with the chopped parsley. Pour the chicken stock over the potatoes and finally sprinkle them with salt and pepper. Cook the casserole, uncovered, on the centre shelf of the preheated oven for 2 hours.

Note: September sees the start of the root vegetable season with the first of the swede crop, but summer produce like spring onions and green peppers is still available. This dish is both useful in overlapping the seasons and economical in using stewing lamb and making 500 g (1 lb) of potatoes go a long way.

Where applicable, frozen vegetables may be used in place of the fresh.

* Suitable for freezing but cook for only 1½ hours.

Vegetable Curry

Serves 4

300 ml	boiling water	½ pint
2 level tbsps	desiccated coconut	2 level tbsps
2 cloves	garlic	2 cloves
250 g	onions	8 oz
3 tbsps	cooking oil or margarine	3 tbsps
1½ level tbsps	curry powder	1½ level tbsps
1 level tsp	turmeric	1 level tsp
1 level tsp	ground ginger	1 level tsp
1 level dsp	curry paste	1 level dsp
1½ level tsps	salt	1½ level tsps
1	bay leaf	1
1 level tbsp	sweet chutney	1 level tbsp
½ tsp	lemon juice	½ tsp
350 g	tomatoes	12 oz
300 ml	stock	½ pint
250 g	small potatoes	8 oz
350 g	swede	12 oz
1	small cauliflower	1
175 g	runner or French beans	6 oz

Place the 300 ml (½ pint) boiling water in a jug or bowl, add the desiccated coconut and leave to infuse for 15 minutes.

Peel and crush the cloves of garlic with a little salt; peel and finely chop the onions. Heat the oil or margarine in a large pan and fry the onion and garlic until soft but not browned. Add the curry powder, turmeric, ginger, curry paste and salt and continue cooking, stirring occasionally, for 2 minutes. Remove from the heat and add the bay leaf, chutney and lemon juice.

Peel the tomatoes (see p. 172), chop roughly and add to the pan.

Return the pan to the heat and cook for a few minutes. Drain the water from the coconut, pressing out as much water as possible. Stir the coconut water into the pan with the stock, bring to the boil, cover and simmer gently for 35 to 40 minutes.

Peel or scrub the small potatoes and leave them whole (if using larger potatoes, peel and cut them into pieces the size of a walnut). Peel and cut the swede into the same size as the potatoes. Wash the cauliflower and cut into small florets. Add the potatoes and swede to the curry sauce and cook, covered, for 15 minutes.

Top, tail and wash the beans; cut the French beans into 3-cm (1-inch) pieces or slice the runner beans fairly thickly. Add the cauliflower florets and beans to the pan and continue to cook, covered, for a further 15 to 20 minutes until all the vegetables are tender.

Serve the curry with boiled rice.

Note: To make a more substantial meal, four hard-boiled eggs can be added with the potatoes and swedes.

* Suitable for freezing.

Swede Patti-Cakes

Makes 8–10

375 g	swede	12 oz
250 g	potatoes	8 oz
	knob of butter	
½ level tsp	salt	½ level tsp
	freshly ground pepper	
1 level tbsp	fresh parsley, chopped	1 level tbsp
175 g	cooked chicken	6 oz
1	egg	1
	dried breadcrumbs	
	fat or oil for frying	

Peel the swede and potatoes and cut into dice. Place in a pan of cold salted water, bring to the boil, cover and cook for 15 to 20 minutes until tender. Drain very well, return to the pan, mash well, then put over a low heat for 2 minutes, turning frequently. Add the butter, salt, pepper and parsley. Mix well and leave to cool slightly.

Finely chop or mince the chicken meat, stir into the swede mixture and leave to cool.

Beat the egg lightly in a bowl. Put the breadcrumbs in another bowl. Divide the swede mixture into eight or ten portions and pat into flat cakes about 7 to 8 cm (3 inches) in diameter. Dip first in the egg and then in the breadcrumbs.

Heat the fat or oil in a frying pan and fry the patti-cakes for about 4 minutes on each side until golden brown.

Note: This is a useful recipe for using up left-over mashed swedes and potatoes and any left-over Sunday joint can be used instead of chicken.

Frozen swede may be used instead of the fresh vegetable.

* Suitable for freezing.

The following recipes also include swedes:

Carrot and lentil soup (p. 55)
January suet pudding (p. 41)

23 Tomatoes

Introduction

Tomatoes are surely the most popular vegetable for the home gardener. There is always room for a few tomato plants in even the smallest garden – e.g. amongst the rose bushes, on the patio in large pots or even in hanging baskets.

Tomatoes are easily grown from seed if warmth and a sterile soil are provided, and once you have succeeded with your plants no shop-bought tomato will ever compare with the sweet taste of a newly picked home-grown fruit.

Another advantage of tomatoes is the great selection of dishes which can be made with them – so many that we have had to restrict ourselves in the number included in this book.

Tomatoes to be grown outdoors should be planted out only when all danger of frosts has passed. Most of the plants, except the dwarf or bush varieties, will require the support of a cane and should have all their side shoots removed. After four or five trusses have formed, the tops should be pinched off, though greenhouse plants can produce up to seven trusses before having their growth stopped. After the first truss has set, all tomatoes benefit from a feed of liquid manure every fortnight.

Green tomatoes, which have not reddened before the first frosts, can be ripened off on a sunny windowsill or in a warm cupboard or drawer.

Preparation and cooking

For most dishes in which tomatoes are to be cooked it is advisable to skin them first. The easiest method is to put the tomatoes into a bowl of boiling water for $\frac{1}{2}$ minute and then drain them; the skins should then peel off easily. If some skins are stubborn, return to the water for a few seconds more, but take care not to leave them in the boiling water longer than recommended otherwise the flesh will start to become mushy.

To grill: Wash the tomatoes, cut in half, dot with butter, season to taste and grill for 5 minutes.

To bake: Wash the tomatoes, make a little slit at the top, to stop the skins from bursting, and bake for 25 to 30 minutes.

To sauté: Wash the tomatoes, then halve or slice them and sauté in butter, margarine or other fat for 5 to 6 minutes.

Serving suggestions: Serve tomatoes raw in salads and sandwiches.

How to deal with a glut

1. Freezing: Frozen whole they lose their texture, but are ideal for cooking. To freeze whole: remove skins, pat dry and pack into polythene bags in 250-g (8-oz) and 500-g (1-lb) quantities. Seal, label and freeze. Storage time: 9 to 12 months.

Tomatoes may also be frozen as purée: skin, chop roughly and cook for 5 minutes; then sieve, cool and pack into cartons, plastic containers or polythene bags. Seal, label and freeze. Storage time: 9 months.

Also freeze tomato soup (p. 174), French provincial tart (p. 176), gardener's pizzas (p. 178) and barbecue sauce (p. 181).

2. Preserving: Bottle in brine (p. 325) or make red tomato jam (p. 185), green tomato jam (p. 184), tomato relish (p. 182), green tomato chutney (p. 183) or tomato ketchup (p. 182).

3. Storing: Tomatoes will keep for 3 to 4 weeks in the bottom of the fridge.

Gazpacho

Serves 6

1 kg	red tomatoes	2 lb
125 g	stale white bread	4 oz
1 tbsp	red wine vinegar	1 tbsp
4 tbsps	olive oil	4 tbsps
300 ml	tomato juice (p. 175)	½ pint
½	lemon, juice only	½
1	large onion	1
½	cucumber	½
2 cloves	garlic, peeled	2 cloves
1	red pepper	1
1	green pepper	1

1 level tsp	salt	1 level tsp
	freshly ground black pepper	
450 ml	iced water	¾ pint

For the garnishes

½	cucumber	½
3	tomatoes	3
2	hard-boiled eggs	2
1	green pepper	1
	fried croûtons of bread	
	green or black olives	

Skin the tomatoes (see p. 172) and chop the flesh finely.

Crumble the bread into a large bowl and stir in the vinegar, oil, tomato juice and lemon juice. Mix well together and then stir in the chopped tomato flesh.

Peel and finely chop the onion and the cucumber; crush the cloves of garlic with a little salt; remove the seeds and white pith from the red and green peppers and finely chop the flesh; add all these vegetables to the bowl with the salt, pepper and iced water.

Put the soup through a liquidizer or fine sieve, The gazpacho should now be quite thick and smooth. Test for seasoning and serve well chilled with ice and the garnishes, all finely diced and placed in individual dishes. It is customary for each person to choose his or her own garnishes for the soup.

Note: Frozen tomatoes may be used to make this soup.

* Suitable for freezing.

Tomato Soup

Serves 8–10

1 kg	red tomatoes	2 lb
250 g	potatoes	8 oz
250 g	onions	8 oz
25 g	butter or margarine	1 oz
1 tbsp	olive oil	1 tbsp
1 level tsp	parsley, chopped	1 level tsp

½ level tsp	thyme, chopped	½ level tsp
½ level tsp	salt	½ level tsp
	freshly ground pepper	
2 level tsps	sugar	2 level tsps
¾ litre	chicken stock	1¼ pints
300 ml	milk	½ pint

Skin the tomatoes (see p. 172) and roughly chop the flesh. Peel and dice the potatoes and onions. Heat the butter or margarine and the oil in a large saucepan, add the onions and potatoes and fry for 5 minutes without browning. Stir in the chopped tomatoes, parsley, thyme, salt, pepper and sugar and continue to cook gently for a further 5 minutes.

Stir in the chicken stock, cover the pan and simmer for about 15 minutes until the vegetables are cooked. Put the soup through a fine sieve or liquidize it, return it to the saucepan and stir in the milk. Test for seasoning, reheat and serve hot, garnished with chopped parsley.

Note: This soup is a good way of using soft tomatoes which have passed their peak.

* Suitable for freezing, but omit the milk which is added later when the soup is thawed and ready to serve.

Tomato Juice

Makes 300 ml (½ pint)

500 g	red tomatoes	1 lb
½ tsp	salt	½ tsp
1 tbsp	lemon juice	1 tbsp
	a few shakes of tabasco (optional)	
	a pinch of basil (optional)	
	red colouring, if required	

Chop the tomatoes roughly and place in a saucepan with the rest of the ingredients; cover with a lid and cook gently for 5 to 10 minutes. Rub through a fine sieve or liquidize and then sieve.

If the tomato juice is not red enough in colour, add a few drops of cochineal or red colouring. This doesn't affect the flavour of the juice but will improve its colour.

Note: Frozen or bottled tomatoes may be used to make this juice. Once made, it will keep for about 1 week in the refrigerator.

For how to use the juice in cooking, see baked pork and cauliflower (p. 63) and gazpacho (p. 173).

* Suitable for freezing.

French Provincial Tart

Serves 4

100 g	shortcrust pastry (p. 334)	4 oz
250 g	onions	8 oz
	fat or oil for frying	
250 g	tomatoes	8 oz
6–8	anchovy fillets	6–8
6–8	black olives	6–8
	salt and freshly ground pepper	

a 20-cm (8-inch) round pie dish

Preheat the oven to 190°C, 375°F, gas mark 5.

Prepare the pastry and leave to rest for 15 minutes. Roll out on a floured surface and line the base and sides of the pie dish. Trim the edges and leave to rest a further 15 minutes.

Peel and slice the onions into thin rings. Heat the fat or oil and gently fry the onions until tender but not browned. Allow to cool slightly before spreading over the base of the pastry.

Skin the tomatoes if desired (see p. 172) and slice fairly thickly over the onions. Finally, lay the anchovies and black olives on top, e.g. in a spoke pattern with the anchovies meeting in the centre and the olives placed between the spokes. Season with a little salt and pepper sprinkled over the top.

Bake on the centre shelf of the preheated oven for 25 to 30 minutes.

Note: This tart is extremely popular in France where it can be bought in bakeries and at market stalls as a small pie suitable for one person – the French equivalent of a pork pie or a Scots bridie. It makes a delicious hors d'œuvre, buffet snack or lunch dish, served with a tossed green salad. To remove some of the saltiness from the anchovy fillets, lay them on a saucer in a little milk and leave to stand for 10 minutes before using.

* Suitable for freezing.

Greek Stuffed Tomatoes

Serves 4

4	large tomatoes	4
½	cucumber	½
150 ml	plain yoghurt	¼ pint
	fresh chives	
	salt and pepper	
½	lettuce, shredded	½

Cut the tops off the tomatoes, then, using a teaspoon, remove the centre pulp and use it for another recipe.

Wipe and cut the cucumber into very small dice and stir into the yoghurt. Add the chopped chives, salt and pepper to taste. Now fill the hollowed tomatoes with the cucumber mixture. Put the tomato lids at an angle on top and serve chilled on a bed of shredded lettuce. This makes a very refreshing starter.

Country Lamb and Tomato

Serves 3–4

6–8	lamb chops	6–8
1 tbsp	oil for frying	1 tbsp
175–250 g	onions	6–8 oz
	salt and pepper	
175–250 g	tomatoes	6–8 oz
	sprinkling of basil	
50 g	cheese, grated	2 oz
50 g	fresh white breadcrumbs	2 oz

a 1¾-litre (3-pint) casserole dish

Preheat the oven to 180°C, 350°F, gas mark 4.

Trim any excess fat from the chops. Heat the oil in a frying pan and lightly brown the chops on both sides. Remove them from the pan and lay on the bottom of the casserole dish. Peel and slice the onions and fry in the pan until they are soft and golden. Remove them from the pan, scatter over the chops and season well.

Skin (see p. 172) and slice the tomatoes, lay them on top of the onions and sprinkle with basil if desired.

Finally, grate the cheese and mix well with the breadcrumbs. Sprinkle the cheese/crumb mixture over the top of the casserole and bake on the centre shelf of the preheated oven for 45 minutes until the top is brown and crispy.

Note: To vary the dish, the lamb chops may be sprinkled with chopped mint.

* Suitable for freezing.

Gardener's Pizzas

Makes 2 large pizzas

For the dough

150 ml	tepid water	¼ pint
15 g	fresh yeast	½ oz
	or	
1½ level tsps	dried yeast with a sprinkling of sugar	1½ level tsps
25 g	melted butter	1 oz
200 g	plain flour (preferably strong white flour)	7 oz
1 level tsp	salt	1 level tsp
	freshly ground pepper	

For the tomato sauce

½	large onion	½
500 g	tomatoes	1 lb
1 tbsp	oil	1 tbsp
1 large clove	garlic	1 large clove
¼ tsp	basil or oregano, chopped	¼ tsp
1 level tsp	brown sugar	1 level tsp
1 level tbsp	tomato purée	1 level tbsp
	salt and pepper	

For the toppings

100–175 g	mozzarella, bel paese or Gruyère cheese	4–6 oz
4–6	anchovy fillets	4–6
50 g	mushrooms	2 oz
8 small or 4 large	black olives	8 small or 4 large
100 g	salami	4 oz
1	green pepper	1
1	leek, sautéed (p. 90)	1

2 baking trays, 20–25 cm (8–10 inches) in width

To prepare the yeast dough: Crumble the fresh yeast into the water and stir until it is dissolved and the mixture becomes creamy. If using dried yeast, follow the manufacturer's instructions by dissolving the yeast with a little sugar in the tepid water and leave to stand for about 7 to 10 minutes until the mixture is frothy. Stir the melted butter into the yeast mixture.

Sift the flour and seasonings into a bowl, make a well in the centre and pour in the yeast liquid. Mix thoroughly together and when the dough forms a ball remove it to a lightly floured surface and knead well until the dough is smooth and elastic.

Cover the dough with a piece of oiled polythene and leave in a warm place to 'prove', i.e. rise. When the dough has roughly doubled in size, about 1 hour later, return it to the floured surface and knead again.

Cut the mixture into two equal portions and roll out into two thin circles of about 20 to 25 cm (8 to 10 inches) in diameter. Place the pizza bases on the well-greased baking trays, spread half the tomato sauce mixture over the surface of each pizza and then decorate with a selection of the toppings, as prepared below.

To prepare the tomato sauce: Peel and finely chop the onion. Skin the tomatoes (see p. 172) and chop the flesh. Peel the garlic.

Heat the oil in a saucepan and add the onion and the garlic, crushed with a little salt. Cook gently until soft, then add the chopped tomatoes, chopped basil or oregano, sugar, tomato purée, a little water if needed and the seasonings and cook gently for about 10 minutes until the sauce is thick and the tomatoes are tender. Leave to cool slightly.

To prepare the toppings of your choice: Slice the cheese into long strips to decorate the pizza like the spokes of a wheel. (*Note:* Mozzarella is the most expensive of the cheeses but the one traditionally used in Italian pizzas. You could make do with slices of Cheddar instead.)

Slice the anchovies in half lengthwise; thinly slice the mushrooms; halve the larger black olives; cut the salami into thin rounds; remove the seeds and pith from the pepper and cut the flesh into small strips; cut the leek into thin rounds and sauté gently in butter until tender.

Preheat the oven to 200°C, 400°F, gas mark 6.

Decorate the top of the pizzas in any way you choose, leave to rise for 20 minutes before baking on the centre shelf of the preheated oven for about 20 minutes until the crust is cooked. Serve hot or cold.

Note: You may use frozen or bottled tomatoes and frozen onions to make the tomato sauce.

* Pizzas, ready cooked, freeze very well. You may also freeze quantities of the tomato sauce for making pizzas at a later date.

Green Tomato Casserole

Serves 4

500 g	stewing, braising or leg of beef	1 lb
	oil for frying	
250 g	green tomatoes	8 oz
175 g	leeks	6 oz
½	green pepper	½
	salt and pepper	
150 ml	stock or gravy	¼ pint

a 1¼- to 1¾-litre (2- to 3-pint) ovenproof casserole

Preheat the oven to 190°C, 375°F, gas mark 5.

Remove any excess fat from the beef and cut into cubes. Heat the oil in a frying pan or large saucepan, add the beef and fry quickly, turning frequently, until browned on all sides. Place in the casserole dish.

Chop the green tomatoes roughly (they cannot be skinned by the method used for ripe tomatoes); wash the leeks thoroughly and thinly slice them; remove the seeds from the half pepper and cut the flesh into 2- to 3-cm (1-inch) strips. Add all these vegetables to the pan juices, cover and sauté for 5 minutes, turning occasionally. Add to the casserole, season with salt and pepper and pour the stock or gravy over the top.

Cover the dish and cook on the centre shelf of the preheated oven for
1½ hours.

Note: Don't be put off by the thought of cooked green tomatoes.
This is a really delicious casserole which makes a different way of using
up those unripe tomatoes we all have at the end of the season.

* Suitable for freezing.

Barbecue Sauce

Makes 150 ml (¼ pint)

½	large onion	½
25 g	butter or margarine	1 oz
175 g	tomatoes	6 oz
1 tbsp	soy sauce	1 tbsp
1 level tbsp	brown sugar	1 level tbsp
½ level tsp	paprika	½ level tsp
1½ tbsps	vinegar	1½ tbsps
150 ml	water	¼ pint
	salt and pepper	

Peel and finely chop the onion. Heat the butter or margarine in a
saucepan and sauté the onion until soft and golden. Skin the tomatoes
(see p. 172), roughly chop the flesh and add to the onion. Cook gently
for a further 2 minutes then add the soy sauce, brown sugar, paprika,
vinegar, water, salt and pepper. Leave the saucepan, uncovered, to
simmer gently for 15 to 20 minutes, by which time the sauce will have
reduced and thickened.

Serve hot over minceburgers, grilled chops or baked slices of belly of
pork.

Note: Frozen or bottled tomatoes may be used in this recipe.

* Suitable for freezing.

Tomato Ketchup

Makes about 750 ml (1¼ pints)

3 kg	ripe tomatoes	6 lb
250 g	granulated sugar	8 oz
300 ml	malt vinegar	½ pint
	pinch of cayenne pepper	
1 level tbsp	salt	1 level tbsp
¼ level tsp	ground cinnamon	¼ level tsp
¼ level tsp	ground ginger	¼ level tsp
¼ level tsp	ground cloves	¼ level tsp
½ level tsp	ground mace	½ level tsp

a preserving pan or large saucepan

Wash the tomatoes, cut into quarters and put in a preserving pan. Cook them slowly until they have softened, then boil rapidly to reduce them to a pulp. Put the tomato pulp through a sieve, return to the pan and stir in the sugar, vinegar, and all the spices and seasonings.

Heat slowly over a low heat to allow the sugar to dissolve completely and then bring to the boil and boil rapidly for about 5 minutes until it is a fairly thick sauce.

Pour into clean, warm, dry bottles, leaving 4 cm (1½ inches) unfilled at the top (we used non-returnable tonic-water bottles and old sauce bottles with well fitting tops). Scald the tops and screw on tightly.

To process, place the bottles on a trivet in a large saucepan and fill the pan with water to within 3 cm (1 inch) of the tops of the bottles.

Heat the water to 80°C (170°F) and simmer very gently for 20 minutes.

Remove the bottles and leave to cool before storing. This recipe filled three small tonic bottles.

Note: Frozen or bottled tomatoes may be used to make this sauce.

Red Tomato Relish

Makes about 2 kg (4 lb)

1½ kg	ripe tomatoes	3 lb
250 g	onions	8 oz

½ head	celery	½ head
250 g	seedless raisins	8 oz
1 level tbsp	salt	1 level tbsp
600 ml	malt vinegar	1 pint
375 g	granulated sugar	12 oz

For the pickling spice

1 level tsp	black peppercorns	
1 level tsp	allspice berries	*or* 25 g (1 oz) whole
1 level tsp	mustard seed	pickling spice
3	pieces of root ginger	
4	cloves	

a preserving pan or large saucepan

Skin the tomatoes (see p. 172) and chop the flesh; peel and chop the onions; wipe, trim and dice the celery; chop the raisins. (Alternatively, put all these ingredients through a fine mincer.)

Put the vegetables and fruit into the pan. Tie all the spices in a muslin bag and add to the pan with the salt and half the vinegar. Simmer gently until the relish is thick and the vegetables are soft – about 40 minutes. Remove the muslin bag.

Dissolve the sugar in the remaining vinegar and add to the pan. Return to simmering point and cook until the chutney is thick. Pour into warm, clean, dry jars, cover with thick polythene and preferably screw tops as well, label and store when cold in a cool, dry place.

Note: Frozen tomatoes may be used to make this relish.

Green Tomato Chutney

Makes about 4 kg (8 lb)

2 kg	green tomatoes	4 lb
¾ kg	cooking apples	1½ lb
500 g	onions	1 lb
4–5 cloves	garlic	4–5 cloves
375 g	sultanas	12 oz
125 g	salt	4 oz
1 litre	white vinegar	1½ pints
25 g	root ginger	1 oz

50 g	mustard seeds	2 oz
1 level tbsp	chillies	1 level tbsp
1 kg	demerara sugar	2 lb

a preserving pan or large saucepan

Wash the tomatoes, chop them roughly and place in the preserving pan. Peel and core the apples, peel the onions and garlic cloves and put them all through a coarse mincer. Add to the tomatoes with the sultanas, salt and vinegar.

Crush the root ginger and mustard seeds and shred the chillies. Put all the spices in a muslin bag, tie it securely and add to the pan. Place the pan over a gentle heat and cook until all the ingredients are soft and the chutney is thick and well blended – about 2 hours.

Remove from the heat and stir in the sugar. Over a very low heat allow the sugar to dissolve completely, then bring to the boil and boil for about 20 minutes until thick again. Pour into clean, warm, dry jars, cover with wax discs and polythene and screw tops, label and store when cold in a cool, dry place.

Note: Frozen sliced apples and onions may be used in this chutney.

Green Tomato Jam

Makes 2 kg (4½ lb)

2 kg	green tomatoes	4 lb
1	orange, grated rind and juice	1
½ level tsp	ground ginger	½ level tsp
1½ kg	granulated or preserving sugar	3 lb

a preserving pan or large saucepan

Wash the tomatoes, then chop them into fairly small pieces and place in the pan. Add the grated orange rind, the orange juice and the ground ginger and place the pan over a gentle heat. Bring to the boil and simmer gently for about 1 hour, stirring occasionally, until the tomatoes are tender and becoming pulpy.

Stir in the sugar and allow to dissolve over a low heat. When the sugar has all dissolved, bring to the boil and boil rapidly until setting point is reached – about 15 minutes (see p. 311 for full jam-making instructions). Allow to stand for 10 minutes before pouring into clean, warm, dry jars. Cover, label and, when cold, store in a cool, dry place.

Red Tomato Jam

Makes about 2¼ kg (4 lb)

1¾ kg	red tomatoes	3½ lb
250 g	cooking apples	8 oz
1	lemon, grated rind and juice	1
1½ kg	granulated or preserving sugar	3 lb

a preserving pan or large saucepan

Skin the tomatoes (see p. 172) and chop the flesh fairly finely into the pan. Peel and core the apples and cut into small dice. Add to the tomatoes with the grated lemon rind and juice.

Place the pan over a low heat, bring to the boil and simmer gently for about ½ hour until the tomatoes are pulpy and the apples soft. Stir in the sugar and allow to dissolve over a low heat. When the sugar has completely dissolved, bring to the boil and boil rapidly until setting point is reached – about 15 to 20 minutes (see p. 311 for full jam-making instructions).

Allow to stand for 10 minutes before pouring into warm, clean, dry jars. Cover, label and when cold store in a cool, dry place.

Tomato Sauce

Makes 300 ml (½ pint)

500 g	ripe tomatoes	1 lb
½ large	onion	½ large
1 small	carrot	1 small
2 cloves	garlic, peeled	2 cloves
25 g	margarine	1 oz
2 level tbsps	flour	2 level tbsps
150 ml	stock	¼ pint
1	bay leaf	1
1 level dsp	fresh herbs, chopped	1 level dsp
	salt and pepper	

Wipe the tomatoes and chop them roughly; peel and finely dice the onion and carrot; crush the garlic with a little salt. Heat the margarine in a saucepan and fry the onion, carrot and garlic until soft and lightly browned. Stir in the flour and cook until browned, add the tomatoes and, stirring occasionally, cook for 5 minutes. Add the stock, bay leaf and chopped herbs, season with salt and pepper, bring to the boil, cover and simmer gently for 15 minutes.

Strain the tomato sauce through a sieve, and return to the heat before serving.

* Suitable for freezing.

The following recipes also include tomatoes:

Cornish lamb stew (p. 29)
Eastern parsnip soup (p. 129)
Piquant marrow hors d'œuvre (p. 102)
Baked lamb chops (p. 145)
Fillet of lamb *en croûte* (p. 119)
Chicken in cider (p. 120)
Spanish chicken and rice (p. 138)
Minted lamb kebabs (p. 112)
Smoked cod gougère (p. 137)
Vegetable curry (p. 169)
Kidneys turbigo (p. 121)
Worcestershire beans (p. 88)
Braised runner beans (p. 154)
Baked cabbage and tomato (p. 49)
Celery *à la provençale* (p. 69)
Baked courgettes and tomato (p. 76)
Lettuce with mushrooms and tomatoes (p. 99)
Marrow casserole (p. 105)
Bottled tomatoes (p. 325)

24 Turnips

Introduction

Turnips are another useful winter crop, invaluable in soups, stews and casseroles where they give a distinct, almost peppery, taste. They are much lighter coloured than their close relative, the swede, less sweet in flavour and harvested smaller in size.

Turnips like a fertilized, well-composted, moist soil to help them mature more quickly and to enrich their flavour. If your first sowing fails to form any roots and the tops quickly go to seed, this will be the result of a cold, wet spring. Normally the first sowings for an early crop can be made in early April, and further sowings can be made later in July/August to provide a succession of crops.

There is nothing you can do to save a crop which has gone to seed, so pull up the offending plants and re-sow for a new supply. When the new shoots first appear, dust with an insecticide to kill the devastating flea beetle which will quickly eat through all the roots. Keep the plants well watered in dry weather.

Preparation and cooking

Early turnips have a more delicate flavour and the tiny ones can even be served raw in salads as well as cooked. The tops of young turnips can be cooked and mashed and served like cabbage. One variety we know of – Green Top White – is specially recommended for the usefulness of its green tops.

To prepare, top, tail and peel off the skin. Baby turnips can be left whole, but larger ones are sliced or diced.

To boil: Prepare as above, place in a pan of cold salted water, bring to the boil, cover and cook for 15 to 25 minutes.

To steam: Place the prepared vegetables in a steamer over a pan of boiling water, cover and cook for 20 to 30 minutes.

To braise: See Indian turnips (p. 190); sauté in butter and spices for 10 minutes, then braise in stock for 10 minutes.

To roast: See roast lamb and baby turnips in wine (p. 189); parboil for 5 minutes, drain and roast for 45 minutes to 1 hour.

To sauté: See turnip sauté (p. 191) and herbed turnip (p. 191); sauté in butter for 15 to 20 minutes.

Serving suggestions: Boiled or steamed whole baby turnips may be served in a mornay sauce.

How to deal with a glut

1. Freezing: Peel; leave small turnips whole; slice or dice larger ones into 3- to 5-cm (1- to 2-inch) pieces.

Blanch the prepared turnips for 3 minutes. Chill, drain and pack into polythene bags or wax or foil containers. Storage time: 9 to 12 months.

Also freeze turnip and chicken soup (below).

2. Storing: Turnips may be left in the ground or stored in a cool shed – twist off the tops and store in boxes of sand.

Turnip and Chicken Soup

Serves 6–8

1	chicken carcass and bones	1
1¾ litres	water	3 pints
500 g	young turnips	1 lb
250 g	potatoes	8 oz
½	large onion	½
50 g	butter or margarine	2 oz
	salt and pepper	
100–175 g	left-over chicken pieces	4–6 oz
2	egg yolks	2
4–6 tbsps	single cream	4–6 tbsps
	fried croûtons	

Place the chicken carcass and bones in a large saucepan with the water, bring slowly to the boil, cover and simmer gently for at least 1 hour. Drain the bones from the stock and retain any pieces of chicken left on the carcass. Leave the stock to cool and, when cold, skim off the fat which will have solidified on top.

Peel and dice the turnips and the potatoes; peel and finely chop the onion. Melt the butter or margarine in a large saucepan, add these vegetables, cover and cook over a low heat for about 10 minutes, stir-ring occasionally and taking care that the vegetables do not brown. Add the chicken stock, salt and pepper, but not the pieces of left-over chicken. Bring to the boil, cover and simmer slowly for about 45 minutes. Put the soup through a fine sieve or liquidize it. Now add the chicken, cut into bite-sized pieces.

Finally, beat the egg yolks with the cream in a large bowl and slowly stir in the soup. Return the soup to the saucepan and heat, but do not boil.

To serve, place an extra teaspoon of cream in the middle of each bowl of soup and serve with a bowl of fried croûtons to garnish.

Note: Frozen turnips may be used to make this soup.

* Suitable for freezing before adding the egg yolks and cream. After thawing, thicken the soup with the yolk and cream liaison.

Roast Lamb and Baby Turnips in Wine

Serves 4

1¼–1½ kg	leg or shoulder of lamb	3–3½ lb
	fat for roasting	
500 g	baby turnips	1 lb
150 ml	red wine	¼ pint
	salt and freshly ground black pepper	

a roasting pan

Preheat the oven to 220°C, 425°F, gas mark 7.

Weigh the lamb and calculate the cooking time, allowing 20 minutes per 500 g (1 lb) and 20 minutes extra. Wipe the lamb with a damp cloth.

Heat the fat in the roasting pan in the preheated oven, add the lamb joint and roast for 20 minutes before reducing the oven temperature to 180°C, 350°F, gas mark 4.

Meanwhile, top and tail the baby turnips and remove the skins. Place in a saucepan of cold salted water (with the peeled potatoes if you are also preparing roast potatoes), bring to the boil and cook for 5 minutes. Drain thoroughly, then, when the oven temperature is being reduced, add the turnips to the roasting pan with the lamb (roast the potatoes in a separate pan).

Pour the red wine over the lamb and turnips; continue to cook, basting frequently with the wine, until the lamb is tender. When the meat is cooked, place the turnips in a warm serving dish and sprinkle with salt and pepper. Use the wine and lamb juices in the roasting pan to make a rich gravy.

Indian Turnips

Serves 3–4

300 g	turnips	10 oz
1	small onion	1
1 clove	garlic, peeled	1 clove
25 g	butter or margarine	1 oz
½ level tsp	turmeric	½ level tsp
¼ level tsp	ground coriander	¼ level tsp
¼ level tsp	ground cumin	¼ level tsp
¼ level tsp	fenugreek	¼ level tsp
150 ml	chicken stock	¼ pint
	salt and freshly ground pepper	
2 tbsps	sour cream	2 tbsps

Peel and dice the turnips and onion; crush the garlic with a little salt. Melt the butter or margarine in a large frying pan and add the diced vegetables and crushed garlic. Sauté over a low heat, tossing occasionally until the turnips have absorbed the butter and are browning – about 10 minutes.

Add the turmeric, coriander, cumin and fenugreek and fry for a further 2 minutes. Stir in the stock and seasoning, cover the pan and cook for a further 10 minutes by which time the stock will have been absorbed. Stir in the sour cream, check for seasoning and serve hot as a vegetable accompaniment.

Note: Frozen diced turnips may be used in this recipe.

Turnip Sauté

Serves 3–4

175 g	streaky bacon	6 oz
500 g	turnip	1 lb
½	large onion	½
25 g	butter or margarine	1 oz
	salt and pepper	

Remove the rind and any bone from the bacon and dice the bacon. Put the rinds and bacon in a frying pan and fry gently for 5 minutes. Discard the rinds and put the bacon on a plate.

Meanwhile, peel and dice the turnip; peel and slice the onion thinly. Heat the butter or margarine in the frying pan, add the turnip and onion, cover and sauté gently for 10 minutes, stirring occasionally.

Return the bacon to the pan, mix with the other ingredients and sauté for a further 5 to 10 minutes until the turnip is tender. Season to taste with salt and pepper. Serve as a vegetable accompaniment – it is delicious with roast pork or grilled chops.

Note: Frozen diced turnips may be used in this recipe.

Herbed Turnip

Serves 4

500 g	turnip	1 lb
25 g	butter or margarine	1 oz
1 tbsp	lemon juice	1 tbsp
½ tsp	fresh mixed herbs, chopped	½ tsp
½ tsp	brown sugar	½ tsp

Peel and dice the turnip. Heat the butter or margarine in a large saucepan or frying pan, add the turnip, lemon juice and chopped herbs, cover and sauté gently for 15 to 20 minutes, turning occasionally.

Place the turnips and their juices in a warmed serving dish, sprinkle the brown sugar over them and place under a hot grill until the top is starting to brown. Serve as a vegetable accompaniment.

Note: Frozen diced turnips may be used in this recipe.

Part Two: Fruits

General Introduction to Fruits

The fruit garden can be one of the most rewarding ventures for the home gardener. Once established, fruit trees and bushes will continue cropping for many years, providing supplies of luscious fruits for the family to enjoy.

The best results are only achieved by lavishing care and attention on your fruit crops. The normal tasks include spraying, pruning and protecting from birds. All the fruits are fair prey to the aphids – black and green fly – and all except rhubarb have their own particular pests, e.g. the raspberry beetle, the blackcurrant 'big bud' mite and the gooseberry sawfly caterpillar. To combat attacks from these and other insects, spray your plants with Derris or Malathion.

Pruning is another important chore in caring for the fruit garden. Some fruits, e.g. blackcurrants, raspberries and blackberries, produce their crops on new wood, so pruning back the old stems which have recently borne fruit is very important to encourage the development of new wood. Pruning is also important after planting new bushes or trees as this helps to concentrate growth to produce stronger new shoots or branches.

However, all this hard work can soon turn to bitter disappointment if your fruit garden is not protected from attack by birds. Watching your fruits being systematically stripped by unwelcome invaders is one of the most frustrating and discouraging things that can happen to a gardener. For this reason it is best to protect your fruit crops, especially soft fruits, plums and sweet cherries, by covering them with nets or growing them inside a special fruit cage.

A fruit garden presents the gardener with several advantages. To begin with, there is little need to plant new trees or bushes once your fruit garden is well established. Most will last for at least a decade before needing replacement. Once the initial investment is made, most will reproduce themselves, e.g. strawberries throw out numerous runners to provide new crops, cuttings may be taken from currant and gooseberry bushes, raspberries provide new canes each year to bear their fruit, and rhubarb 'crowns' can be split to form new clumps.

Another advantage of the fruit garden is the attractive display it can provide, especially with the spring blossoms. The fan-tailed or cordon varieties of most fruits make a neat and pleasing spectacle and these also make use of normally unproductive space, e.g. against a garden wall or fence.

A final point in favour of a fruit garden is that some fruits will even tolerate partial shade.

To counteract these advantages there are two main disadvantages to fruits. First, with some varieties it may take several years after planting before you begin to reap the full benefit of their crops.

The other problem is that of storage – only apples and pears can be stored raw and, to store successfully, they require careful handling and packing. Soft fruits do not store at all well and should be eaten as soon after picking as possible. All fruits deteriorate faster if kept in a centrally heated room and should ideally be kept in a cool larder (but not a fridge).

However, freezer owners can easily overcome the problem of storage as most fruits freeze well without even needing to be blanched first.

Even if you do not own a deep freeze, all fruits make excellent jams, jellies, chutneys, pickles, sauces, drinks and home-made wines to fill the store cupboard.

25 Apples

Introduction

Apples are by far and away the most common fruit grown in British gardens. Every garden, however small, benefits from the presence of a tree, and apple trees not only provide fruit to eat but attractive spring blossom and summer shade from the sun.

There are dozens of varieties and most thrive happily in the temperamental British climate. Some, however, like Cox's Orange Pippins, require a fertile soil and the warmer weather of the south to be successful.

After first planting, most trees will take a number of years to establish themselves before they start to yield a good crop. Thereafter, the quantity and quality of the fruit will be greatly improved by pruning in late autumn/early winter and by spraying against pest attack.

For the small garden, the bush or dwarf varieties or the cordon (trained) trees are real space-savers. They are also more easily pruned, sprayed with insecticides and protected with netting from birds.

Preparation and cooking

There are a wealth of recipes using apples – they feature not only in sweet puddings but also in almost all chutneys and many preserves and salads, and they also add an extra dimension to casseroles. However, we have had to restrict ourselves in the number of recipes used in this book.

When apples are being prepared for cooking they are usually peeled, cored and sliced or quartered. Occasionally, the skins are not removed, e.g. for baked apples or when red-skinned eating apples are required to add colour contrast in a recipe.

To stew: Prepare 500 g (1 lb) of fruit as above and slice thinly into a pan with 2 tablespoons of water. Cover and simmer for 7 to 10 minutes until tender, then add enough sugar to sweeten – approximately 100 to 125 g (3 to 4 oz) for every 500 g (1 lb) of fruit.

Alternatively, apples may be stewed in butter – 25 g (1 oz) butter for every 500 g (1 lb) of fruit, with 2 tablespoons sugar added to the pan. First melt the butter, then add the apples and sugar, cover and cook very gently for 7 to 10 minutes, stirring occasionally, until tender. This is a tastier if more expensive way of stewing them.

To steam: Prepare as above, slice the apples into a steamer (no water is necessary) over a pan of boiling water, cover and cook for 7 to 10 minutes.

To bake: See baked stuffed apples (p. 200) and apple dumplings (p. 201); bake for about 30 minutes.

To deep fry: See apple dough rings (p. 202); coat in batter and fry for 3 to 4 minutes.

Serving suggestions: The stewed or steamed apples may be served with custard, cream or ice-cream. To use raw apple slices for decoration, first dip in lemon juice to prevent discoloration.

How to deal with a glut

1. Freezing: Choose fresh, undamaged, just-ripe fruits. Peel, core and slice. If freezing without sugar, blanch in boiling water for 2 minutes; cool, drain and dry. Pack into polythene bags or wax containers. To freeze in sugar, prepare as above and pack in layers with dry sugar – 125 g (4 oz) sugar for every 500 g (1 lb) fruit – or pour over the apples a cold syrup solution of 375 g (13 oz) sugar in 600 ml (1 pint) water. Pack into containers or polythene bags, seal, label and freeze. Storage time: 9 to 12 months.

To freeze apple purée, prepare the apples and stew or steam as above, using 1 tablespoon of water. Sieve them and sweeten if desired. It is a good idea to sweeten some of the purée and leave the rest unsweetened to be used for savoury sauces, etc. Storage time: 9 months.

Apple and gingerbread pudding (p. 203), apple cake (p. 207) and apple brown betty (p. 203) all freeze well, cooked or uncooked.

2. Preserving: The following are ways of preserving apples: sliced apples bottled in syrup (p. 323) or bottled with blackberries (p. 324); onion and apple pickle (p. 330); apples pickled in spiced vinegar syrup (p. 323); apple mincemeat (p. 208); apple jelly (p. 318); apple and ginger jam (p. 312); blackberry and apple jam (p. 218); damson and apple jam (p. 265); apple and date chutney (p. 208); and all other chutneys listed in the index.

3. Storing: Only undamaged fruit can be stored successfully on trays, and it is essential to ensure that the apples are not touching (a good idea is to ask your greengrocer for one of the apple boxes, with special polystyrene layers, in which his apples were delivered to him). Otherwise, each apple should be individually wrapped, e.g. in newspaper. Store in a cool, dry place – a shed or garage is ideal. If stored indoors where there is central heating, you will find that the skins will soon start to shrivel. Occasionally check that none of the apples have become rotten and, if there are rotten ones, discard these immediately or they will turn the others bad.

Breast of Lamb with Apple Stuffing

Serves 3–4

½–1 kg	breast of lamb	1–2 lb
1 tbsp	dripping or fat	1 tbsp

For the stuffing

175 g	cooking apples	6 oz
25 g	butter or margarine	1 oz
4	mint leaves	4
1 level tbsp	nuts, chopped finely	1 level tbsp
50 g	fresh breadcrumbs	2 oz
1 tsp	lemon juice	1 tsp
½ level tsp	salt	½ level tsp
	cayenne pepper, to taste	

Preheat the oven to 180°C, 350°F, gas mark 4.

Wipe the lamb and trim off as much fat as possible. Remove any bones. Either get your butcher to do this or use a small, sharp, pointed knife to cut down each side of the bones and ease them out.

Peel, core and finely dice the apples. In a saucepan heat the butter or margarine, add the apple, cover the pan and cook gently for 5 minutes. Finely chop the mint leaves and the nuts and add them all to the pan along with the breadcrumbs, lemon juice, salt and a sprinkling of cayenne. Mix all the ingredients well together.

Lay the breast of lamb out and spread the stuffing mixture over the inside surface of the meat. Carefully roll up the meat and secure the joint in several places with some string.

Roast with the dripping or fat in the preheated oven for 1 to 1½ hours, basting occasionally.

* Suitable for freezing – stuffed and uncooked.

Liver Casserole

Serves 2–3

300 g	liver	10 oz
25 g	flour seasoned with salt and pepper	1 oz
25 g	butter or margarine	1 oz
½	lemon, juice only	½
100 g	onions	4 oz
100 g	cooking apples	4 oz
4	rashers of streaky bacon	4

a 1¼-litre (2-pint) casserole

Preheat the oven to 180°C, 350°F, gas mark 4.

Wipe the liver with damp kitchen paper, then coat the slices with seasoned flour. Melt the butter or margarine in a frying pan and fry the liver for a minute on each side. Lay the slices in the base of the casserole dish and squeeze the juice of the half lemon over them.

Peel and finely chop the onions; peel, core and chop the apples. Fry both in the fat in the frying pan until soft and golden. Spread the apple and onion mixture on top of the liver slices. Finally, remove the rinds and any bone from the bacon and lay the rashers on top of the casserole. Bake, uncovered, on the centre shelf of the preheated oven for 45 minutes until the liver is cooked.

* Suitable for freezing.

Monday Pancakes

Serves 3–4

300 ml	pancake batter (p. 344)	½ pint

For the filling

350 g	cooking apples	12 oz
50 g	onion	2 oz
	knob of butter or margarine	
3 tbsps	pork gravy	3 tbsps
300–350 g	cooked pork, minced	10–12 oz
1 level tsp	salt	1 level tsp
	freshly ground pepper	
1 level tbsp	fresh sage, chopped	1 level tbsp
600 ml	celery sauce (p. 70)	1 pint

Prepare and make the pancakes (see p. 344) and keep warm, wrapped in a clean tea towel.

To prepare the filling, peel, core and finely chop the apples and peel and finely chop the onion. Heat the butter or margarine in a saucepan and sauté the onion gently until it is soft but not browned. Add the diced apple and the pork gravy, cover the pan and cook gently for a further 10 minutes. Stir in the minced pork, salt, pepper and chopped sage and heat until the meat is hot.

Lay the pancakes out flat and divide the pork stuffing evenly among them; place the filling at one end of the pancake, then roll it up. Lay the hot pancake rolls in an ovenproof serving dish and pour the celery sauce over them. Serve hot.

Note: This is a good recipe for stretching any left-over meat from the Sunday joint (chicken or lamb can also be used).

* Suitable for freezing.

Baked and Stuffed Apples

Serves 4

4	medium-sized cooking apples	4
	knob of butter	

Stuffings	*1*	
4 tbsps	mincemeat (p. 208)	4 tbsps
	or 2	
50 g	brown sugar	2 oz
50 g	butter	2 oz

	pinch of ground cloves *or 3*	
4 tbsps	blackcurrant, blackberry or plum jam *or 4*	4 tbsps
4 tbsps	lemon curd	4 tbsps
1 level tbsp	chopped walnuts	1 level tbsp

Preheat the oven to 190°C, 375°F, gas mark 5.

Wipe the apples and, keeping them whole, remove the centre core using an apple corer or a small knife. If baking the apples beside a joint of pork, leave the apples unstuffed or use stuffing no. 2 to fill the centre cavities. Make a thin cut around the middle of each apple to just break the skin. Place the apples beside the joint and baste with the fat juices. There is no need to use the butter given in the ingredients.

For stuffed apples as a sweet, fill the centres with one of the four stuffings and brush with melted butter. Place the apples on a greased baking sheet or tray and bake on the centre shelf of the preheated oven for about 30 minutes until cooked but still whole. Serve hot with custard, cream or brandy butter.

Apple Dumplings

Serves 4

200 g	puff, rough puff or shortcrust pastry (pp. 336, 337, 334)	8 oz
4	medium-sized apples a filling for the centres (see stuffed apples, p. 200) egg glaze	4

Preheat the oven to 190°C, 375°F, gas mark 5.

Prepare the pastry and leave to rest. Wipe the apples and, keeping them whole, remove the centre cores. Choose one of the stuffings from the baked and stuffed apples recipe opposite and fill the cavity of each apple.

Roll out the pastry on a floured surface and cut three circles about 17 to 18 cm (7 inches) in diameter. Re-roll the trimmings to make the fourth circle. Place the top end of one of the apples down on the centre of one of the circles and fold up the pastry to envelop the apple completely. Damp the edges well and seal. Turn the dumpling upside down so that the seal is underneath and place on a baking sheet or tray.

Repeat this process with the other apples. Re-roll the pastry trimmings again and cut eight pastry leaves to decorate the dumplings. Place two leaves on each dumpling, and brush them with egg glaze. Bake on the centre shelf of the preheated oven for about 30 minutes until the pastry is lightly browned. Serve hot with custard or cream.

Apple Dough-Rings

Serves 4

150 ml	fritter batter (p. 343)	¼ pint
350 g	apples	12 oz
	oil for deep frying	
	caster sugar	

a deep-fat frying pan

Prepare the batter and leave to stand for ½ hour before use.

Peel the apples and, keeping them whole, remove the centre core, using an apple corer. Cut into 1-cm (¼- to ½-inch) rings and dip into the coating batter to cover completely.

Meanwhile, heat the oil in the frying pan until it is hot enough to turn a cube of bread golden brown almost immediately. Deep fry the apple rings two or three at a time, taking care they do not stick together. When browned underneath – about 1 to 2 minutes – turn over to brown the other side. Drain well and then toss in a bowl of caster sugar to coat generously. Serve hot with melted syrup, custard or cream.

Note: This recipe can be made with either cooking or eating apples. The cooking apples will be rather more tart when cooked.

Apple Brown Betty

Serves 4–6

500 g	cooking apples	1 lb
175 g	fresh brown breadcrumbs	6 oz
½	lemon, grated rind and juice	½
75 g	demerara sugar	3 oz
2 tbsps	golden syrup	2 tbsps
1 tbsp	water	1 tbsp
	knob of butter or margarine	

a 1-litre (1½-pint) ovenproof dish

Preheat the oven to 160°C, 325°F, gas mark 3.

Grease the ovenproof dish well around the base and sides. Peel, core and finely slice the apples. Sprinkle some of the breadcrumbs in the bottom of the dish and turn around to coat the sides as well. Lay half of the sliced apples on top of the crumbs, another layer of crumbs and then the remaining apples. Reserve the rest of the crumbs for the topping.

Put the grated lemon rind and juice in a saucepan with the sugar, syrup and water and heat to melt the sugar and syrup, but do not boil. Pour the sauce evenly over the dish and cover the top with the remaining breadcrumbs. Dot with the butter or margarine and bake on the centre shelf of the preheated oven for 1¼ to 1½ hours until the apples are tender and the top of the pudding is nicely browned.

* Suitable for freezing.

Apple Gingerbread Pudding

Serves 5

125 g	butter	4 oz
125 g	dark, soft brown sugar	4 oz
125 g	black treacle	4 oz
1	large egg	1
175 g	plain flour	6 oz

2 level tsps	ground ginger	2 level tsps
1½ level tsps	ground cinnamon	1½ level tsps
150 ml	milk	¼ pint
1 level tsp	bicarbonate of soda	1 level tsp
500 g	cooking apples	1 lb

a 1-kg (2-lb) loaf tin, greased and base-lined

Preheat the oven to 150°C, 300°F, gas mark 2.

Put the butter, sugar and treacle in a saucepan over a low heat to allow the butter to melt, but do not allow it to become too hot.

Beat the egg lightly, add to the warm treacle mixture and mix well. Sift the flour, ginger and cinnamon into a medium-sized bowl. Warm the milk to blood heat, pour it onto the bicarbonate of soda, stir into the flour with the treacle mixture and mix well together.

Quickly peel, quarter and core the apples and slice thinly into the greased loaf tin (it is not necessary to arrange them neatly).

Pour the gingerbread mixture over the apples and bake at once on the centre shelf of the preheated oven for about 50 minutes, until the centre is firm to the touch. Cool slightly in the tin, then run a knife down the sides of the tin before turning the pudding onto a serving plate. Serve hot with custard.

* Suitable for freezing.

Veiled Country Girl

Serves 4–5

1 kg	cooking apples	2 lb
175 g	sugar	6 oz
2 tbsps	water	2 tbsps
25 g	butter or margarine	1 oz
50 g	plain chocolate	2 oz
150 g	fresh brown breadcrumbs	5 oz
150 ml	double cream	¼ pint
	a little grated chocolate	

Peel and core the apples and slice into a pan with the sugar and water; cover and cook until soft. Put the apples through a sieve, or liquidize them. Leave to cool, then check to see if extra sugar is needed.

Melt the butter in a pan with the chocolate. Stir in the breadcrumbs and, stirring continuously, cook until all the butter mixture is absorbed and the breadcrumbs are crispy. Pour the cream into a bowl and whip until thick.

In a glass serving dish, first spread a layer of apple purée, then crumb mixture, whipped cream and another layer of apples. Repeat the layers, ending with the cream. Smooth over the surface and decorate with a little grated chocolate. Leave for 2 hours before serving.

Note: Frozen sweetened apple purée can be used.

Swiss Dessert

Serves 4

¾ kg	cooking apples	1½ lb
1 tbsp	water	1 tbsp
	pinch of ground cloves	
1 well-rounded tsp	honey	1 well-rounded tsp
½	lemon, grated rind and juice	½
150 ml	double cream	¼ pint
50 g	Swiss muesli	2 oz
	a little grated chocolate	

4 individual glass dishes

Peel, core and slice the apples and place in a saucepan with the water and ground cloves. Cover the pan and cook gently until the apples are soft and pulpy. Pass them through a sieve or purée them in a liquidizer. Stir in the honey and leave to chill.

When the apple is cold, stir in the grated lemon rind and 1 teaspoon of lemon juice. Whip the double cream until thick then fold it into the apple. Finally, stir in the muesli and divide the mixture among the four serving dishes. Decorate with a little grated chocolate and serve at once while the muesli is still quite crunchy.

Apple Soufflé Cake

Serves 8

¾ kg	cooking apples	1½ lb
75 g	butter or margarine	3 oz
50–75 g	sugar	2–3 oz
½	lemon, grated rind and juice	½
175 g	sweet biscuits, e.g. digestive, oatmeal	6 oz
3 level tsps	powdered gelatine (1 sachet)	3 level tsps
150 ml	double cream	¼ pint
2	egg whites	2

a 20-cm (8-inch) loose-based cake tin

Peel, core and slice the apples. Heat 25 g (1 oz) of the butter or margarine in a saucepan and add the apples, sugar, grated lemon rind and juice. Cook gently until tender, stirring occasionally to prevent the apples from sticking to the pan. Purée in a liquidizer or through a fine sieve. Leave to cool.

Place the sweet biscuits in a polythene bag and crush with a rolling pin. Melt the rest of the butter in a saucepan, remove from the heat and add the crumbs, stirring well to mix with the butter. Press the crumb mixture onto the base of the cake tin.

Dissolve the gelatine in 3 tablespoons of water over a low heat, but do not boil; then add to the apple purée. Lightly whip the cream and fold almost all of it into the apple mixture, keeping a little for decoration.

Finally, stiffly beat the egg whites and gently fold them into the soufflé. Pour the mixture onto the cooled biscuit base and leave in a cool place, e.g. the refrigerator, for several hours to set.

When ready to serve, carefully ease the soufflé cake out of the tin and decorate the top with whirls of whipped double cream.

Note: Frozen apple slices or sweetened apple purée, with the lemon rind and juice added, can be used.

Apple Cake

Serves 6–8

175 g	self-raising flour	6 oz
	pinch of salt	
1 level tsp	mixed spice	1 level tsp
50 g	rolled oats	2 oz
100 g	margarine	4 oz
100g	light, soft brown sugar	4 oz
2	large eggs	2
3 tbsps	milk	3 tbsps
500 g	cooking apples	1 lb
50 g	demerara sugar	2 oz

a 20-cm (8-inch) loose-based cake tin

Preheat the oven to 190°C, 375°F, gas mark 5.

Grease the tin and line the base with greased greaseproof paper. Sift the flour and salt into a bowl with the mixed spice, then add the rolled oats. Rub the margarine into the flour, using the fingertips only, until the mixture resembles fine breadcrumbs. Stir in the sugar. Beat the eggs lightly together and stir into the mixture with the milk. Mix well together, then spoon the mixture into the greased tin and smooth over the surface.

Peel, quarter and core the apples and slice them fairly thinly. Lay the apple slices overlapping each other to cover the entire surface of the cake in a neat pattern. Sprinkle the demerara sugar over the apple slices and bake on the centre shelf of the preheated oven for 55 minutes to 1 hour, until the cake is springy to the touch and the apples are golden brown. Remove from the tin and serve, hot or cold, as a pudding with custard or as a tea-time cake.

* Suitable for freezing.

Apple Mincemeat

Makes about 1 kg (2 lb)

250 g	currants	8 oz
250 g	raisins	8 oz
100 g	dates, chopped	4 oz
100 g	chopped mixed peel	4 oz
75 g	chopped mixed nuts, almonds or walnuts	3 oz
175 g	shredded suet	6 oz
350 g	soft brown sugar	12 oz
1	lemon, juice and grated rind	1
25 g	crystallized ginger, finely chopped	1 oz
150 ml	sherry	¼ pint
1 level tsp	ground mace	1 level tsp
1 level tsp	ground cinnamon	1 level tsp
1 level tsp	ground mixed spice	1 level tsp
¾ kg	cooking apples	1½ lb

In a large bowl mix together all the ingredients except the apples.

Peel, core and grate the apples into the mincemeat mixture. Stir well to combine all the ingredients evenly. Bottle, label, seal and store for about 1 month before using.

Note: See baked stuffed apples (p. 200) for a use of apple mincemeat.

Apple and Date Chutney

Makes about 3 kg (6½ lb)

¾ kg	demerara sugar	1½ lb
900 ml	malt vinegar	1½ pints
1 kg	cooking apples	2 lb
500 g	onions	1 lb
500 g	cooking dates	1 lb
500 g	currants	1 lb
2 tbsps	black treacle	2 tbsps

1 tbsp	salt	1 tbsp
1 tbsp	curry paste	1 tbsp
1 level tsp	ground ginger	1 level tsp
½ level tsp	ground cloves	½ level tsp

a preserving pan or large saucepan

Put the demerara sugar in a bowl and add 300 ml (½ pint) of vinegar. Leave in a warm place to dissolve the sugar partially, stirring occasionally.

Meanwhile, place the remaining 600 ml (1 pint) of vinegar in a preserving pan. Peel, core and thinly slice the apples into the pan and cook them gently for 20 minutes. Peel and finely chop the onions; and chop the dates roughly, and add them both to the pan. When the contents are bubbling, simmer gently for 15 minutes, then remove from the heat.

Add the rest of the ingredients – the currants, treacle, salt, curry paste, ginger and cloves. Finally, stir in the sugar and vinegar mixture.

Return the pan to a low heat and allow the sugar to dissolve completely, stirring occasionally. Now bring the contents to the boil and boil for 30 minutes, stirring occasionally, by which time the chutney should be dark and fairly thick.

Remove from the heat and pour into warm, clean, dry jars. Cover with wax discs, seal with thick polythene, label and store for a month in a cool place before using.

Note: Frozen sliced apples may be used.

The following recipes also include apples:

Blackberry and apple squares (p. 215)
Blackberry and apple jam (p. 218)
Harvest tart (p. 212)
Damson and apple jam (p. 265)
Mock mango chutney (p. 264)
Blackberry and apple jelly (p. 318)
Elderberry and apple jelly (p. 318)
Apple or crab apple jelly (p. 318)
Apple and ginger jam (p. 312)
Mint and apple jelly (p. 318)
Bottled apples (p. 323)
Pickled apples (p. 332)
Cucumber and apple salad (p. 81)

September lamb hotchpotch (p. 168)
Parsnip and apple rolls (p. 131)
Braised red cabbage (p. 50)
Waldorf salad (p. 70)
Bramble chutney (p. 217)
Beetroot chutney (p. 26)
Cucumber relish (p. 83)
Late summer chutney (p. 106)
Green tomato chutney (p. 183)
Red tomato jam (p. 185)
Beetroot jam (p. 26)

Try substituting apples for the main fruit in the following recipes:

Rhubarb and gooseberry crumble (p. 286) (both fruits or just the gooseberry)
Cherry batter pudding (p. 231)

26 Blackberries

Introduction

You do not need to grow cultivated blackberries to find this chapter of interest, as during the late summer months the countryside teems with wild blackberry bushes laden with fruit. It is mainly on this free produce that we have based most of the following recipes, but remember that the wild berries tend to be more bitter in taste and smaller in size than the cultivated varieties.

There are now thornless bushes on the market, which make picking the fruit a less prickly task, and these plants need not take up much space in the garden as they can be planted against a shed, wall or fence. Blackberries are not fussy about the quality of soil they grow on and will also tolerate a shady position which helps make them easy plants to grow. However, the addition of manure or well-rotted compost to the soil will improve the quality of the crops and, once established, each bush can provide up to 10 kg (20 lb) of berries.

When the old canes have borne their fruit, they should be cut right down at the end of the year to allow new stalks to take over. Plant new canes from October to mid winter.

Preparation and cooking

As most people know, blackberries and apples team very well together, complementing each other in colour, flavour and texture.

To prepare blackberries, the leaves and hulls are removed, but only road-side berries need to be washed.

To stew: Prepare 500 g (1 lb) fruit as above and place in a saucepan with 1 to 2 tablespoons water; cover and simmer gently for about 10 minutes until soft. To purée, put through a sieve while still hot. Add enough sugar to sweeten – about 125 to 150 g (4 to 6 oz) for every 500 g (1 lb) fruit.

Serving suggestions: Serve hot or cold as a sauce for ice-cream, melbas, etc.

How to deal with a glut

1. Freezing: Prepare as above; if they need washing, then gently pat dry afterwards. Place in polythene bags or containers in handy quantities. Alternatively, pack into containers layered with dry sugar, allowing 125 g (4 oz) per 500 g (1 lb) berries. Storage time: 9 to 12 months.

Blackberry and apple squares (p. 215) and blackberry purée also freeze very well.

2. Preserving: Bottle in spiced vinegar syrup (p. 332) or in syrup or water (p. 324); or make blackberry jelly (p. 318) or blackberry and apple jam (p. 218).

3. Storing: They will keep in the bottom of the fridge for up to 10 days, provided that they have not been washed first.

Harvest Tart

Serves 5–6

200 g	sweet shortcrust pastry (p. 335)	8 oz

For the filling

350 g	cooking apples	12 oz
250 g	blackberries	8 oz
40 g	butter	1½ oz
75 g	caster sugar	3 oz
25 g	plain flour	1 oz
2	large eggs	2
150 ml	milk	¼ pint
	a little extra caster sugar	

a 22-cm (9-inch) fluted flan dish

Preheat the oven to 190°C, 375°F, gas mark 5.

Make the pastry and roll it out on a floured surface to line the flan dish. Trim the top edges and then leave the flan to rest for 15 minutes.

Peel, quarter and core the apples and slice them thinly. Hull the blackberries, rinse under cold water and drain well. Heat the butter in a large frying pan and toss the apples in the butter for a few minutes to soften them slightly, then stir in the blackberries and heat for a minute until the colour of the blackberries starts to run into the apples. Fold in 50 g (2 oz) of the sugar, then turn the fruit into the pastry flan case.

In a bowl mix together the remaining 25 g (1 oz) caster sugar, the flour and the eggs; then gradually beat in the milk. Pour this mixture over the fruit and bake at once on the centre shelf of the preheated oven for 40 to 45 minutes, until the filling is cooked and the pastry lightly golden.

Before serving, either hot or cold, sprinkle over it a little extra caster sugar.

Note: Frozen apple slices and blackberries can be used.

* Suitable for freezing.

Blackberry and Orange Pudding

Serves 4

300 g	blackberries	10 oz
	a little caster sugar	
25 g	butter or margarine	1 oz
100 g	caster sugar	4 oz
1	orange, grated rind and juice	1
25 g	plain flour	1 oz
	pinch of salt	
2	large eggs, separated	2
150 ml	milk	¼ pint

a 20-cm (8-inch) deep pie dish, greased

Preheat the oven to 160°C, 325°F, gas mark 3.

Hull and, if necessary, rinse the blackberries and place in the base of the greased pie dish. Sprinkle with a little caster sugar if the berries are bitter.

Cream together the butter and sugar, add the grated orange rind and juice, and beat the mixture, which will be runny. Beat in the flour, salt and egg yolks. Stir in the milk and, finally, fold in the stiffly beaten egg whites.

Pour the mixture over the top of the blackberries and bake on the centre shelf of the preheated oven for 45 minutes, by which time the topping will have risen and become browned. Dredge the top with caster sugar and serve immediately, otherwise, like a soufflé, the sponge will soon start to sink. The blackberries should be cooked in a lovely creamy orange sauce. Serve with cream or custard.

Blackberry Roll

Serves 4–5

For the pastry

200 g	self-raising flour	8 oz
	pinch of salt	
75 g	margarine	3 oz
½	orange, grated rind	½
25 g	caster sugar	1 oz
1	small egg	1
2 tbsps	milk	2 tbsps

For the filling

75 g	cream cheese	3 oz
1 tbsp	orange juice	1 tbsp
50 g	caster sugar	2 oz
250 g	blackberries	8 oz

a greased baking sheet

Preheat the oven to 190°C, 375°F, gas mark 5.

Sift the flour and salt into a bowl and rub in the margarine, using the fingertips only, until the mixture resembles fine breadcrumbs. Add the grated orange rind and the sugar. Mix the egg with the milk and add to the dry ingredients to form a firm dough. Leave to rest for 15 minutes.

Beat the cream cheese lightly in a bowl with the orange juice and sugar. Hull and, if necessary, rinse the blackberries, drain well and pat dry to remove any excess moisture. Stir them gently into the cheese mixture.

On a floured surface, roll out the pastry to a rectangle 30 by 25 cm (12 by 10 inches). Spread the filling over the pastry to within 3 cm (1 inch) of the edges. Damp the edges and roll up carefully.

Place the roll on the baking sheet with the join underneath. Make two slits in the top and brush the surface with a little milk.

Bake on the centre shelf of the preheated oven for 40 minutes. Sprinkle with a little extra caster sugar before serving hot with custard or cream.

Note: Frozen blackberries can be used.

* Suitable for freezing.

Blackberry and Apple Squares

Makes about 12 large slices

| 200 g | flaky pastry (p. 338) | 8 oz |

For the filling

400 g	cooking apples	1 lb
2 tbsps	water	2 tbsps
50–75 g	sugar	2–3 oz
200 g	blackberries	8 oz
	egg white or milk	
	caster sugar	

a 30- by 20-cm (12- by 8-inch) swiss roll tin, greased

Preheat the oven to 190°C, 375°F, gas mark 5.

Prepare the flaky pastry and leave in a cool place for at least ½ an hour before use.

Peel, core and slice the apples. Put in a pan, cover and cook gently in the water and sugar for 5 minutes. Hull and, if necessary, rinse the blackberries, stir them into the apple mixture, remove from the heat and add more sugar to taste.

Divide the flaky pastry into two portions. Roll out the first piece, on a lightly floured surface, large enough to fit the base of the greased swiss roll tin (this should be easily achieved as the preparation of the flaky pastry leaves it in a neat rectangular shape).

Line the base of the tin with the pastry. Spoon the apple and blackberry mixture over it evenly, to within 2 cm (¾ inch) of the edges.

Roll out the second piece of pastry to fit the top of the baking tin and place on top of the fruit. Damp and seal the edges, brush the top of the pastry with lightly beaten egg white or milk and sprinkle generously with caster sugar.

Bake on the centre shelf of the preheated oven for about 25 minutes until the top is nicely frosted and browned. Serve hot or cold, cut into squares.

Note: You can use a smaller-size baking tin if necessary, but the pastry will be thicker and may need longer to cook. Frozen apple slices and blackberries can be used.

* Suitable for freezing.

Blackberry Charlotte

Serves 6

500 g	blackberries	1 lb
1	blackcurrant jelly	1
24–26	sponge finger biscuits	24–26
1 rounded tbsp	custard powder	1 rounded tbsp
50 g	caster sugar	2 oz
300 ml	milk	½ pint
1 level tsp	powdered gelatine	1 level tsp
2 tbsps	water	2 tbsps
150 ml	double cream	¼ pint

an 18-cm (7-inch) straight-sided charlotte mould or cake tin

Rinse the blackberries gently, drain and reserve 10. Put the remainder through a fine sieve to give a purée.

Dissolve the jelly in 150 ml (¼ pint) boiling water, add a further 150 ml (¼ pint) cold water and leave the jelly until it is quite cold. Pour 150 ml (¼ pint) of jelly into the base of the mould or tin, arrange the 10 blackberries around the edge of the jelly and leave to set in a cold place. Stir the remaining jelly into the blackberry purée.

When the jelly in the tin has set, arrange the sponge fingers around the edge of the tin, resting on the jelly, with the sugared sides touching the tin. They should fit closely together and support each other.

In a bowl, blend the custard powder with the sugar and a little milk. Heat the remaining milk in a saucepan and, when nearly boiling, pour over the custard mixture. Return the custard to the saucepan and, stirring constantly, bring to the boil and cook for 2 minutes; allow it to cool. Dissolve the gelatine in the water in a saucepan over a low heat, but do not allow it to boil. Add the gelatine to the custard and then stir the custard into the blackberry purée.

When the mixture is almost at setting point, whip the double cream until stiff and fold it into the blackberry mixture. Carefully pour the mixture into the lined tin, taking care not to dislodge the biscuits. Leave to set.

To serve, trim the biscuits level with the filling, then dip the tin quickly in hot water and turn out onto a flat serving plate.

Note: Frozen blackberries may be used.

Bramble Chutney

Makes about 3 kg (6 lb)

1½ kg	blackberries	3 lb
500 g	cooking apples	1 lb
350 g	onions	12 oz
3-cm	piece of root ginger ⎫ tied in	1-inch
5-cm	cinnamon stick ⎬ a muslin	2-inch
8	whole cloves ⎭ bag	8
600 ml	malt vinegar	1 pint
1 level tsp	ground mace	1 level tsp
1 level tbsp	salt	1 level tbsp
500 g	dark, soft brown sugar	1 lb

a preserving pan or large saucepan

Hull and rinse the blackberries if necessary; peel, core and roughly chop the apples; peel and dice the onions. Place all these ingredients in the preserving pan with the spices, half the vinegar, the ground mace and the salt and bring to the boil. Simmer gently, uncovered, for about 1 hour until the fruits are soft. Remove the muslin bag and add remaining vinegar. Add the sugar and allow it to dissolve, then boil rapidly for 20 to 30 minutes until the chutney is starting to thicken.

Pour into clean, warm, dry jars. Seal with thick polythene and lids if available, label and store in a cool, dry place.

Note: Frozen blackberries can be used.

Blackberry and Apple Jam

Makes 5 kg (10 lb)

2 kg	blackberries	4 lb
300 ml	water	½ pint
1 kg	cooking apples	2 lb
3 kg	granulated or preserving sugar	6 lb

a preserving pan or large saucepan

Hull and rinse the blackberries, if necessary. Place them in a preserving pan with 150 ml (¼ pint) of the water and stew gently over a low heat until tender – about 20 minutes.

Peel, core and thinly slice the apples. Add them to the pan with the remaining water and cook gently until the apples are quite tender and pulpy.

Add the sugar and heat slowly until all the sugar is dissolved. Then bring to the boil and boil rapidly until setting point is reached – about 10 to 15 minutes (see p. 311 for full jam-making instructions).

Leave the jam to stand for 10 minutes before pouring into warm, clean, dry jars. Cover with wax discs and seal. Label the jars and store in a cool, dry place.

Note: Frozen blackberries and apple slices can be used.

The following recipes also include blackberries:

Blackberry jam (p. 312)
Blackberry jelly (p. 318)
Blackberry and apple jelly (p. 318)
Bottled blackberries (p. 324)
Pickled blackberries (p. 332)

Try substituting blackberries for the main fruit in the following recipes:

Raspberry sponge pudding (p. 269)
Gooseberry soufflé (p. 240)
Blackcurrant juice (p. 225)

27 Blackcurrants

Introduction

Blackcurrants are ideal plants to grow in small gardens where the larger fruit trees would take up too much space. They are also very rich in vitamin C, and in pectin which means they make successful jams and jellies.

The bushes are easy to grow, thriving on a generous supply of manure and compost, especially if well fed during the autumn and spring. The best crops will be produced on bushes in a sunny, sheltered position, but the plants will survive happily in partial shade.

The biggest danger to the bushes comes from the 'big bud' mite – so called because it swells the buds. It can transmit reversion disease and once your plants become diseased they must be dug up immediately and destroyed.

Like blackberries, blackcurrants produce their best fruits on young canes, so once the old stems have fruited they should be cut off to encourage new young ones.

New bushes should be planted out in the winter months, deep into the ground, and then pruned right down to within an inch of the soil. Experts recommend that the bushes should not be allowed to fruit until the second summer after planting to encourage the plant to grow as strong as possible.

The number of bushes in your garden can be increased by taking cuttings from established bushes.

Preparation and cooking

Blackcurrants enhance the flavour and appearance of many puddings with their dark, rich, red colour, especially when mixed with fruits like apples and pears. But, unlike redcurrants, they cannot be eaten raw because of their tough skins and slightly sharp acid taste.

To prepare, run the stalks through a fork and this will remove the berries from their stems without damaging the fruit.

The currants are best used within 24 hours of picking as they quickly deteriorate with storage.

To stew: Prepare 250 g (8 oz) currants as above. Place in a saucepan with 2 to 3 tablespoons of water and 75 to 100 g (3 to 4 oz) sugar, cover and simmer gently for about 10 minutes. To purée, press through a sieve.

Serving suggestions: The stewed currants may be served hot or cold as a sauce for ice-cream – especially vanilla – and plain steamed puddings.

How to deal with a glut

1. Freezing: Strip currants from their stalks. Wash, dry and pack into containers, either on their own or in a sugar syrup – 600 g (1¼ lb) sugar and 600 ml (1 pint) water for every 500 g (1 lb) fruit. Storage time: 9 to 12 months.

Lemon cheesecake with blackcurrant topping (p. 223), blackcurrant crumble pie (p. 221) and blackcurrant and pear cobbler (p. 222) all freeze well.

2. Preserving: Bottle in syrup (p. 324); or make blackcurrant jam (p. 312), blackcurrant juice (p. 225) or blackcurrant jelly (p. 318).

Minstrel Pudding

Serves 5–6

250 g	blackcurrants	8 oz
1 tbsp	water	1 tbsp
100 g	granulated sugar	3 oz

For the filling

50 g	margarine	2 oz
150 g	caster sugar	6 oz
2	large eggs, separated	2
25 g	plain flour	1 oz
450 ml	milk	¾ pint
	vanilla essence	

a shallow 1¼-litre (2-pint) ovenproof dish

Preheat the oven to 150°C, 300°F, gas mark 2.

Wash the blackcurrants and remove the stalks. Place in a saucepan with the tablespoon of water and the sugar and poach, uncovered, for about 10 minutes until the blackcurrants are tender but still whole. Pour into the base of the ovenproof dish.

To make the filling: Cream the margarine with 50 g (2 oz) of caster sugar until light and fluffy. Beat in the egg yolks then stir in the sifted flour.

Warm the milk to blood heat and pour onto the mixture, stirring to blend to a smooth consistency. Return to the pan and add a few drops of vanilla essence.

Bring slowly to the boil to thicken, stirring all the time, then pour the mixture over the blackcurrants in the dish.

Whisk the egg whites until stiff, then whisk in half the remaining caster sugar and, using a metal spoon, fold in the rest. Spread the meringue over the filling and rough the surface into little peaks.

Bake on the shelf below the centre of the preheated oven for about 30 minutes until the meringue is lightly golden.

This pudding is delicious served either hot or cold, with cream.

Note: Frozen or bottled blackcurrants can be used.

Blackcurrant Crumble Pie

Serves 6–8

For the pastry and crumble topping

200 g	plain flour	8 oz
	pinch of salt	
100 g	butter or margarine	4 oz
50 g	sugar	2 oz
1	small egg yolk	1

For the filling

500 g	blackcurrants	1 lb
125–150 g	sugar	4–5 oz
2 level tbsps	cornflour	2 level tbsps
2 tbsps	water	2 tbsps

a 20-cm (8-inch) round pie dish

Preheat the oven to 190°C, 375°F, gas mark 5.

Sift the flour and salt into a bowl and rub the butter or margarine into the flour, using the fingertips only, until the mixture resembles fine breadcrumbs. Divide this crumb mixture in half and place in separate bowls.

Into one half, stir 1 rounded tablespoon of sugar. Lightly beat the egg yolk with a little cold water and add to the mixture to make a smooth pastry dough. Leave the pastry to rest for 15 minutes before use.

Add the remainder of the 50 g (2 oz) sugar to the other half of the crumb mixture and mix well. Leave aside for the topping.

Strip the blackcurrants from their stalks and place in a saucepan with 1 tablespoon of water and the sugar. Bring slowly to the boil and simmer gently for 5 minutes until most of the blackcurrant juice has run from the fruit. Remove from the heat.

Blend the cornflour with 2 tablespoons of water, then stir the blended cornflour into the blackcurrants. Return the pan to the heat and, stirring constantly, cook until the mixture is thick. Leave to cool slightly.

Roll out the pastry on a lightly floured surface to line the pie dish, and trim the edges. Pour the thickened blackcurrants into the pastry case and sprinkle the crumble topping over them.

Bake on the centre shelf of the preheated oven for 30 to 35 minutes until the pastry and topping are lightly browned. Serve hot with custard or cream.

Note: Do not try to make this sweet without thickening the blackcurrant mixture, as the enormous amount of juice the blackcurrants produce will make both the pastry and the topping soggy. Frozen blackcurrants can be used.

* Suitable for freezing.

Blackcurrant and Pear Cobbler

Serves 6–8

500 g	blackcurrants	1 lb
1 tbsp	water	1 tbsp
125–150 g	sugar	4–5 oz
250 g	ripe pears	8 oz

For the topping

200 g	plain flour	8 oz
1 level tbsp	baking powder	1 level tbsp
50 g	margarine	2 oz

| 50 g | sugar | 2 oz |
| 150 ml | milk | ¼ pint |

a 20-cm (8-inch) deep ovenproof dish, buttered
a 5-cm (2-inch) plain round cutter

Preheat the oven to 200°C, 400°F, gas mark 6.

Strip the blackcurrants from their stalks, place in a saucepan with the water and stew gently for about 10 minutes to extract most of the juice from the berries. Drain the fruit from the juice and return the juice to the saucepan with the sugar. Bring slowly to the boil and then boil rapidly for 5 minutes. Remove from the heat and return the currants to the syrup.

Peel, quarter and core the pears and lay them in the buttered dish. Pour over them the blackcurrants and their syrup.

To prepare the scone topping, sift the flour and baking powder into a bowl and rub in the margarine, using the fingertips only, until the mixture resembles fine breadcrumbs.

Stir in the sugar, then mix in the milk to give a soft dough. Roll out on a lightly floured surface to 1 cm (½ inch) thick, then, using the cutter, cut out about 18 scones.

Lay the scones, overlapping each other, around the edge and in the centre of the dish to cover the whole surface of the fruit.

Bake the cobbler on the shelf above the centre of the preheated oven for 20 to 25 minutes until the top is brown and the scone mixture is completely cooked. Serve hot with custard.

Note: The secret of making perfect scones and therefore a light topping to this pudding is to handle the dough as little as possible. It should not be kneaded until smooth like pastry.

Frozen blackcurrants can be used.

* Suitable for freezing.

Lemon Cheesecake with Blackcurrant Topping

Serves 6

For the base

150 g	digestive biscuits	6 oz
50 g	butter	2 oz
1 level tbsp	sugar	1 level tbsp

For the filling

1	large egg, separated	1
150 ml	milk	¼ pint
1	lemon, grated rind and juice	1
3 level tsps	powdered gelatine (1 sachet)	3 level tsps
75 g	caster sugar	3 oz
225 g	cottage cheese	8 oz
150 ml	double cream	¼ pint

For the topping

250 g	blackcurrants	8 oz
175 g	sugar	6 oz
150 ml	water	¼ pint
1 rounded tsp	arrowroot	1 rounded tsp

a 20-cm (8-inch) spring-clip tin or a loose-based flan tin, greased

Crush the biscuits with a rolling pin. Melt the butter in a small saucepan, remove from the heat and add the sugar and the biscuit crumbs. Mix well, press into the base of the greased tin and smooth over with the back of a wooden spoon.

To make the filling: Beat together the egg yolk, milk and lemon rind (this can best be done in a liquidizer). Dissolve the gelatine in 2 table-spoons of water in a pan over a very low heat, but do not allow it to boil. Add the gelatine to the milk with the lemon juice and sugar, then, if you are not using a liquidizer, sieve the cottage cheese before beating it into the mixture. If using a liquidizer, add the cottage cheese without sieving and beat or blend until smooth. Pour into a mixing bowl.

Whip the double cream until stiff and fold it into the mixture, then gently fold in the egg white, whisked until it stands in peaks. Spoon the filling into the tin, smooth over the surface and leave to set for 2 to 3 hours.

Meanwhile, for the topping, strip the currants from their stalks, wash and put into a pan with the sugar and the water. Cover and simmer gently for 10 minutes to soften the currants and dissolve the sugar. Strain off the blackcurrants, then blend the arrowroot with a little cold water and stir into the blackcurrant syrup to thicken it. Return to the pan and cook for ½ minute. Stir in the blackcurrants and leave to get cold.

To serve, turn out the cheesecake and spread the blackcurrants and thickened juice over the top.

Note: Frozen or bottled blackcurrants can be used.

* Suitable for freezing.

Blackcurrant Juice

1 kg	ripe blackcurrants	2 lb
600 ml	cold water	1 pint
	warmed cube or preserving sugar	

Rinse the currants and strip them from their stalks into a large saucepan. Add the water and bring quickly to the boil, stirring constantly. Boil for 1 minute, remove from the heat and crush the currants against the sides of the pan using a wooden spoon.

Pour the currants and their juice into a jelly bag or muslin bag and leave to drain overnight. The next day, squeeze out as much juice as possible from the bag and measure the juice into a large saucepan.

Allow 350 g (12 oz) sugar to each 600 ml (1 pint) of fruit juice and add to the pan. Leave over a low heat, stirring occasionally, until the sugar has dissolved but do not allow to boil.

Strain the fruit juice through clean muslin into clean, dry bottles (e.g. sauce bottles or small tonic bottles which have screw tops), to within 3 cm (1 inch) of the top. If the bottles do not have screw tops then corks, which first need to be sterilized in boiling water, should be used and tied down securely after processing.

To sterilize the bottles of juice: Place them, with screw tops or corks loosely fitted, on a trivet in a large pan. Pour in enough water to come to within 3 cm (1 inch) of the tops of the bottles, bring to the boil and simmer gently for about 20 minutes (or maintain at a temperature of 90°C, 190°F).

Remove from the pan and tighten the tops at once. Leave to get cold before labelling and storing. (If corks have been used, they and the tops of the bottles must be covered with melted wax to give an airtight seal.)

Once a bottle of juice is opened it will keep for up to 2 or 3 weeks. Dilute with water in the same way as commercial concentrated fruit juice.

Note: Home-made fruit juice is a useful recipe for using up slightly overripe fruit.

The following recipes also include blackcurrants:

Blackcurrant jam (p. 312)
Blackcurrant jelly (p. 318)
Bottled blackcurrants (p. 324)

Try substituting blackcurrants for the main fruit in the following recipes:

Gooseberry soufflé (p. 240)
Raspberry sorbet (p. 274)
Rhubarb charlotte (p. 285)

28 Cherries

Introduction

The cherry tree provides one of the most beautiful of spring blossoms and its crops of bright red cherries make a colourful addition to any garden. The trouble with cherries is that they are not only attractive to humans – birds find them irresistible, too.

If you are thinking of planting a cherry tree you would be best advised to grow one of the self-pollinating varieties, e.g. Morello or Kentish Red, as these are fairly sour and the birds tend to ignore them. They also crop better and younger than the sweet ones and can even be grown against a high wall in a fan-shape.

The sweet or eating cherries are unfortunately difficult to protect from pecking beaks as they are the tallest of the fruit trees and, unlike the bush or fan-tailed cooking cherries, they cannot easily be covered with protective netting.

These sweet cherries also take up more room in the garden because of their size and usually require the proximity of other cherry trees to cross-pollinate. They are happiest grown in a chalky or sandy soil with good drainage.

Cherries should be picked the moment they ripen but not before. Cooking cherries should not be pulled off the tree by their stalks but carefully cut off.

Preparation and cooking

It is best to use the acid cooking cherries like Morello for jam-making (rather than using the dessert varieties) as they contain more pectin and thus give a better set to the jam.

To prepare, remove the stalks, wash and stone, using the round end of a clean hairpin – this keeps the cherry whole. However, if your trees crop well we would advise you to invest in a cherry stoner.

To stew: Prepare 500 g (1 lb) cherries as above and place in a saucepan with 3 tablespoons water and 125 g (4 oz) sugar; cover and simmer for 10 minutes until the cherries are tender.

To prepare a cherry compôte to serve with cold meats such as ham and poultry, stew the cherries with 25 g (1 oz) sugar and serve cold.

Cherries can be stewed in red wine syrup – 150 ml (¼ pint) red wine and 150 ml (¼ pint) water to each 100 g (4 oz) demerara sugar. Stew gently, covered, for 15 to 20 minutes, strain off the fruit and reduce syrup by half.

Serving suggestions: The stewed cherries can be served with ice-cream, cream or syllabub.

How to deal with a glut

1. Freezing: Wash and, if preferred, stone the cherries. Cooking cherries are packed either in dry sugar – 125 g (4 oz) for every 500 g (1 lb) fruit – or in a syrup – 250 g (8 oz) sugar in 600 ml (1 pint) water to each 500 g (1 lb) of fruit. Store in polythene bags or wax containers. Storage time: 9 to 12 months.

We do not recommend freezing the sweet dessert cherries as their flesh becomes brown thus defeating the object of keeping them. However, they can be frozen without sugar or syrup – wash and stone if desired and pack into polythene bags or wax containers. Storage time: 3 to 4 months.

Cherry ice-cream (p. 234) is a good way of storing a glut crop.

2. Preserving: Cherries can be made into cherry jam (p. 312), pickled in spiced vinegar (p. 332) or bottled in syrup, water or wine syrup (p. 324).

Roast Duck with Cherry Sauce

Serves 4

2 kg	duck	4–5 lb

For the sauce

250 g	dark cherries	8 oz
150 ml	port (sweet sherry can be used as an alternative)	¼ pint
	duck giblets	

1	onion	1
1	carrot	, 1
1	bay leaf	1
1 sprig	fresh sage	1 sprig
1 blade	mace	1 blade
5	peppercorns	5
1 level tsp	salt	1 level tsp
450 ml	water	¾ pint
1 level tbsp	cornflour	1 level tbsp
	a bunch of watercress	

a roasting tin

Preheat the oven to 200°C, 400°F, gas mark 6.

If the duck is frozen, make sure that it is completely thawed before cooking. Remove the giblets and any excess fat. Wipe the duck and place in the roasting tin (no extra fat is necessary when roasting duck). Prick the skin well with a fork and rub salt into the outside. Calculate the cooking time, allowing 55 minutes per kilogram or 25 minutes to the pound.

Roast the duck on the centre shelf of the preheated oven for 30 minutes, then reduce the heat to 180°C, 350°F, gas mark 4, for the remainder of the cooking time.

Meanwhile, wash and stone the cherries, leaving them whole (see p. 227). Place them in a bowl with the port and leave to marinate.

Wash the giblets and place in a pan with the peeled and halved onion and carrot, the bay leaf, sage, mace, peppercorns and salt. Add the water and bring to the boil, then cover and simmer for about 1½ hours. Strain off the giblets and seasonings and, if necessary, boil the stock until it has reduced to 300 ml (½ pint). Check the flavour and season to taste if necessary.

When the duck is cooked, remove it onto a board and cut into quarters. To do this, cut across the centre and down between the leg and wing on each side. Cut along the centre of the breast bone and slip the knife down between the flesh and the bone. Cut the legs and the wings from the carcass at their joints to give four good quarters, place on a hot serving dish and keep warm.

Strain off almost all the fat from the roasting pan. Add the stock to the sediment left in the pan and stir in the stoned cherries and port. Simmer gently for 5 minutes and turn off the heat. Blend the cornflour with a tablespoon of water and stir into the sauce. Bring back to the

boil and cook for 1 minute. Pour the sauce and cherries over the duck
and garnish with the watercress. Serve with roast potatoes, new carrots
and peas.

Note: Bottled cherries can be used.

* Suitable for freezing.

Hot Cherry Soufflé

Serves 3–4

200 g	cherries	6 oz
20 g	butter or margarine	¾ oz
3 level tbsps	plain flour	3 level tbsps
300 ml	milk	½ pint
50 g	sugar	2 oz
¼ tsp	rum essence	¼ tsp
2	large eggs, separated	2

a 1¼- to 1¾-litre (2- to 3-pint) soufflé dish

Preheat the oven to 200°C, 400°F, gas mark 6.

Butter the base and sides of the soufflé dish.

Wash and stone the cherries, leaving them whole (see p. 227).

Heat the butter or margarine in a saucepan, add the flour and cook
for 1 minute. Remove the pan from the heat and slowly blend in the
milk. Return to the heat and, stirring constantly, cook until the mixture
thickens. Remove from the heat again and stir in the sugar, the rum
essence, the egg yolks and lastly the cherries.

Whisk the egg whites until they are stiff and, using a metal spoon,
carefully fold them into the cherry mixture. Pour the soufflé into the
greased dish and bake on the centre shelf of the preheated oven for
25 minutes until the soufflé has risen and the top is browned. Serve
immediately with cream as the soufflé will soon start to sink.

Cherry Batter Pudding

Serves 4–5

500 g	cherries	1 lb
450 ml	milk	¾ pint
	knob of butter	
3	large eggs	3
50 g	plain flour	2 oz
	pinch of salt	
100 g	caster sugar	4 oz
	pinch of ground cinnamon	

a 1¼-litre (2-pint) shallow ovenproof dish

Preheat the oven to 200°C, 400°F, gas mark 6.

Wash and stone the cherries, leaving them whole (see p. 227).

Lightly butter the dish and lay the cherries in it. Heat the milk with the butter to blood heat. Beat the eggs lightly together in a bowl and beat in the flour, salt and 75 g (3 oz) of the caster sugar. Gradually blend in the warm milk, then pour the batter over the cherries and bake at once on the shelf above the centre of the preheated oven for 35 to 40 minutes, until the batter is cooked. (The base of the pudding should be like a firm custard when cooked.)

Sprinkle the remaining 25 g (1 oz) sugar, mixed with the cinnamon, over the top of the pudding and place it under a hot grill to caramelize lightly. Serve at once with cream.

Note: Frozen or bottled cherries can be used.

Cherry and Melon Coronet

Serves 2

250 g	dark sweet cherries	8 oz
1	Charentais or Canteloupe melon	1
1 tbsp	kirsch	1 tbsp
150 ml	double cream	¼ pint
25 g	caster sugar	1 oz

a few drops vanilla essence
a few flaked almonds

2 individual serving dishes

Wash and stone the cherries, leaving them whole (see p. 227).

Place the stoned cherries in a bowl. Using the point of a sharp knife, cut the melon in half in a zig-zag pattern, making the points of the zig-zag fairly large to look like the points of a coronet. Scoop out the pips and discard them. Use a melon-scoop to remove most of the melon in small balls and add these to the cherries. Leave the remaining melon flesh in the shells.

Add the kirsch to the fruit and chill in the refrigerator for at least 1 hour. Chill the melon shells as well. About ½ hour before serving, whip the cream until thick, then fold in the caster sugar and vanilla essence. Fold the cherries and melon balls very gently into the cream and spoon into the shells. Brown the almonds under a hot grill and scatter over the top of the coronets. Serve chilled.

Quick Black Forest Cherry Gâteau

Serves 8

100 g	soft margarine	4 oz
100 g	caster sugar	4 oz
100 g	self-raising flour	4 oz
1 level tsp	baking powder	1 level tsp
1 level tbsp	cocoa powder	1 level tbsp
2	large eggs	2

For the syrup

250 g	caster sugar	8 oz
300 ml	water	½ pint
2 tbsps	kirsch	2 tbsps

For the filling

500 g	dark red cherries	1 lb
450 ml	double cream	¾ pint
	or	
300 ml	double cream ⎱ mixed	½ pint
150 ml	single cream ⎰	¼ pint

| 2 level tbsps | icing sugar | 2 level tbsps |
| 50 g | grated chocolate | 2 oz |

three 18-cm (7-inch) sandwich tins

Preheat the oven to 160°C, 325°F, gas mark 3.

Grease the bases and line the three sandwich tins with greased greaseproof paper. Place the soft margarine and sugar in a large mixing bowl, sift in the flour, baking powder and cocoa, and add the eggs. Using a wooden spoon, beat well until the mixture is soft and creamy. Divide evenly between the three tins, smooth over the tops and bake on the centre shelf of the preheated oven for about 30 minutes until springy to the touch.

Turn the cakes out onto a cooling rack, remove the greaseproof paper bases and leave to cool.

Meanwhile, place the sugar and water in a pan and dissolve the sugar over a low heat. Add the kirsch, bring the syrup to the boil and boil for 5 minutes.

Wash and stone the cherries, leaving them whole (see p. 227) Reserve a few bunches of the best cherries for decorating the cake. Reduce the heat under the syrup, add the cherries and poach for 5 to 7 minutes. Strain the fruit from the syrup and leave both to cool.

When cool, prick the bases of the sponges all over and carefully spoon the syrup over them until the sponges have absorbed the liquid and become quite moist.

Whip the double cream or the mixture of double and single cream until stiff, stir in the sifted icing sugar and spread some of the cream on top of two of the sponges. Divide the cherries between these two cakes, spreading them evenly over the layer of cream. Lay one sponge on top of the other and finally place the third sponge on top of the cake. Spread the rest of the cream over the top and sides of the gâteau and decorate the sides with grated chocolate. Place the bunches of reserved cherries on the top of the cake for decoration.

Note: This beautifully rich gâteau is traditionally made with a whisked egg sponge and twice the quantity of double cream and chocolate to decorate it. We have cut down on these expensive ingredients and on the cooking time by using an all-in-one sponge. Bottled cherries can be used with their syrup, thus eliminating the preparation and poaching of the cherries as given in the recipe.

* Suitable for freezing. Freeze undecorated, without the grated chocolate and bunches of cherries.

Frosted Cherries

500 g	dark red or Morello cherries	1 lb
125 g	caster sugar	4 oz
1	large egg white	1

Wash the cherries and dry thoroughly, but leave on their stalks in bunches.

Place the caster sugar in a bowl. Lightly beat the egg white, then, holding the cherries by their stalks, brush them with egg white to cover completely. Dip the cherries in caster sugar to coat them thoroughly and then lay them on a wire cooling rack to dry. The sugar will have hardened on the outside when they are dry, giving a frosted appearance.

To serve, pile the cherries on a dish and serve as an alternative to fresh fruit after dinner.

Note: Many other fruits can be prepared in the same way, e.g. red- or green-skinned apples, plums, pears, redcurrants, dessert gooseberries and grapes. A bowl made up of a selection of frosted fruits makes an attractive centre piece on a dinner table.

Cherry Ice-Cream

Makes about 1 litre (1½ pints)

500 g	cherries	1 lb
300 ml	water	½ pint
125 g	sugar	4 oz
1–2 tbsps	cherry brandy	1–2 tbsps
1 dsp	lemon juice	1 dsp
2 level tbsps	custard powder	2 level tbsps
1 level tbsp	sugar	1 level tbsp
600 ml	milk	1 pint
150 ml	double cream	¼ pint

an ice-cream freezing tray

Turn the refrigerator to its coldest setting or turn on the fast-freeze section of the home freezer.

Wash and stone the cherries, leaving them whole (see p. 227).

Place the cherries in a saucepan with the water and sugar, bring to the boil and cook for 10 minutes. Remove from the heat and stir in the cherry brandy and the lemon juice.

Place the custard powder and sugar in a bowl and blend with a little milk. Put the remaining milk in a saucepan and bring to the boil. When the milk is almost at boiling point, pour it onto the custard mixture, stirring, and then return the custard to the pan and the heat.

Stirring constantly, cook until the mixture has thickened and is bubbling. Reduce to a low heat for a further 2 minutes, then pour the custard into a bowl and slowly stir in the cherries and their syrup. Mix together well and allow to cool, stirring occasionally to prevent a skin forming.

Lightly whip the double cream and fold it into the cooled cherry mixture. Pour the cream into an ice-cream tray and put it in either the freezing compartment of the refrigerator or the fast-freeze section of the home freezer. Leave until it has started to set around the edges, then remove from the freezer and beat lightly with a fork to break up the ice crystals which have formed. Return the ice-cream to the freezer until it has set completely.

Before serving, remove from the freezer for 10 minutes to thaw slightly. Remember to turn the refrigerator or home freezer back to its normal setting.

Note: Frozen cherries can be used.

The following recipes also feature cherries:

Cherry jam (p. 312)
Bottled cherries (p. 324)
Pickled cherries (p. 332)

Try substituting cherries for the main fruit in the following recipes:

Chocolate pear flan (p. 253)
American plum pie (p. 260)
Raspberry sponge pudding (p. 269)
Strawberry shortbread dessert (p. 303)

29 Gooseberries

Introduction

Gooseberries grow on thorny bushes and can be hairy or hairless and green, yellow or red in colour. But whatever their shape or hue, they are a most useful fruit to grow in any garden.

They have the longest cropping season of all the soft fruits and some dessert varieties, e.g. Leveller, can produce fruit the size of plums which is harvested in mid to late summer and can be eaten raw. However, most other varieties are too tart and require cooking first.

Gooseberries will grow on almost any well-drained soil and cordon varieties can be grown against walls, fences or sheds. To improve your crops, manure should be added to the soil as well as plenty of potash, otherwise the leaves will start to wither and brown. Dig some of your bonfire ash into the soil to help supply this need.

The smaller cooking gooseberries are picked when required for use, but the larger dessert varieties should be left on the bushes until fully ripe.

Preparation and cooking

Wipe the fruit and snip off the tops and tails with a pair of scissors.

To stew: Prepare 500 g (1 lb) gooseberries as above and place in a saucepan with 1 tablespoon of water; cover and simmer gently for 10 to 15 minutes until tender but whole. Stir in 100 to 150 g (4 to 6 oz) sugar, depending on the tartness of the fruit.

Serving suggestions: Purée stewed and sweetened gooseberries through a sieve and use as a sauce for ice-cream or sponge puddings. Use unsweetened gooseberry purée cold as a sauce to go with roast pork or lamb.

How to deal with a glut

1. Freezing: Prepare as above, wash and dry, then pack without sugar in wax containers or polythene bags. Alternatively, pack with dry sugar

– about 125 g (4 oz) per 500 g (1 lb) fruit. Storage time: 9 to 12 months.

Freeze sweetened or unsweetened gooseberry purée in 300-ml (½-pint) quantities. Leave to get cold, then pack into polythene bags or wax or foil containers. Also freeze gooseberry and raisin slice (p. 245). Frozen gooseberry cream (p. 243) is a good recipe for using and storing a bumper crop.

2. *Preserving:* Make gooseberry jam (p. 312), gooseberry chutney (p. 244) or gooseberry jelly (p. 318); or bottle in water or syrup (p. 324).

3. *Storing:* Like all soft fruits, gooseberries do not store well, but if the bushes are covered with nets or grown in a fruit cage, the berries may be left on the plants until just before the first frosts.

Pork and Gooseberry Casserole

Serves 4

1 kg	spare rib of pork	2 lb
25 g	flour seasoned with salt and pepper	1 oz
	knob of butter or margarine	
1 tbsp	cooking oil	1 tbsp
250 g	onions	8 oz
75 g	streaky bacon	3 oz
½ head	celery	½ head
1 level tbsp	fresh parsley, chopped	1 level tbsp
300 ml	dry cider	½ pint
150 ml	stock	¼ pint
250 g	gooseberries	8 oz

a 2¼-litre (4-pint) flameproof casserole

Wipe the meat and trim off any bone, skin and excess fat; cut into cubes and toss in the seasoned flour. Heat the butter and oil in the casserole or a large saucepan, add the meat and cook quickly, turning frequently, to brown lightly for 2–3 minutes.

Peel the onions and slice thinly; remove the skin and any bone from the bacon and cut into pieces; trim and wipe the celery, then slice it. Add these ingredients to the meat and continue cooking for a further 3 minutes. Stir in the chopped parsley, cider and stock, bring to the boil, stirring, then cover and simmer gently for 1¼ hours.

Top, tail and wash the gooseberries and add to the casserole. Cover and cook for a further 20 minutes until the gooseberries are tender but still whole. Serve with creamed potatoes.

* Suitable for freezing – but only cook the gooseberries for 10 minutes.

Gooseberry Meringue Pie

Serves 5–6

200 g	*pâte sucrée* (sweet pastry) (p. 335)	8 oz

For the filling

500 g	gooseberries	1 lb
2 tbsps	water	2 tbsps
2 tbsps	single cream or top of the milk	2 tbsps
1	egg yolk	1
75 g	caster sugar	3 oz
50 g	cake crumbs	2 oz

For the meringue

2	egg whites	2
100 g	caster sugar	4 oz

a 20-cm (8-inch) fluted flan ring on a baking sheet

Preheat the oven to 190°C, 375°F, gas mark 5.

On a floured surface, roll out the prepared pastry and line the flan ring. Trim the top edge and bake blind (for a detailed explanation of baking blind, see p. 334) in preheated oven for 15 minutes until light golden brown. Remove from the oven and turn the oven down to 160°C, 325°F, gas mark 3.

To make the filling: top, tail and wash the gooseberries. Place in a saucepan with the water, cover and cook until tender, about 10 to 15 minutes. Stir in the cream, egg yolk, sugar and cake crumbs, and pour the filling into the flan case.

Whisk the egg whites until stiff and dry, then beat in half the sugar until thick and glossy. Fold in the remaining sugar with a metal spoon and spread the meringue over the top of the filling to the edge of the flan.

Bake the flan on the centre shelf of the oven at 160°C, 325°F, gas mark 3, for 25 minutes.

Serve hot or cold with single cream.

Note: Frozen gooseberries can be used.

* Suitable for freezing without the meringue topping.

Gooseberry Summer Pudding

Serves 5–6

1 kg	gooseberries	2 lb
1 tbsp	water	1 tbsp
8	thin slices white bread with crusts removed	8
175 g	caster sugar	6 oz

a ¾-kg (1½-lb) pudding basin or fluted mould

Top, tail and wash the gooseberries, put in a saucepan with the water, cover and cook gently until tender, about 10 minutes. Leave to cool slightly.

Line the pudding basin or mould with the bread. To do this, place 1 slice in the base and trim 6 slices to fit round the sides, overlapping slightly. Mix the sugar with the gooseberries and spoon into the basin. Put the remaining slice of bread on top of the basin or mould, cover with a plate and stand a heavy weight or large tin of fruit on top. Leave overnight in the refrigerator.

Turn out onto a plate and serve chilled, with whipped cream.

Gooseberry Soufflé

Serves 4–5

500 g	gooseberries	1 lb
2 tbsps	water	2 tbsps
150 g	caster sugar	5 oz
2	large eggs, separated	2
3 level tsps	powdered gelatine (1 sachet)	3 level tsps
3 tbsps	water	3 tbsps
150 ml	double cream	¼ pint
	green colouring, optional	
1 level tbsp	chopped walnuts	1 level tbsp

a 1-litre (1¾-pint) soufflé dish
a no. 8 large star pipe and piping bag

Tie a double band of foil or greaseproof paper round the outside of the soufflé dish to come 5 to 6 cm (2 to 3 inches) above the dish. Top, tail and wash the gooseberries and place in a saucepan with the 2 table-spoons water. Cover and simmer gently for 10 to 15 minutes until tender. Purée the gooseberries through a sieve or in a liquidizer and leave to cool.

Place the sugar and egg yolks in a bowl over a pan of simmering water, and whisk together until thick and creamy. Remove from the heat and continue beating for a further few minutes to cool. Add the gooseberry purée to this mixture. Dissolve the gelatine in the 3 table-spoons water over a very gentle heat but do not allow to boil. Stir the slightly cooled, dissolved gelatine into the soufflé mixture. Beat the cream until thick and fold in three quarters of it. Add green colouring if desired.

Beat the egg whites until stiff and dry and, when the mixture is beginning to set, fold them into it, using a metal spoon. Finally, pour the soufflé into the prepared dish. Smooth over the surface and leave in a cool place to set completely.

When set, gently remove the collar of foil or greaseproof paper. Press the chopped walnuts onto the sides of the soufflé, using a palette knife. Place the remaining quarter of the whipped cream in the piping bag with the star nozzle attached. Decorate the top with stars of cream and scatter a few remaining chopped nuts over the top.

Note: Frozen gooseberries can be used.

Gooseberry and Banana Pie

Serves 4–5

200 g	shortcrust pastry (p. 334)	8 oz
500 g	gooseberries	1 lb
1	large banana	1
	or	
2	small bananas	2
	a few drops of lemon juice	
75 g	sugar	3 oz
	milk or egg white to glaze	

a 20-cm (8-inch) round pie dish, greased

Preheat the oven to 190°C, 375°F, gas mark 5.

Roll out two thirds of the prepared pastry on a lightly floured surface, shape into a round and line the base and sides of the greased pie dish. Roll out the remaining one third to cover the top of the pie. Gather up the pastry trimmings.

Top, tail and wash the gooseberries and pile into the pie dish. Chop the banana, sprinkle the slices with a little lemon juice and add them to the pie. Sprinkle the sugar over the top. Cover the pie with the remaining pastry, damp the edges and seal well. Roll out the pastry trimmings and cut four pastry leaves to place on the centre of the pie, to decorate. Brush the pie with milk or egg white and bake on the centre shelf of the preheated oven for 30 to 35 minutes until the pastry is cooked.

Serve hot or cold with custard or cream.

Note: Frozen gooseberries can be used.

Gooseberry Crunch

Serves 4

¾ kg	gooseberries	1½ lb
150 g	sugar	5 oz
1 tbsp	water	1 tbsp
	green colouring, if desired	
150 g	digestive biscuits	6 oz
50 g	butter or margarine	2 oz

25 g	sugar	1 oz
1 level tsp	ground ginger	1 level tsp
150 ml	whipped cream	¼ pint

4 glass sundae dishes or tall glasses

Top, tail and wash the gooseberries and place them in a saucepan with the 150 g (5 oz) sugar and the water. Cover and simmer for 10 minutes until tender. Purée the fruit in a liquidizer or through a sieve, add a few drops of green colouring, if desired, and leave to cool.

Put the digestive biscuits in a polythene bag and crush with a rolling pin. Melt the butter or margarine in a saucepan, remove from the heat and add the 25 g (1 oz) sugar and the ground ginger. Then add the biscuit crumbs and mix together well.

Spread a layer of gooseberry purée in the base of each dish, then some of the crumb mixture, and continue to layer them, ending with a layer of crumbs. Decorate with whipped cream.

Note: This dish can be varied by using chocolate-coated digestive biscuits.

Gooseberry Ring with Ice-Cream

Serves 6–8

500 g	gooseberries	1 lb
1 tbsp	water	1 tbsp
150 g	sugar	5 oz
½	lemon, grated rind and juice	½
3 level tsps	powdered gelatine (1 sachet)	3 level tsps
300 ml	water	½ pint
	green colouring	
1	egg white	1
	a block of vanilla ice-cream	

a ¾-litre (1¼-pint) ring mould, lightly oiled

Top, tail and wash the gooseberries and put in a saucepan with the 1 tablespoon water, the sugar and the rind and juice of the half lemon. Cover and cook until tender.

Dissolve the gelatine in 2 tablespoons water (taken from the 300 ml /½ pint water) over a low heat, but do not allow to boil. Add the remainder of the water to the gelatine and stir it into the fruit. Add a little green colouring and leave to cool. Just before the mixture is set, beat the egg white until stiff and gently fold it into the gooseberry mixture. Pour into the lightly oiled ring mould and leave to set in a cool place.

To serve, turn the gooseberry ring out of the mould onto a serving dish, pile scoops of vanilla ice-cream into the centre of the ring and serve immediately.

Note: Frozen or bottled gooseberries can be used.

Frozen Gooseberry Cream

Serves 5–6

500 g	gooseberries	1 lb
150 g	sugar	5 oz
2 tbsps	water	2 tbsps
2 level tbsps	custard powder	2 level tbsps
450 ml	milk	¾ pint
2	large eggs, separated	2
150 ml	natural yoghurt (small carton)	¼ pint
	green colouring	

Turn the refrigerator to its coldest setting or turn on the fast-freeze section of the home freezer.

Top, tail and wash the gooseberries, and place them in a saucepan with the sugar and water. Cover and simmer gently for about 10 minutes until tender. Purée the gooseberries through a sieve or in a liquidizer and leave to cool.

In a saucepan, blend the custard powder with a little milk, add the rest of the milk and, stirring continuously, bring to the boil and cook for 1 minute. Separate the egg yolks and whites into two bowls. Stir the hot custard into the yolks. Add the gooseberry purée, yoghurt and a few drops of green colouring to give the mixture a soft green colour. Leave to cool.

Pour the gooseberry cream into a plastic container or tray and place either in the freezing compartment of the refrigerator or in the fast-freeze section of the freezer for about 30 minutes or until it is beginning to set around the edges.

Remove the gooseberry cream, turn into a bowl and beat lightly to break up the ice crystals. Whisk the egg whites until stiff and then fold into the cream mixture. Return to the container and put it back in the freezer or the ice-making compartment of the refrigerator for a further 30 minutes until it is beginning to set.

Again remove the gooseberry cream and beat gently to break down the ice crystals that are forming. Put the mixture back into the container, return to the freezer or refrigerator and leave to freeze completely.

Before serving, leave at room temperature for 10 minutes, then serve with wafers or shortbread biscuits.

Note: Frozen gooseberries can be used.

Gooseberry Chutney

Makes about 2¾ kg (5–6 lb)

1 kg	gooseberries	2 lb
500 g	onions	1 lb
250 g	dates	8 oz
250 g	raisins	8 oz
650 ml	vinegar	1 pint
350 g	demerara sugar	12 oz
25 g	salt	1 oz
1 heaped tsp	ground ginger	1 heaped tsp
1 level tsp	turmeric	1 level tsp
1 level tsp	coriander	1 level tsp
	freshly ground black pepper	

a preserving pan or large saucepan

Top, tail and wash the gooseberries, then chop them. Peel and chop the onions finely, and chop the dates. Put them and all the remaining ingredients into the preserving pan and heat gently, stirring occasionally, until the sugar is dissolved. Bring to the boil and then simmer gently for an hour until thick.

Bottle in clean, warm, dry jars; cover with wax discs and seal with thick polythene and lids if available. Label and store in a cool place for 1 month before use.

Note: Frozen gooseberries can be used.

The following recipes also include gooseberries:

Rhubarb and gooseberry crumble (p. 286)
Gooseberry jam (p. 312)
Gooseberry jelly (p. 318)
Bottled gooseberries (p. 324)

Try substituting gooseberries for the main fruit in the following recipes:

Frosted cherries (p. 234)
Plum cheesecake (p. 262)
Raspberry sorbet (p. 274)
Rhubarb and raisin slice (p. 288)

30 Pears

Introduction

Pear trees, like the apple and cherry, provide magnificent spring blossom. But, as they flower earlier than apple trees, they are more liable to frost damage and so prefer the warmer climate of the south of England.

They grow best when protected in a sheltered though sunny garden or trained against a wall. Many varieties need to be planted with a suitable tree for cross-pollination, although there are self-pollinating or family trees.

Pears differ from most other fruits in one important respect – they are best left to ripen in cool storage and not left on the tree. The timing of and care taken in picking the fruit is very important. Early varieties, like the William pears, should be picked when they are still green and hard. It is better to pick these too early than too late.

Later varieties, on the other hand, should never be picked too early as they will fail to mature to their best quality.

One other problem to guard against is drought. Pears are less tolerant of dry spells than apples and so should be kept well watered during such periods.

Preparation and cooking

Ripe dessert pears are simply delicious eaten raw on their own, but cooking pears need to be stewed in a vanilla syrup first before being turned into a tasty sweet. Because of their rather bland taste they are best combined with some other flavour, e.g. chocolate, apples or black-currants. Chocolate and pear make a particularly delicious combination and we have included two out of many possible recipes in this chapter.

To prepare, peel, halve and remove the centre core, using a teaspoon; then slice, quarter or leave in halves. Some recipes require the pears to be left whole, e.g. hazelnut pear parcels (p. 249).

To stew: Peel, slice or halve the pears, remove the core and stew

500 g (1 lb) fruit in 150 ml ($\frac{1}{4}$ pint) water with 125 g (4 oz) sugar; simmer for 15 minutes until tender. Vanilla essence may be added to make a vanilla syrup.

Pears may also be stewed in a red wine syrup – 150 ml ($\frac{1}{4}$ pint) red wine and 150 ml ($\frac{1}{4}$ pint) water to each 100 g (4 oz) demerara sugar. Stew gently, covered, for 45 minutes to 1 hour, strain off fruit and reduce syrup by half.

To bake: See hazelnut pear parcels (p. 249); the pears are wrapped in hazelnut pastry and baked for 30 minutes.

Serving suggestions: The stewed pear halves combine well with ice-cream and raspberry sauce to make desserts like *poire belle Hélène*. They can also be used to make sherry trifle or can be served by themselves with a cold or hot chocolate sauce, fresh cream or a caramel or butterscotch sauce.

How to deal with a glut

1. Freezing: Prepare as above, quarter or slice and pack immediately or they discolour. If freezing large amounts, sprinkle the prepared pears with lemon juice to help prevent discoloration. Pack in syrup – 250 g (8 oz) sugar and 600 ml (1 pint) water to every 500 g (1 lb) fruit and some lemon juice to help keep the fruit white during storage. Storage time: 9 to 12 months.

Chocolate and pear sponge ring (p. 250) and Normandy pear tart (p. 252) freeze well. Pear and kirsch ice-cream (p. 254) is a good way of freezing a glut crop.

2. Preserving: Make pear and plum jam (p. 256), pear chutney (p. 255) or late summer chutney (p. 106). Pickle in spiced vinegar syrup (p. 332) or bottle in syrup, water or red wine (p. 324).

3. Storing: It is very important to handle the pears carefully and not throw or drop them into boxes or buckets. Once picked, they will quickly ripen if left in a fruit bowl at room temperature. Ideally, the pears should be stored in a cool place on trays where they are not touching one another. Leave the fruit unwrapped so it can be easily inspected, as once pears have ripened they soon pass their best and begin to ferment.

To check if early or mid-season pears are ready to be picked, lift the fruit and twist gently and they should come away easily from the branch. The later varieties are ready to pick when they come off the tree easily without having to be twisted.

Stuffed Pear Hors d'Œuvre

Serves 4

100 g	cream cheese	4 oz
1 level tbsp	walnuts, chopped	1 level tbsp
1	large stick celery	1
1	red-skinned apple	1
	salt	
2	ripe pears, large	2
4	lettuce leaves, large	4
	paprika	

Put the cream cheese, chopped walnuts and finely diced celery into a small bowl. Leaving the skin on the apple, grate it into the bowl. Season with salt to taste and then stir until the mixture is well combined.

Peel, halve and core the pears. Place each half on a lettuce leaf on a serving plate and then divide the stuffing equally between the pear halves. Sprinkle the top of the mixture with paprika and serve cold, as a first course, with brown bread and butter.

Summer Cocktail

Serves 4

2	large oranges	2
250 g	ripe eating pears	8 oz
125 g	cucumber	4 oz
75–100 g	peeled prawns	3–4 oz
1–2 dsps	mustard dressing (p. 147)	1–2 dsps
	salt and pepper	
4	small sprigs of fresh parsley	4

Cut the oranges in half in a 'vandyke' pattern (use the point of a small sharp knife to make a series of small V-shaped cuts around the circumference of the fruit). Cut out the orange flesh from the shells, using a grapefruit knife, and remove the pips and the membrane. Place the orange flesh and juice in a bowl and reserve the orange cups.

Peel, quarter and core the pears, cut them into small dice and place in the bowl with the oranges. Wipe the cucumber, peel off the skin only if desired, cut the flesh into small cubes and add to the rest of the fruit in the bowl.

Reserve four of the best prawns for decoration and cut the remainder in half. Add to the cocktail and stir gently to combine the ingredients. Cover the bowl with an air-tight seal, e.g. cling-wrap or a piece of dampened greaseproof paper, and leave in a cool place.

Just before serving, drain the cocktail mixture to remove the excess orange juice, stir in the mustard dressing and season to taste with salt and pepper.

Spoon the filling into the four orange shells and decorate with the four reserved prawns and the small sprigs of parsley. Serve as a refreshing dinner-party first course.

Hazelnut Pear Parcels

Serves 4

For the pastry

250 g	plain flour	8 oz
125 g	butter or margarine	4 oz
60 g	ground hazelnuts	2 oz
1 level tbsp	caster sugar	1 level tbsp
1	large egg	1

For the filling

4	ripe pears	4
4 level tsps	demerara sugar	4 level tsps

an 18-cm (7-inch) plate or flan ring to cut the pastry

Preheat the oven to 190°C, 375°F, gas mark 5.

Sift the flour into a bowl and rub in the butter or margarine, using the fingertips, until the mixture resembles fine breadcrumbs. Stir in the ground hazelnuts and caster sugar. Mix the egg with a little cold water and add enough to make a fairly firm dough. Reserve the rest of the egg for the glaze. Leave the pastry in a cool place for 15 minutes.

Peel the pears but leave on the stalks. Using a teaspoon, scoop out the centre core through the base of the pears. Fill each of the cavities with a teaspoon of demerara sugar.

On a floured surface, roll out the pastry to a 36-cm (14-inch) square. Cut four 18-cm (7-inch) rounds of pastry and stand a pear, cavity side down, in the centre of each round of pastry. Damp the edges, gather up the pastry around the pears and seal well. Roll out the pastry scraps and cut out four leaves. Damp one side of the leaves and stick one onto each pear near the stalk.

Place the pear parcels on a baking sheet and brush the pastry with the egg glaze. Bake on the shelf above centre of the preheated oven for 30 minutes until the pears are cooked and the pastry is golden. Serve hot or cold with cream.

* Suitable for freezing – cooked or uncooked.

Chocolate and Pear Sponge Ring

Serves 4–6

3	ripe dessert pears	3
50 g	butter or margarine	2 oz
50 g	caster sugar	2 oz
1	large egg	1
50 g	self-raising flour	2 oz
1 level tbsp	cocoa powder	1 level tbsp
1 tbsp	milk	1 tbsp

a 1-litre (1¾-pint) ring mould

Preheat the oven to 190°C, 375°F, gas mark 5.

Brush the inside of the ring mould with oil. Peel and halve the pears lengthwise and remove the cores, using a teaspoon. Lay the pear halves in the base of the mould with the scooped-out centre facing upwards.

In a bowl, cream together the butter or margarine and the sugar. Beat in the egg and lastly fold in the sifted flour and cocoa powder with a little milk to give the mixture a dropping consistency. Spoon the sponge into the ring mould on top of the pears, smooth over the surface and bake on the centre shelf of the preheated oven for 25 to 30 minutes until the sponge is cooked.

Loosen around the edges before turning the pudding out onto a serving dish. Serve with a chocolate cornflour sauce.

* Suitable for freezing.

Port Pears and Raspberry Flan

Serves 6–8

100 g	*pâte sucrée* (sweet pastry) (p. 335)	4 oz
350 g	small ripe pears (3–4)	12 oz
75 g	granulated sugar	3 oz
5 tbsps	water	5 tbsps
1	small sherry glass of port (about 3 tbsps)	1
½ level tsp	arrowroot	½ level tsp
250 g	raspberries	8 oz

an 18- to 20-cm (7- to 8-inch) fluted flan ring on a baking sheet

Prepare the *pâte sucrée* and leave to rest for ¾ hour before using.

Preheat the oven to 190°C, 375°F, gas mark 5.

Roll out the pastry on a floured surface and line the greased flan ring. Bake blind for 15 minutes until browned lightly (for a detailed explanation of baking blind, see p. 334). Remove the flan ring and leave the pastry to cool.

Peel, quarter and core the pears. Dissolve the sugar in the water in a saucepan. Then add the pears and simmer gently until they are soft. Add the port and continue to simmer for a few minutes more. Drain the pears from the liquid and leave to cool. Blend the arrowroot with a little water and stir into the port syrup; return to the heat and stir to thicken. Leave to cool slightly.

Lay the pears around the edge of the flan case and pile the hulled raspberries in the centre. Finally, pour the thickened port syrup over the flan to cover the top and chill in the refrigerator.

Serve cold with whipped cream.

* Suitable for freezing.

Normandy Pear Tart

Serves 6

For the pastry

200 g	plain flour	8 oz
	pinch of salt	
	pinch of ground cinnamon	
100 g	margarine	4 oz
50 g	caster sugar	2 oz
25 g	chopped walnuts	1 oz
1	large egg	1

For the filling

3	medium, ripe dessert pears	3
25 g	butter	1 oz
2 level tbsps	clear honey	2 level tbsps
1 level tsp	lemon juice	1 level tsp
150 ml	double cream	¼ pint

a 20-cm (8-inch) flan ring on a greased baking sheet
a 9-cm (3½-inch) plain round cutter

Preheat the oven to 200°C, 400°F, gas mark 6.

To make the pastry: Sift the flour, salt and cinnamon into a mixing bowl and rub in the margarine, using the fingertips only, until the mixture resembles fine breadcrumbs. Stir in the sugar and chopped walnuts and mix well. Lightly beat the egg and add it with a little cold water to give a firm dough. Leave to rest for a few minutes before using.

Divide the pastry into two pieces, one slightly larger than the other. Roll out the larger piece on a floured surface, line the flan ring and trim the edges. Roll out the other piece of dough into a 20-cm (8-inch) round for the top. Using the cutter, cut out the centre.

Peel, halve and core the pears and lay them, core side down, in the flan case, with the thinner stalk ends towards the centre. Melt the butter in a pan, remove from the heat and stir in the honey and the lemon juice. Spoon the sauce over the pears, then cover the tart with the pastry top, sealing the edges.

Brush the pastry with lightly beaten egg white or milk and dust with caster sugar. Bake on the centre shelf of the preheated oven for 35 minutes until golden brown.

If serving hot, just before serving whip the cream until thick and pile it in the centre of the flan. If serving cold, leave the flan to get cold before piling the whipped cream in the centre.

* Suitable for freezing – cooked or uncooked, but without the cream in the centre.

Chocolate Pear Flan

Serves 6

100 g	sweet shortcrust pastry (p. 335)	4 oz
4	ripe dessert pears	4
100 g	plain chocolate	4 oz
150 ml	single cream	¼ pint

To decorate

4 tbsps	double cream	4 tbsps
1 level tbsp	chopped nuts	1 level tbsp

a 20-cm (8-inch) fluted or plain flan ring on a baking sheet

Preheat the oven to 190°C, 375°F, gas mark 5.

Prepare the pastry, roll out on a lightly floured surface and line the flan ring. Bake 'blind' in the preheated oven for 15 to 20 minutes until the pastry is golden brown. Remove from the oven and allow to cool. (For a detailed explanation of baking blind, see p. 334.)

Meanwhile, peel, quarter and core the pears, and place them in a bowl of water with a few drops of lemon juice to prevent discoloration.

Break the chocolate into pieces and melt in a bowl over a pan of simmering water, stir in the single cream, then place the bowl in a basin of cold water to cool.

Drain the pears well and place them in the pastry case. Pour the chocolate cream mixture over the top, leave in a cool place to set and serve cold, decorated with swirls of whipped double cream sprinkled with a few chopped nuts.

* Suitable for freezing, cooked but undecorated.

Pear and Kirsch Ice-Cream

Makes 600 ml (1 pint)

500 g	pears	1 lb
100 g	sugar	4 oz
150 ml	water	¼ pint
2	large eggs, separated	2
1 tbsp	kirsch	1 tbsp
½	lemon, juice only	½
150 ml	double cream	¼ pint

an ice-cream tray

Turn the refrigerator to its coldest setting or turn on the fast-freeze section of the home freezer.

Peel, quarter and core the pears. In a saucepan, dissolve the sugar in the water over a gentle heat. Slice the pears into the pan, cover and poach gently until the fruit is very soft – about 15 to 20 minutes. Purée the pears with their syrup in a liquidizer or press through a sieve.

Beat the egg yolks in a bowl until frothy; slowly beat in the pear purée, a little at a time, then put the bowl over a pan of simmering water and, stirring constantly, cook until the mixture is becoming thick.

Remove the pan from the heat, stir in the kirsch and lemon juice and leave the mixture to get cold.

Whip the cream until it is thick and fold it into the pear mixture. Beat the egg whites until stiff, then, using a metal spoon, fold carefully into the cream and pour the mixture into the ice-cream tray. Place in the freezing section of the refrigerator or in the fast-freeze compartment of the home freezer.

After about 30 minutes remove the ice-cream and beat lightly with a fork to break up the ice crystals which have formed. Return the cream to the freezer until it is frozen solid.

Before serving, remove the ice-cream from the freezer for 10 minutes to allow it to thaw slightly.

Remember to turn off the fast-freeze section of the home freezer or return the refrigerator to its normal setting.

Note: Windfall and overripe pears can be used, as may frozen pears.

Pear Chutney

Makes 1¼ kg (3 lb)

250 g	onions	8 oz
½	a green pepper	½
450 ml	cider vinegar	¾ pint
1 kg	pears	2 lb
	a small piece root ginger	
6	whole cloves	6
1 tbsp	mustard seed	1 tbsp
1 level tsp	salt	1 level tsp
175 g	demerara sugar	6 oz

a preserving pan or large saucepan

Peel and finely chop the onions; remove the seeds and white pith from the half pepper and cut the flesh into thin 5-cm (2-inch) strips. Place these vegetables in the preserving pan with the vinegar.

Peel, core and dice the pears; bruise the piece of root ginger, e.g. in a pestle and mortar or with a rolling pin, and tie in a muslin bag with the 6 cloves. Add the pears and muslin bag to the pan with the mustard seed and salt, bring the mixture to the boil, cover and simmer gently for about 30 minutes until the pears are soft. Remove the muslin bag.

Add the demerara sugar, dissolve over a low heat, then bring to a rapid boil and boil for 10 minutes, uncovered, until the chutney is beginning to thicken. Pour into clean, warm, dry jars, cover with thick polythene, seal (with screw lids if available), label and store in a cool, dry place for 3 months before use.

Note: Frozen pears may be used for this chutney.

Pear and Plum Jam

Makes about 2–2¾ kg (4–5 lb)

1 kg	pears	2 lb
1 kg	plums	2 lb
300 ml	water	½ pint
1½ kg	granulated or preserving sugar	3 lb
1 level tsp	ground ginger	1 level tsp

a preserving pan or large saucepan

Peel and core the pears and cut into very small dice. Wash and halve the plums and remove the stones. Place the fruit in the preserving pan with the water and simmer gently until it is tender.

Add the sugar and ground ginger and, over a gentle heat, allow the sugar to dissolve completely before bringing to the boil. Boil rapidly until setting point is reached (see p. 311 for full jam-making instructions).

Leave the jam to stand for about 10 minutes before pouring into clean, warm, dry jars. Then cover with wax discs, seal with cellophane covers, label and store in a cool, dry place.

Note: Frozen pears and plums can be used.

The following recipes also include pears:

Blackcurrant and pear cobbler (p. 222)
Late summer chutney (p. 106)
Bottled pears (p. 324)
Pickled pears (p. 332)

Try substituting pears for the main fruit in the following recipes:

Apple gingerbread pudding (p. 203)
Raspberry sponge pudding (p. 269)

31 Plums (including Greengages and Damsons)

Introduction

A bumper crop of plums can present quite a problem to the cook, as we discovered one memorable year. A champion tree can yield up to 70 kg (150 lb) of fruit and such heavy crops can damage the tree's branches. In these cases it is advisable to thin the fruits as this will help produce bigger and tastier plums than a large, heavy cluster can yield.

One of the problems with plums is that they become overripe very quickly and are invaded by swarms of wasps and flocks of pecking birds.

To avoid this, fruit required for jams, bottling and cooking may be picked earlier, when not quite fully ripe. Eating plums should be left on the tree until they can be eaten straight from the tree.

The plum family, which includes gages and the small bluish-purple damsons, thrives best in a well-drained and manured soil and requires plenty of room to grow. However, dwarf and fan-trained varieties are more suitable for the smaller garden.

Plums suffer damage from late spring frosts, silver-leaf infection – a troublesome disease which can be avoided by pruning at the right time – and wet weather, which causes the plums to split and develop brown rot. Diseased fruit must be removed and destroyed.

Pruning should be done in the spring or in the summer after the trees have fruited, but never in the winter when the trees are most vulnerable to infection.

Preparation and cooking

When cooking plums, remember that they are very juicy and so little water is needed. If you require a less juicy dish, cook the plums first without any sugar, strain off some of the excess plum juice and then add the sugar and dissolve it. Also bear in mind that even the sweetest plums become more tart in taste after cooking, so the fruit requires more sugar than you might expect.

To prepare, wash, halve and stone.

To stew: Place the prepared fruit in a saucepan with 1 tablespoon water and 125 g (4 oz) sugar for every 500 g (1 lb) fruit; cover the pan and simmer gently for 10 to 15 minutes until tender.

To purée, press the plums through a sieve.

Serving suggestions: The stewed or puréed plums may be served as a sauce with ice-cream or poured over steamed and sponge puddings.

How to deal with a glut

1. Freezing: Plums and gages should be washed, halved and stoned. Damsons should be washed, and stoned if desired.

Plums can be packed in dry sugar – 125 g (4 oz) dry sugar to every 500 g (1 lb) fruit – or in a sugar syrup – 600 g (1¼ lb) sugar in 600 ml (1 pint) water for every 500 g (1 lb) fruit.

Damsons are best packed without sugar, although they can be packed with dry sugar – 125 g (4 oz) sugar for every 500 g (1 lb) fruit.

Gages are packed in sugar syrup – 600 g (1¼ lb) sugar in 600 ml (1 pint) water for every 500 g (1 lb) fruit.

All these fruits can be packed in polythene bags or wax containers. Storage time: 9 to 12 months.

The following are successful freezer recipes: plum purée (see above), American plum pie (p. 260) and plum cheesecake (p. 262).

Damson sorbet (p. 263) and frozen plum cream (p. 267) are useful ways of storing a glut crop.

2. Preserving: Plum jam (p. 312), pear and plum jam (p. 256), plum and orange jam (p. 266), damson jam (p. 312), damson jelly (p. 318), damson and apple jam (p. 265) and mock mango chutney (p. 264); pickle plums and damsons (p. 332); bottle damsons or plums in syrup or water (p. 324).

3. Storing: Plums will store for 2 to 3 weeks in a cool place if picked when dry, with their stalk intact, and then carefully covered in wrapping paper. Otherwise the plums will only keep a short time.

Rabbit and Damson Stew with Dumplings

Serves 4–6

¾ kg	rabbit, cut into joints by the butcher	1¼–1½ lb
25 g	flour	1 oz

1 level tsp	salt	1 level tsp
	freshly ground pepper	
25 g	cooking fat or dripping	1 oz
175 g	onions	6 oz
100 g	small button mushrooms	4 oz
250 g	carrots	8 oz
1 litre	good light stock	1½ pints
1	*bouquet garni* (sprigs of thyme and parsley, and a bay leaf, tied in muslin)	1
200 g	damsons	6 oz

For the dumplings

150 g	plain flour	6 oz
1½ level tsps	baking powder	1½ level tsps
½ level tsp	salt	½ level tsp
	pepper	
1 level tbsp	parsley, chopped	1 level tbsp
1 level tsp	thyme and marjoram, chopped	1 level tsp
75 g	shredded suet	3 oz

a 2¼-litre (4-pint) flameproof casserole

Preheat the oven to 160°C, 325°F, gas mark 3.

Wipe the rabbit and toss it in the flour, seasoned with the salt and pepper. Heat the cooking fat or dripping in the casserole and fry the joints until browned on all sides, about 5 minutes. Remove onto a plate.

Peel and slice the onions and fry in the casserole for 2 minutes until browned lightly. Wipe and trim the mushrooms and leave whole. Peel and slice the carrots. Add the carrots to the pan, with the mushrooms, and cook for a minute. Stir in any remaining flour, then gradually blend in the stock and bring to the boil. Add the *bouquet garni* and return the rabbit to the dish. Stir well, cover and cook on the centre shelf of the preheated oven for about 1½ hours.

Then wash and stone the damsons and stir them into the stew.

To make the dumplings: Sift the flour and baking powder into a bowl, stir in the salt, pepper, parsley, herbs and suet. Mix in enough cold water to give a soft but not sticky dough. Divide into 6 to 10 dumplings and place on top of the casserole after adding the damsons. Cover with the lid and return to the oven for a further 20 to 30 minutes, until the dumplings are cooked and the rabbit is tender.

* Suitable for freezing – cooked to the stage before the dumplings are added.

American Plum Pie

Serves 5–6

For the pastry

150 g	margarine	5 oz
40 g	butter	1½ oz
225 g	self-raising flour	8 oz
½ level tsp	salt	½ level tsp
3 tbsps	cold water	3 tbsps

For the filling

¾ kg	Victoria plums	1½ lb
100 g	soft brown sugar	4 oz
¼ level tsp	ground cinnamon	¼ level tsp
	egg white	
	caster sugar	

a 20-cm (8-inch) pie plate

Preheat the oven to 200°C, 400°F, gas mark 6.

Beat the margarine and butter together and gradually beat in the sifted flour and salt with a wooden spoon. Finally, add the cold water to make a dough which will be rather sticky, so leave in a cool place for at least ½ hour.

Roll out half the pastry on a well-floured surface and line the pie plate with it; trim the edges. Roll out the remainder for the top of the pie.

Halve and stone the plums and lay them on the pastry, cut sides facing upwards. Sprinkle the sugar and cinnamon over them. Damp the pastry edges and place the second piece of pastry on the top. Seal, trim and crimp the edges. Brush the top with lightly beaten egg white and sprinkle caster sugar over it. Leave to stand for 15 minutes before baking on the centre shelf of the preheated oven for 35 to 40 minutes. Serve with single cream or ice-cream.

* Suitable for freezing.

Rum Plum Pancakes

Serves 6

300 ml	pancake batter (p. 344)	½ pint
	a little oil for frying	

For the filling

500 g	ripe plums	1 lb
1–2 tbsps	rum	1–2 tbsps
1 tbsp	water	1 tbsp
4 level tbsps	sugar	4 level tbsps

Make the pancake batter, leave to stand for 15 minutes, then cook the pancakes and keep them warm.

Wash the plums, halve them and remove the stones. Place the halved plums in a pan with the rum, water and sugar; cover and cook very gently for a few minutes until the plums are soft. Take care not to reduce the plums to a pulp.

To serve, place two hot plum halves on one corner of a pancake and fold up the pancake around it like an envelope. Place two filled pancakes on each plate and pour over them a little of the hot rum juice from the plums. Serve with whipped cream.

* The pancakes, unfilled, can be frozen.

Pam's Plum Pudding

Serves 4

500 g	plums	1 lb
125 g	soft brown sugar	4 oz
450 ml	milk	¾ pint
25 g	butter	1 oz

100 g	fresh breadcrumbs	4 oz
2	large eggs	2
50 g	caster sugar	2 oz

a 1¼-litre (2-pint) ovenproof dish, lightly buttered

Preheat the oven to 190°C, 375°F, gas mark 5.

Wipe and halve the plums and remove the stones. Toss the plums in the soft brown sugar and lay them in the base of the dish.

Warm the milk to blood heat with the butter. Place the breadcrumbs in a bowl, pour the warm milk over them and leave to stand for 15 minutes.

Lightly beat together the eggs and stir into the breadcrumb mixture, with the sugar. Pour the mixture over the plums and bake on the centre shelf of the preheated oven for 1 hour. Remove from the oven and sprinkle a little extra caster sugar over the surface.

Plum Cheesecake

Serves 6–8

For the crumb base

150 g	sweet biscuits, e.g. digestive, Nice, Lincoln	6 oz
75 g	butter or margarine	3 oz
½ level tsp	ground cinnamon	½ level tsp

For the filling

¾ kg	red plums	1½ lb
150 g	sugar	5 oz
1 tbsp	water	1 tbsp
225 g	cream cheese	8 oz
3 level tsps	powdered gelatine (1 sachet)	3 level tsps
2 tbsps	water	2 tbsps
150 ml	double cream, whipped	¼ pint
2	egg whites	2
	chopped nuts	

a 20-cm (8-inch) cake tin with removable base

Crush the biscuits in a polythene bag, using a rolling pin. Melt the butter or margarine in a saucepan, remove from the heat, add the biscuits and the ground cinnamon and stir to mix. Press the crumb mixture onto the base of the cake tin.

Wash the plums, remove the stalks and halve them to remove the stones. Place the fruit in a saucepan with the sugar and 1 tablespoon water and simmer for about 10 to 15 minutes. Purée the fruit in a liquidizer or through a sieve. The purée should make a good ½ litre (1 pint).

Beat the cream cheese in a bowl until smooth and carefully fold into the plum purée, beating after each addition.

Dissolve the gelatine in the 2 tablespoons water in a saucepan over a gentle heat, but do not allow to boil; add to the cheese and plums. Whip the cream and add two thirds of it to the mixture. Mix well.

Whisk the egg whites until stiff and fold into the cheesecake mixture, using a metal spoon. Pour the mixture onto the crumb base in the tin, smooth over the surface and leave to set.

To serve, lift the plum cheesecake out of the tin onto a plate, still on the base of the tin; decorate with the remaining whipped cream and scatter a few chopped nuts over the top.

Note: Damsons or gages can also be used for this recipe.

* Suitable for freezing.

Damson Sorbet

Makes about 1 litre (1½–1¾ pints)

500 g	damsons	1 lb
125 g	granulated sugar	4 oz
300 ml	water	½ pint
½	small lemon, juice only	½
2	large egg whites	2

Set the refrigerator to the coldest setting or turn on the fast-freeze section of the home freezer.

Wash the damsons, remove any stalks and place in a pan with 3 tablespoons of water. Cover and simmer gently for 10 to 12 minutes until the damsons are tender. Cool slightly, then press through a sieve.

Put the sugar and water in a pan and heat gently without boiling

264 Part Two: Fruits

until the sugar has all dissolved. Bring to the boil and simmer for about 10 minutes. Pour into a 600-ml (1-pint) measuring jug and stir in the lemon juice and damson purée. (If necessary make up to 600 ml/1 pint with cold water.) Leave to get cold.

Pour the liquid into a shallow container and place either in the freezing compartment of the refrigerator or in the fast-freeze section of the home freezer. Leave until it has started to set around the edges (about 30 minutes).

Whisk the egg whites until stiff. Beat the damson mixture lightly with a fork to break up the ice crystals, then fold the egg whites into it, using a metal spoon. Mix well, return to the freezer and, when it is completely frozen, turn the refrigerator or the home freezer back to its normal setting. Remove from the freezer about 10 minutes before serving.

Note: Frozen damson purée may be used.

Plum Sauce

Makes over 300 ml (½ pint)

500 g	plums	1 lb
125 g	sugar	4 oz
1 tbsp	water	1 tbsp
¼ level tsp	ground cinnamon	¼ level tsp

Wipe the plums, halve them and remove the stones. Place in a saucepan with the sugar, water and cinnamon and bring to the boil. Cook for 10 minutes until the plums are soft enough to pass through a sieve. Leave the plum purée to get cold.

Serve poured over vanilla ice-cream or with spicy plum pudding (p. 267).

Mock Mango Chutney

Makes about 2½ kg (5–6 lb)

1 kg	plums	2 lb
¾ kg	cooking apples	1½ lb
175 g	dates, chopped	6 oz
1	lemon, juice only	1

125 g	onion	4 oz
125 g	sultanas	4 oz
¼ level tsp	ground nutmeg	¼ level tsp
1½ level tbsps	salt	1½ level tbsps
1 level tsp	crushed chillies	1 level tsp
3	bay leaves	3
600 ml	malt vinegar	1 pint
1 kg	demerara sugar	2 lb
2 level tbsps	lime juice	2 level tbsps

a preserving pan or large saucepan

Wash, halve and remove the stones from the plums; peel, core and chop the apples; place both fruits in a large bowl. Add the stoned, chopped dates and the lemon juice. Peel and chop the onion and add to the bowl with the sultanas, nutmeg, salt, chillies and bay leaves.

Stir in the vinegar, mix all the ingredients together and leave to stand for 3 hours. Transfer to a preserving pan, bring to the boil and simmer gently, uncovered, until tender, stirring frequently.

Add the sugar and lime juice and continue to simmer, uncovered, until the chutney thickens, about 15 minutes. Bottle in warm, clean, dry jars, cover with wax discs and seal with thick polythene and lids if available. Label and store in a cool, dry place for at least 3 months to mature before using.

Note: This chutney makes a marvellous substitute for the increasingly expensive real mango chutney, and is delicious with curry dishes.

Damson and Apple Jam

Makes 5 kg (10 lb)

1½ kg	damsons	3 lb
600 ml	water	1 pint
1½ kg	apples	3 lb
about 3 kg	granulated or preserving sugar	about 6 lb
	a knob of butter	

a preserving pan or large saucepan

Place the damsons and water in the preserving pan, cover and simmer gently until soft – 20 minutes. Meanwhile peel, core and roughly chop the apples.

Sieve the damsons and return the pulp to the pan with the apples. Cover and simmer until the apples are pulpy – 20 to 25 minutes. Then measure the pulp and add 500 g (1 lb) sugar to every 600 ml (1 pint) of pulp. Return to the pan and, over a low heat, dissolve the sugar. When all the sugar is completely dissolved, add a knob of butter, bring to the boil and boil rapidly for about 5 minutes, stirring occasionally to prevent it sticking, until setting point is reached. (For full jam-making instructions, see p. 311.) Remove from the heat and pour the jam into warm, clean, dry jars. Cover with wax discs, seal, label and store in a cool, dry place.

Note: Frozen damsons and apple slices can be used.

Plum and Orange Jam

Makes about 2 kg (4 lb)

1½ kg	red plums	3 lb
2	medium-sized oranges	2
300 ml	water	½ pint
1½ kg	granulated or preserving sugar	3 lb
	a knob of butter	

a preserving pan or large saucepan

Wipe and halve the plums and place in the preserving pan (you may remove the stones after halving the fruit or skim them off the jam later).

Squeeze the juice from the oranges; roughly chop the peel and then mince it finely. Add the orange juice and minced peel to the pan, along with the water.

Bring the fruit to the boil and simmer very gently for about 30 minutes until the plums and peel are very tender. During this time the plum stones will rise to the surface and should be scooped out of the pan with a draining spoon.

Add the sugar and heat slowly until all the sugar is dissolved, but do not boil. Add a knob of butter, then boil rapidly for about 15 minutes until the jam has reached setting point (see p. 311 for full jam-making instructions). Skim off any scum from the surface of the jam.

Leave the jam to stand for 10 minutes before pouring into warm, clean, dry jars. Cover with wax discs, seal, label and store in a cool, dry place.

Note: Frozen plums can be used.

The following recipes also include plums:

Pear and plum jam (p. 256)
Damson jam (p. 312)
Greengage jam (p. 312)
Plum jam (p. 312)
Damson jelly (p. 318)
Bottled damsons (p. 324)
Bottled plums (p. 324)
Pickled plums and damsons (p. 332.)

Try substituting plums for the main fruit in the following recipes:

Blackcurrant and pear cobbler (p. 222.)
    (substitute for both fruits)
Frosted cherries (p. 234)
Frozen gooseberry cream (p. 243)
Spicy redcurrant pudding (p. 277)
Rhubarb and raisin slice (p. 288)

32 Raspberries and Loganberries

Introduction

The raspberry is a magnificent fruit, second only to the strawberry in popularity. The canes are quick to fruit and, once established, will provide up to a decade's worth of raspberries before they pass their best.

They can be grown in partial shade and will grow on most soils if provided with a good supply of organic material like manure or compost, but, ideally, they should be grown in a sheltered position as the young canes are vulnerable to high winds.

Raspberries bear their fruit on new young canes, so once the old canes have fruited they should be cut back to the ground. Most varieties require the support of wires tied to stakes, but autumn varieties are normally self-supporting, though they do not crop so abundantly.

To ward off the raspberry beetle maggots, spray the flowers with Derris about one week after flowering and repeat this two weeks later.

Loganberries are said to have originated in the United States of America and are thought to be a cross between a blackberry and a raspberry. They are larger fruits than raspberries, but are used in the same ways. They can be grown against a wall and, like raspberries, should be covered with a net or grown in a fruit cage for protection against birds.

All the recipes below can be successfully made using loganberries.

Preparation and cooking

It seems sacrilegious to do anything to fresh raspberries other than eat them as they are. They certainly need no cooking, not even to make a purée.

To prepare, remove any hulls that may be left on the fruit. It is not usually necessary to wash them.

To purée: Press the prepared fruit through a sieve, sweeten with a little icing sugar and use as a sauce for desserts like peach melba.

Serving suggestions: Fresh whole raspberries can be served with sugar and cream (or condensed milk for a children's sweet); with kirsch for a special sweet; with ice-cream; in fruit salads, trifles and compôtes, etc.

How to deal with a glut

1. Freezing: Select firm but not overripe berries and do not wash them. Pack either with or without sugar – allowing 125 g (4 oz) dry sugar for every 500 g (1 lb) fruit. Storage time: 9 to 12 months.

There is no need to freeze raspberry purée as, once frozen berries are thawed, they can easily be puréed through a sieve.

Raspberry sorbet (p. 274) is a good recipe for using up a bumper crop or overripe fruit.

2. Preserving: Bottle in syrup or water (p. 324); or make raspberry jam (p. 312) or loganberry jam (p. 312).

Raspberry Sponge Pudding

Serves 5–6

100 g	sweet shortcrust pastry (p. 335)	4 oz
350 g	raspberries	12 oz
25 g	granulated sugar	1 oz
50 g	margarine	2 oz
50 g	caster sugar	2 oz
1	large egg	1
	vanilla essence	
50 g	self-raising flour	2 oz
1 dsp	milk	1 dsp
3 level dsps	icing sugar, sifted	3 level dsps

an 18-cm (7-inch) square sandwich tin

Preheat the oven to 190°C, 375°F, gas mark 5.

Make the pastry and roll out to a 20-cm (8-inch) square. Line the base and sides of the sandwich tin. Hull the raspberries and scatter over the pastry base, sprinkle the granulated sugar over them and leave to rest for 15 minutes.

To make the sponge topping: Cream the margarine and caster sugar together in a bowl until light and fluffy. Beat in the egg and vanilla essence, and lastly fold in the sifted flour with the milk to give a soft dropping consistency.

Spread the sponge mixture over the raspberries and bake the pudding on the centre shelf of the preheated oven for about 35 minutes until the sponge is cooked and springy to the touch and the pastry crisp and golden. Dredge the top with sifted icing sugar and serve hot or cold with custard.

Note: Frozen raspberries may be used.

* Suitable for freezing, cooked or uncooked.

Raspberry Cream Tart

Serves 6–8

200 g	sweet shortcrust pastry (p. 335)	8 oz
350 g	raspberries	12 oz
50 g	caster sugar	2 oz
1	egg white, reserved from the egg yolk used to make the pastry	1
1 level tbsp	caster sugar	1 level tbsp
150 ml	single cream	¼ pint

an 18- to 20-cm (7- to 8-inch) pie dish

Preheat the oven to 190°C, 375°F, gas mark 5.

Prepare the sweet shortcrust pastry and leave it to rest for 15 minutes before using.

Divide the pastry into two equal portions. Roll out one piece, lay the pie dish upside down on top of the pastry and cut round the edge to give a circle of pastry the same size as the dish. Leave this on one side.

Add the pastry trimmings to the second piece of pastry and roll it out to line the base and sides of the pie dish, but not the outside rim.

Hull the raspberries, if necessary, place in a bowl with the 50 g (2 oz) caster sugar and toss gently to coat all the fruit with the sugar.

Place the sugared raspberries in the pastry case and lay the pastry circle gently on top of the pie, but do not press it down and do not seal the edges.

Brush the top of the pastry gently with the lightly beaten egg white and sprinkle the tablespoon of caster sugar evenly over the top. Bake on the centre shelf of the preheated oven for 30 to 35 minutes until the pastry is cooked and the top is frosted.

Remove from the oven and leave the pie to cool for *at least 10 minutes*. (This is important, for the pastry is inclined to break if the pie has not been left long enough to cool.) Run a knife carefully underneath the rim of the pastry lid and, using a fish slice, gently lift the whole pastry lid off the pie and place it on a warm plate. Pour the single cream evenly over the hot raspberries and then replace the lid. Serve immediately with extra cream if desired.

Note: Frozen raspberries can be used.

* Suitable for freezing before adding the cream.

Hazelnut Meringue

Serves 6

For the meringue

3	large egg whites	3
175 g	caster sugar	6 oz
60 g	ground hazelnuts	2 oz
¼ tsp	vanilla essence	¼ tsp
½ tsp	white vinegar	½ tsp

For the filling

350 g	raspberries	12 oz
300 ml	double cream	½ pint
1 level tsp	icing sugar	1 level tsp

two 20-cm (8-inch) sandwich tins, greased and base-lined

Preheat the oven to 160°C, 325°F, gas mark 3.

Break the egg whites into a mixing bowl and whisk until stiff and dry. Gradually beat in half the sugar, until the meringue is thick and glossy and stands in peaks. Then fold in the remaining caster sugar with the ground hazelnuts, the vanilla essence and the vinegar.

Divide the meringue between the two greased and lined sandwich tins. Smooth over the surface and bake on the shelf below centre of the preheated oven for 25 minutes. Turn the oven temperature down to 140°C, 275°F, gas mark 1, for a further 35 minutes, then turn off the heat and leave for 30 minutes before removing the tins. When they are cool, turn the meringues out onto a cooling rack and peel off the base paper.

About 1 to 1½ hours before serving, hull the raspberries if necessary. Whip the cream until stiff and fold in the icing sugar. Spread three quarters of the cream onto one meringue piece, cover with two thirds of the raspberries and place the second layer of meringue on top. Press down lightly, then spread the rest of the cream over the top of the meringue and decorate with the remaining raspberries. Sift a little extra icing sugar over the top before serving.

Note: Frozen raspberries may be used.

Raspberry Ratafia Cream

Serves 4

250 g	raspberries	8 oz
1	large egg white	1
60 g	caster sugar	2 oz
4 tbsps	single cream	4 tbsps
150 ml	plain yoghurt (small carton)	¼ pint
50 g	ratafia biscuits	2 oz

4 individual glass serving dishes

This pudding must be made not more than 1 hour before serving.

Remove any hulls from the raspberries. Beat the egg white until it is stiff and dry, add the sugar and cream and continue to beat for a little longer. Fold in the plain yoghurt.

Divide the raspberries between the 4 dishes, reserving 4 of the best ones for decoration, and divide the ratafia biscuits between the glasses. Pour the creamy topping over the puddings, dividing the mixture evenly between the dishes. Place a raspberry in the centre of each sweet, to decorate.

Note: Frozen raspberries may be used.

Raspberry Flan

Serves 4–5

1	20-cm (8-inch) ready-made sponge flan case	1
1	raspberry jelly	1
250 g	raspberries	8 oz
4 tbsps	double cream	4 tbsps
150 ml	raspberry yoghurt (small carton)	¼ pint
1 level tbsp	sugar	1 level tbsp

Place the sponge flan case on a flat serving dish. Dissolve the jelly in 450 ml (¾ pint) hot water and leave until it has almost set. Remove any hulls from the raspberries and put aside 8 of the best ones for decoration.

Whip the double cream until thick and fold in the yoghurt and sugar. Stir the jelly into the cream until well mixed, then carefully fold in the raspberries. Spoon the setting mixture into the sponge case and place the 8 raspberries around the edge of the flan to decorate. Leave the dessert to set for 1 hour before serving.

Note: Frozen raspberries may be used.

Raspberry Mould

Serves 4

350 g	raspberries	12 oz
75 g	caster sugar	3 oz
2 rounded tsps	powdered gelatine	2 rounded tsps
6 tbsps	water	6 tbsps
2 tsps	lemon juice	2 tsps
2	large egg whites	2

a 1-litre (1½-pint) mould

Hull the raspberries, if necessary, and press through a sieve. Stir in the caster sugar.

Place the gelatine in a saucepan with the water and lemon juice and heat very gently until it has completely dissolved. Add the mixture to the raspberry purée.

Place the egg whites in a bowl and whisk until stiff. Lightly fold them into the raspberry mixture. Pour the pudding into a mould and leave to set in a cool place. When set, the pudding will have separated into two layers, with a raspberry jelly on the base of the mould and a fluffy layer on top.

To serve, dip the mould quickly into a basin of hot water to loosen the sides and turn it onto a serving plate. Serve immediately with cream or evaporated milk, or keep in the refrigerator as the jelly will become soft on a warm day and soon collapse.

Note: This pudding is a good way of using raspberries which have become soft and overripe. Frozen raspberries may be used also.

Raspberry Sorbet

Makes about ¾ litre (1–1¼ pints)

250 g	raspberries	8 oz
125 g	granulated sugar	4 oz
300 ml	water	½ pint
½	small lemon, juice only	½
2	large egg whites	2

Set the refrigerator to the coldest setting or turn on the fast-freeze section of the home freezer.

Press the raspberries through a sieve into a bowl and discard the pips. Put the sugar and water in a pan and heat gently without boiling until the sugar has all dissolved. Bring to the boil and simmer for about 10 minutes. Pour into a 600-ml (1-pint) measuring jug and stir in the lemon juice and the raspberry purée. If necessary make the liquid up to 600 ml (1 pint) with a little cold water. Leave to get cold.

Pour the liquid into a shallow container and place either in the freezing compartment of the fridge or the fast-freeze section of the home freezer. Leave until it has started to set around the edges (about 30 minutes).

Whisk the egg whites until stiff. Beat the raspberry mixture lightly with a fork to break up the ice crystals which have formed, then fold the beaten egg whites into it, using a metal spoon. Mix well, return to the freezer and, when it has frozen completely, turn the refrigerator back to normal setting or turn off the fast-freeze section of the home freezer. Remove from the freezer about 10 minutes before serving.

Note: Frozen raspberries can be used.

The following recipes also include raspberries:

Linzer torte (p. 278)
Redcurrant and raspberry summer pudding (p. 279)
Port pears and raspberry flan (p. 251)
Raspberry jam (p. 312)
Loganberry jam (p. 312)
Bottled loganberries and raspberries (p. 324)

Try substituting raspberries for the main fruit in the following recipes:

Cherry batter pudding (p. 231)
Cherry and melon coronet (p. 231)
Blackcurrant juice (p. 225)
Gooseberry soufflé (p. 240)
Strawberry baked Alaska (p. 299)
Strawberry gâteau(p. 304)
Strawberry éclairs (p. 298)
Strawberry ice-cream (p. 306)

33 Redcurrants

Introduction

Redcurrants and blackcurrants are often thought to be the same kind of plant, only bearing different coloured fruit. In fact the two are dissimilar in several ways and this should be remembered when caring for them in the garden and in cooking.

Redcurrant bushes are not as strong as blackcurrant bushes and their stems are more likely to snap in high winds – so stake the young shoots to give them some support.

Redcurrants grow their berries on the old wood so these branches are only occasionally cut out. The bushes also like a well-manured soil, but not the surfeit that blackcurrants thrive on.

On the other hand, redcurrants are prone to a deficiency of potash which can be counteracted by digging in your bonfire ash in the spring.

To protect the fruit from birds, grow the bushes under netting or in a cage with other fruits. Cuttings may be taken from established plants to increase the number of bushes in your garden.

Preparation and cooking

Redcurrants are delicious eaten raw with a sprinkling of caster sugar and cream. They also make a colourful addition to a fresh fruit salad or as part of a red fruit salad with raspberries, strawberries and cherries. Also, they make a tasty summer compôte with fresh raspberries.

To prepare, run the stalks through a fork and this will remove the berries from their stems without damaging the fruit.

The currants are best used within 24 hours of picking as they quickly deteriorate with storage.

There is no need to pre-cook redcurrants. To purée, press the fruit through a sieve and sweeten to taste. For redcurrant sauce, add 100 g (4 oz) sugar to each 300 ml ($\frac{1}{2}$ pint) fruit purée and place in a pan over a low heat to dissolve the sugar but do not boil.

How to deal with a glut

1. Freezing: Strip the currants from their stalks, wash and dry. Pack into containers in layers with dry sugar – 125 g (4 oz) for every 500 g (1 lb) of fruit. Storage time: 9 to 12 months.

Redcurrant sorbet (p. 281) is a good recipe for using up and storing a bumper crop.

2. Preserving: Make redcurrant jelly (p. 318); or bottle in syrup (p. 325).

Spicy Redcurrant Pudding

Serves 5–6

For the suet pastry

50 g	shredded suet	2 oz
50 g	plain flour	2 oz
50 g	brown wheatmeal flour	2 oz
	a pinch of salt	
50 g	fresh breadcrumbs	2 oz
25 g	soft brown sugar	1 oz
1 level tsp	mixed spice	1 level tsp
1 level tsp	bicarbonate of soda	1 level tsp
1 tsp	golden syrup	1 tsp
6 tbsps	milk	6 tbsps

For the filling

350 g	redcurrants	12 oz
60 g	soft brown sugar	2 oz
¼ level tsp	ground cinnamon	¼ level tsp

a 500-g (1-lb) pudding basin, greased

Put the shredded suet, sifted flours, salt, breadcrumbs, sugar, spice and bicarbonate of soda in a large bowl. Mix well together, then add the syrup and milk to make a soft dough. Knead the dough a little to make it smooth and divide it into three portions.

Roll out the first piece of dough on a lightly floured surface and fit into the base of the pudding basin.

Strip the currants from their stalks, wash, if necessary, in cold water and drain thoroughly. Mix them with the sugar and ground cinnamon.

Place half the sugared redcurrants on top of the suet dough in the basin. Roll out the second piece of dough to fit neatly over the redcurrants and cover this second layer of dough with the remaining redcurrants.

Finally, roll out the last piece of dough to a larger circle to fit over the top of the pudding. Cover the basin with a double layer of greaseproof paper, with a small pleat in the centre to allow for expansion of the pudding, and secure it tightly with string.

Place the basin in a steamer over a large saucepan of simmering water. Cover and slowly steam the pudding for 2½ hours; check the water occasionally and, if necessary, replenish the saucepan with boiling water.

To serve, remove the string and greaseproof paper, loosen the sides of the pudding carefully with a knife and then turn the pudding out onto a warm serving plate. Serve with cold redcurrant sauce (see p. 276) and hot custard.

Note: Frozen redcurrants can be used.

Linzer Torte

Serves 6

For the pastry

150 g	plain flour	6 oz
	a good pinch of ground cloves and ground cinnamon	
	a pinch of salt	
1	lemon, grated rind only	1
75 g	butter, softened	3 oz
75 g	caster sugar	3 oz
50 g	ground almonds	2 oz
1	large egg	1

For the filling

300 g	redcurrants	12 oz
100 g	raspberries	4 oz
75 g	caster sugar	3 oz

a 22-cm (9-inch) fluted flan dish, lightly buttered

Preheat the oven to 190°C, 375°F, gas mark 5.

Sift the flour, spices, and salt into a bowl. Mix in the grated lemon rind. Cut the butter into small pieces and, using the fingertips only, rub into the flour until the mixture resembles fine breadcrumbs. Stir in the sugar and ground almonds. Lightly beat the egg, then, using a fork, mix the egg into the dry ingredients until a dough has formed. Knead the dough lightly, wrap it in greaseproof paper and put in a cool place for 1 hour.

On a floured surface roll out the pastry into a round and carefully line the flan dish (*Note:* This is a fairly short pastry and so needs careful handling). Trim the top edges and then roll up the trimmings, re-roll them and cut into ten 1-cm (½-inch) wide strips for the lattice top.

Wash the redcurrants and remove them from their stalks, using a fork. Mix the currants with the hulled raspberries and place in the flan case. Sprinkle the caster sugar over them and lay the strips of pastry over the tart to give a lattice effect. Leave to rest for 15 minutes before baking.

Bake on the centre shelf of the preheated oven for 35 to 40 minutes until the pastry is golden brown and both it and the filling are cooked. Serve hot or cold with fresh cream.

* Suitable for freezing.

Redcurrant and Raspberry Summer Pudding

Serves 4–5

500 g	redcurrants	1 lb
250 g	raspberries	8 oz
1 tbsp	water	1 tbsp
125 g	caster sugar	4 oz
8	thin slices of white bread	8

a ¾-kg (1½-lb) pudding basin or fluted mould

Wash and strip the redcurrants from their stalks, hull the raspberries, if necessary, and place both fruits in a pan with the water and sugar. Cover the pan and cook gently for 2 to 3 minutes; leave to cool slightly.

Line the pudding basin or mould with the slices of bread. Place 1 slice in the base and arrange 6 slices overlapping round the sides (they may need trimming to fit closely together). Pour the fruit and its syrup into the lined basin and cover with the remaining slice of bread. Cover with a plate and stand a heavy weight or large tin of fruit on top. Leave overnight in the refrigerator.

Turn out onto a plate and serve chilled with whipped cream.

Redcurrant and Orange Tart

Serves 6

For the biscuit base

150 g	shortbread biscuits, e.g. Royal Scot	6 oz
75 g	unsalted butter	3 oz
1 level tbsp	sugar	1 level tbsp

For the filling

1	large orange, juice only	1
25 g	cornflour	1 oz
1	egg yolk	1
25 g	sugar	1 oz
	a knob of unsalted butter	
250 g	redcurrants	8 oz
2 tbsps	redcurrant jelly (p. 318)	2 tbsps

a 20-cm (8-inch) pie or flan dish

Put the biscuits in a polythene bag and crush them with a rolling pin. Melt the butter in a saucepan, remove from the heat and stir in the biscuit crumbs and sugar. Mix well, then press the mixture onto the base of the flan dish. Leave in a cool place to set.

Squeeze the juice from the orange and make it up to 180 ml (6 fl oz) with water. Place the cornflour in a small saucepan and blend in the orange juice. Bring the mixture to the boil, stirring constantly, until it becomes thick and opaque. Remove from the heat and beat in the egg yolk and the sugar.

Finally, stir in the butter a little at a time until it has been absorbed. Cover the pan with an air-tight seal, e.g. cling-film or a damp piece of greaseproof paper, and leave to cool.

Before the mixture sets, spread it evenly over the biscuit base. Strip the currants from their stalks and wash in cold water. Drain well before laying over the top of the orange filling.

Melt the redcurrant jelly in a saucepan over a low heat and brush the hot jelly over the top of the fruit to glaze the tart. Serve cold with cream.

* Suitable for freezing.

Redcurrant Sorbet

Makes about ¾ litre (1–1¼ pints)

250 g	redcurrants	8 oz
125 g	granulated sugar	4 oz
300 ml	water	½ pint
½	small lemon, juice only	½
2	large egg whites	2

Set the refrigerator to its coldest setting or turn on the fast-freeze section of the home freezer.

Remove the redcurrants from their stalks, rinse in cold water and place in a pan with 2 tablespoons of water. Cover and simmer gently for 10 minutes. Cool slightly then press the fruit through a sieve and add a little red colouring if necessary.

Put the sugar and 300 ml (½ pint) water in a pan and heat gently without boiling until the sugar has all dissolved. Bring to the boil and simmer for about 10 minutes. Pour into a 600-ml (1-pint) measuring jug and stir in the lemon juice and redcurrant purée. If necessary, make up to 600 ml (1 pint) with cold water. Leave to get cold.

Pour the liquid into a shallow container and place either in the freezing compartment of the refrigerator or in the fast-freeze section of the home freezer. Leave until it has started to set around the edges (about 30 minutes).

Whisk the egg whites until stiff. Beat the redcurrant mixture lightly with a fork to break up the ice crystals, then fold in the egg whites, using a metal spoon. Mix well, return to the freezer and, when it is completely frozen, turn the refrigerator or home freezer back to its normal setting. Remove the sorbet from the freezer about 10 minutes before serving.

Note: Frozen redcurrant purée may be used.

The following recipes also include redcurrants:

Redcurrant jelly (p. 318)
Bottled redcurrants (p. 325)

Try substituting redcurrants for the main fruit in the following recipes:

Rhubarb and gooseberry crumble (p. 286)
    (substitute for the rhubarb)
Raspberry flan (p. 273)
Frosted cherries (p. 234)

34 Rhubarb

Introduction

Continentals think of rhubarb as a weed and, judging by its prolific growth, they are partially justified in this verdict – for if left unchecked it will soon threaten to take over the garden.

To confuse matters further, it is usually classed as a vegetable and not a fruit. But weed or no weed, rhubarb has the advantage of being the first fruit of the year that the home gardener can enjoy from his plot.

Rhubarb also has the distinction of being one of the very few crops that will grow in the shade, although it is at its best in an open sunny patch enriched with compost or manure.

To force rhubarb for early cropping at the start of the year, choose the strongest crowns, cover them with a large bucket or box and protect from frosts by surrounding these with straw or leaves.

If at any stage your rhubarb starts to go to seed, cut out the seeded stems as they are of no use. To increase the number of plants, lift an established crown and split it into new plants each with a good piece, of root and a rounded bud on it.

Always pull the rhubarb stalks gently from the base and never cut them. The large leaves at the top of the stalks must never be used as they contain oxalic acid and are therefore poisonous.

A good tip for cleaning stained cooking pans is to stew a little rhubarb in them. The acidity of the rhubarb soon removes the stains.

Preparation and cooking

Rhubarb combines well with oranges, gooseberries, apples and spices – rhubarb and ginger is one of the most popular preserves. Unlike most other fruits, it is never eaten raw because it is so acid.

To prepare, wipe the stalks, remove the base and leaves and cut into 2- to 3-cm ($\frac{1}{2}$- to 1-inch) slices. Very little water is required, if any, as the rhubarb is so juicy.

To stew: Place 500 g (1 lb) prepared rhubarb in a pan with 1 tablespoon water and 75 to 100 g (3 to 4 oz) sugar; cover the pan and simmer gently for 5 to 7 minutes until tender.

Alternatively, the rhubarb can be stewed with golden syrup instead of sugar and water. Melt 1 to 2 tablespoons syrup in a saucepan, add the prepared rhubarb, cover and simmer gently for 5 to 7 minutes until tender. Sweeten with a little extra sugar if necessary.

Serving suggestions: The stewed rhubarb can be served with baked custard, ice-cream or custard.

How to deal with a glut

1. Freezing: Choose young tender stalks. Cut off the leaves and base, wash and cut into 3-cm (1-inch) pieces. There is no need to blanch. Pack into containers either with or without sugar – use 125 g dry sugar for every 500 g rhubarb (4 oz for every 1 lb), or prepare a syrup of 600 g (1¼ lb) sugar in 600 ml (1 pint) water for every 500 g (1 lb) rhubarb. Storage time: 9 to 12 months.

Stewed rhubarb can also be frozen, e.g. in 600 ml (1 pint) quantities. Allow to cool first. Rhubarb and raisin slice (p. 288) is also good for freezing.

2. Preserving: Make rhubarb and orange jam (p. 291), rhubarb, peel and ginger jam (p. 291), rhubarb chutney (p. 289), rhubarb pickled in spiced vinegar (p. 332), rhubarb bottled in syrup or water (p. 325) or spiced rhubarb (p. 290).

3. Storing: Once picked it will keep in the bottom of the fridge for 2 to 3 weeks providing that it is left whole with just the leaves cut off.

Rhubarb Fruit Pie

Serves 6–8

| 200 g | sweet shortcrust pastry (p. 335) | 8 oz |

For the filling

500 g	rhubarb	1 lb
125 g	sugar	4 oz
2	oranges	2
1	large banana	1

a 20-cm (8-inch) deep pie dish

Preheat the oven to 190°C, 375°F, gas mark 5.

Make the pastry and leave to rest for 15 minutes.

Meanwhile, wipe and trim the rhubarb, cut into 3-cm (1-inch) pieces and put in a saucepan with the sugar. Cook for 5 to 10 minutes, depending on the thickness of the rhubarb. If the rhubarb makes a lot of juice, blend 1 tablespoon cornflour with 1 tablespoon water and stir it into the rhubarb. Bring to the boil and, stirring, cook until thickened. Leave the rhubarb to cool slightly.

Keeping the oranges whole, use a small sharp knife to cut off a circle of peel from the base, and then peel off the skin and pith leaving the orange itself whole. Slice the orange thinly.

Roll out half the pastry on a lightly floured surface to fit the base and sides of the pie dish. Roll out the second half to cover the top of the pie. Gather up the trimmings.

Spoon the rhubarb into the pastry case, cover with the sliced oranges and, finally, the peeled and sliced banana. Cover the fruit with the pastry lid, seal and crimp the edges and decorate the pie with pastry leaves made from the trimmings.

Bake on the centre shelf of the preheated oven for 30 to 35 minutes until the pastry is golden brown. Serve hot with custard.

Note: Frozen rhubarb can be used.

Rhubarb Charlotte

Serves 4–5

500 g	rhubarb	1 lb
1	medium orange, grated rind and juice	1
150 g	soft brown sugar	5 oz
150 g	fresh brown breadcrumbs	5 oz
40 g	shredded suet	1½ oz

a 1- to 1¼-litre (1½- to 2-pint) soufflé dish or ovenproof glass dish

Preheat the oven to 180°C, 350°F, gas mark 4.

Trim off the top and base of the rhubarb, wipe well and cut into 3-cm (1-inch) pieces. Place the rhubarb in a pan with the orange juice and 60 g (2 oz) of the sugar, cover the pan and cook for 5 minutes.

In a bowl, mix together the remaining 90 g (3 oz) of sugar, the grated orange rind, the fresh breadcrumbs and the suet.

Butter the soufflé dish or glass dish and lay half the rhubarb in the base. Scatter half the breadcrumb mixture over it, then the rest of the rhubarb and end with a layer of the remaining crumb mixture.

Press the layers down lightly, cover the dish with a lid or cooking foil and bake on the centre shelf of the preheated oven for about 1 hour. Serve with custard.

* Suitable for freezing, cooked or uncooked.

Rhubarb and Gooseberry Crumble

Serves 4

250 g	rhubarb	8 oz
250 g	gooseberries	8 oz
2 tbsps	water	2 tbsps
75 g	sugar	3 oz

For the topping

150 g	plain flour	6 oz
¼ level tsp	ground cinnamon (optional)	¼ level tsp
75 g	butter or margarine	3 oz
50 g	sugar	2 oz

a 1- to 1¼-litre (1½- to 2-pint) pie dish

Preheat the oven to 190°C, 375°F, gas mark 5.

Wash and trim the rhubarb and cut into 3-cm (1-inch) pieces; top, tail and wash the gooseberries and mix the fruits together. Put in the pie dish, add the water and sprinkle the sugar over the top.

Prepare the crumble by sifting the flour and cinnamon into a bowl; add the butter or margarine cut into pieces and rub into the flour, using the fingertips only, until the mixture resembles fine breadcrumbs. Add the sugar and spread the topping over the fruit.

Bake on the centre shelf of the preheated oven for 35 to 40 minutes. Serve hot or cold with custard or cream.

Note: For a plain rhubarb crumble, use 500 g (1 lb) rhubarb and omit the gooseberries. Frozen rhubarb and gooseberries may be used.

Rhubarb Meringue Pie

Serves 5–6

| 100 g | sweet shortcrust pastry (p. 335) | 4 oz |

For the filling

500 g	rhubarb	1 lb
125 g	granulated sugar	4 oz
1 tbsp	water	1 tbsp
	pinch of ground cinnamon	
25 g	cornflour	1 oz
2	large eggs, separated	2
100 g	caster sugar	4 oz

a 20-cm (8-inch) fluted flan ring on a baking sheet

Preheat the oven to 200°C, 400°F, gas mark 6.

Make the pastry, using a whole egg yolk from the separated eggs in the filling. Roll out on a floured surface and line the flan ring. Trim the top edge and leave to rest for 15 minutes before baking blind in the pre-heated oven for 15 minutes (see p. 334 for explanation of baking blind). Remove the pastry case from the oven and reduce the heat to 160°C, 325°F, gas mark 3.

Meanwhile, make the filling. Wipe and trim the rhubarb and cut it into 3-cm (1-inch) pieces. Place in a saucepan with the sugar, water and cinnamon, cover and cook until tender – about 10 to 12 minutes. Drain well, reserving the juice in a measuring jug. If necessary make up to 300 ml ($\frac{1}{2}$ pint) with cold water. Return the pan to the heat.

Blend the cornflour with a little cold water, then gradually stir in the rhubarb juice. Bring to the boil in the saucepan, stirring until thick, and cook for 2 minutes. Remove from the heat and beat in the remaining egg yolk from the separated eggs. Pour the mixture into the cooked flan case.

Whisk the egg whites until stiff, then beat in half the caster sugar and continue whisking until the mixture is stiff and glossy. Fold in the remaining sugar and spread over the filling. Rough the surface into little peaks and bake on the centre shelf of the cooler oven (160°C, 325°F, gas mark 3) for 25 minutes until a light golden brown.

Note: Frozen or bottled rhubarb can be used.

Rhubarb and Raisin Slice

Serves 4–6

For the base and top

150 g	self-raising flour	6 oz
	pinch of salt	
¼ level tsp	ground cinnamon	¼ level tsp
100 g	margarine	4 oz
100 g	granulated sugar	4 oz
1	large egg	1
2 tbsps	milk	2 tbsps

For the filling

500 g	rhubarb	1 lb
50 g	stoned raisins	2 oz
125 g	granulated sugar	4 oz

an 18-cm (7-inch) square sponge tin, greased and base-lined

Preheat the oven to 190°C, 375°F, gas mark 5.

Sift the flour, salt and cinnamon into a bowl. Rub in the margarine, using the fingertips only, until the mixture resembles fine breadcrumbs. Stir in the sugar and divide the mixture in half for the base and top of the slice.

Wipe and trim the rhubarb and cut into 3-cm (1-inch) pieces. Place in a saucepan with the raisins and sugar and cook gently for 10 to 15 minutes until the rhubarb is tender. Leave to cool slightly.

Using one half of the rubbed-in mixture, add the lightly beaten egg and milk to give a soft dropping consistency and spread it over the lined base of the tin. Gently cover the top of this with the cooked rhubarb, then sprinkle the remaining rubbed-in mixture over the rhubarb.

Bake the slice on the centre shelf of the preheated oven for about 40 minutes until the sponge is cooked and the topping is crunchy.

Cut the slice into four or six pieces and serve hot with custard.

Note: Frozen or bottled rhubarb can be used.

* Suitable for freezing – cooked or uncooked.

Rhubarb Gluwein

Makes 600 ml (1 pint)

500 g	rhubarb	1 lb
150 ml	water	¼ pint
50–100 g	demerara sugar	2–4 oz
300 ml	red wine	½ pint
1-cm	piece of cinnamon stick	½-inch
4	whole cloves	4
	pinch of ground nutmeg	
1–2 tbsps	Cointreau	1–2 tbsps

Wipe and trim the rhubarb and cut into 1-cm (½-inch) pieces. Place in a saucepan with the water and sugar (50 g/2 oz if using a sweet wine, 75–100 g/3–4 oz if the wine is dry), cover and bring to the boil. Simmer gently for 10 minutes, then strain the rhubarb juices through a sieve into a bowl, pressing well to extract all the liquid.

Return the rhubarb juice to the saucepan, add the wine, spices and Cointreau, bring to the boil, cover and simmer very gently for 15 minutes. Strain off the spices with a draining spoon and serve the gluwein hot as a party punch.

Rhubarb Chutney

Makes about 1½ kg (3 lb)

1 kg	rhubarb	2 lb
250 g	onions	8 oz
250 g	sultanas	8 oz
600 ml	malt vinegar	1 pint
1 level tsp	salt	1 level tsp
¼ level tsp	cayenne pepper	¼ level tsp
½ level tsp	ground ginger	½ level tsp
½ level tsp	ground mixed spice	½ level tsp
400 g	demerara sugar	12 oz
	a preserving pan or large saucepan	

Trim and wipe the rhubarb and cut it into 1-cm (½-inch) pieces. Peel the onions and mince them coarsely with the sultanas. (Alternatively, chop the onions and the sultanas.)

Place all the ingredients except the sugar in the pan, bring slowly to the boil and cook, uncovered, over a medium heat for 40 minutes until the rhubarb is well-cooked. Add the sugar and cook for a further 10 to 15 minutes until the chutney is thick, stirring occasionally.

Pour into clean, warm, dry jars, label and seal with thick polythene and lids if available. Store in a cool, dry place.

* Frozen sliced rhubarb may be used.

Spiced Rhubarb

Makes 1¼ kg (2½–3 lb)

1½ kg	rhubarb	3½ lb
150 ml	malt vinegar	¼ pint
150 ml	water	¼ pint
1 level tsp	whole pickling spice	1 level tsp
¼ level tsp	ground nutmeg	¼ level tsp
¼ level tsp	ground cloves	¼ level tsp
¼ level tsp	ground cinnamon	¼ level tsp
1 kg	demerara sugar	2 lb
250 g	stoned raisins	8 oz

a preserving pan or large saucepan

Wipe and trim both ends of the rhubarb and cut into 3-cm (1-inch) pieces.

Put the vinegar, water, spices and sugar in the pan, heat gently to dissolve the sugar, then bring to the boil and simmer for about 20 minutes. Strain off the spices and return the syrup to the pan. Add the rhubarb pieces and raisins and cook gently, uncovered, until the mixture is thick.

Pour the spiced rhubarb into clean, warm, dry jars and cover with wax discs and a double layer of thick polythene (and lids if available). Label and store, when cold, in a cool, dry place.

Note: This makes a pleasant change from redcurrant jelly when served with roast meats, especially lamb. It can also be served as a rich, highly flavoured sauce with ice-cream.

Rhubarb and Orange Jam

Makes 2 kg (4 lb)

1 kg	rhubarb	2 lb
3	oranges	3
½	lemon	½
1 kg	granulated or preserving sugar	2 lb
	knob of butter	

a preserving pan or large saucepan

Cut off the leaves and base from the stalks of rhubarb, wipe, cut into 3-cm (1-inch) pieces and put in the preserving pan.

Grate the orange rind into the pan. Cut the oranges in half and squeeze their juice, and the juice of the half lemon, into the pan. Put over a low heat and cook gently for 10 minutes to soften the rhubarb slightly.

Add the sugar and, over a low heat, allow it to dissolve. When it has completely dissolved, add a knob of butter and bring to the boil. Boil rapidly until setting point is reached, about 5 minutes (see p. 311 for full jam-making instructions).

Pour into warm, clean, dry jars, cover with wax discs and seal. Label and store in a cool, dry place.

Rhubarb, Peel and Ginger Jam

Makes about 1½ kg (3 lb)

1 kg	rhubarb	2 lb
50 g	chopped mixed peel	2 oz
50 g	crystallized ginger, chopped	2 oz
	or	
2	pieces of root ginger	2
1	lemon, grated rind and juice	1
150 ml	water	¼ pint
125 ml	liquid pectin	4 fl oz

| 1 kg | preserving or granulated sugar | 2 lb |

a preserving pan or large saucepan

Wipe the rhubarb, top and tail and cut the stalks into 1-cm (½-inch) pieces. Place in the preserving pan with the chopped peel and ginger. If you are using root ginger, bruise the pieces (e.g. in a pestle and mortar or with a rolling pin) and tie them in a small piece of muslin or a muslin bag. Add the grated lemon rind, lemon juice and water to the pan and bring to the boil; cover and simmer gently for 10 to 15 minutes until the rhubarb is soft. Remove the muslin bag.

Stir the liquid pectin into the rhubarb, add the sugar and, over a low heat, allow it to dissolve completely. Bring the jam to a rapid boil and boil until setting point is reached – about 15 minutes (see p. 311 for full jam-making instructions).

Remove from the heat and leave the jam to stand for 10 minutes before pouring into clean, warm, dry jars. Cover with wax discs and cellophane seals, label and store in a cool, dry place.

The following recipes also include rhubarb:

Bottled rhubarb (p. 325)
Pickled rhubarb (p. 332)

Try substituting rhubarb for gooseberries in gooseberry soufflé (p.240).

35 Strawberries

Introduction

The British are famous for their strawberries and cream and it is only regrettable that the strawberry season is the shortest of all the fruit seasons – as little as 2 weeks if the weather is cold and wet. Normally, though, the berries are harvested over a 4-week period and, once picked, should be eaten immediately. At best the fruits will keep for only 2 to 3 days before becoming soft and mouldy.

Strawberry plants should be planted out in mid to late summer in a soil rich in manure. Unlike all other fruits, the strawberry will produce its crops the first summer after planting, and each plant will reproduce itself many times over by throwing out runners to provide new stock.

However, early flowers are susceptible to frost damage and should be covered overnight with cloches or straw and uncovered the next day. Later the fruits should be carefully laid on a bed of straw or on special strawberry mats to stop them becoming muddy and wet.

The berries also need protection from marauding squirrels, slugs, blackbirds, etc., which will decimate the crops unless the strawberries are covered with netting and slug pellets laid down.

Preparation and cooking

Like raspberries, strawberries are best eaten fresh and uncooked, but can enhance many different desserts with their colour and flavour.

To prepare, remove the hulls and leaves and, just before use, gently rinse in cold water. Drain well.

To purée, press the prepared fruit through a sieve – there is no need to cook it first – and sweeten with icing sugar if liked.

Serving suggestions: Serve with sugar and cream; ice-cream; syllabub; in a fruit salad; or as a fruit filling, with cream, in a cake or gâteau.

How to deal with a glut

1. Freezing: This is not very successful as the strawberries lose their texture. However, frozen strawberries, after thawing, are useful in cooked dishes. Select firm berries, hull, rinse and drain well. Leave whole, or halve, and pack in dry sugar – 125 g (4 oz) sugar for every 500 g (1 lb) fruit – or unsweetened, in polythene bags or wax containers. Storage time: 9 to 12 months.

Strawberry purée, sweetened or unsweetened, can also be frozen in polythene bags or wax containers. Also freeze strawberry gâteau (p. 304). Strawberry ice-cream (p. 306) is a good recipe for storing a glut crop.

2. Preserving: Bottle strawberries in syrup or water (p. 325); or make strawberry sauce (p. 307) and strawberry jam (p. 312).

Pavlova Gâteau

Serves 5–6

For the meringue

2	large egg whites	2
125 g	caster sugar	4 oz
	a few drops of vanilla essence	
½ tsp	white vinegar	½ tsp
1½ level tsps	cornflour	1½ level tsps

For the filling

300 ml	double cream	½ pint
	or	
150 ml	single cream ⎱ mixed	¼ pint
150 ml	double cream ⎰	¼ pint
1 level tsp	caster sugar	1 level tsp
500 g	strawberries	1 lb
	or	
500 g	mixed fruit, e.g. sliced apple, sliced pear, halved grapes without pips,	1 lb

	sliced banana, orange	
	segments	
1 level tbsp	desiccated coconut, toasted	1 level tbsp

a baking tray

Preheat the oven to 110°C, 225°F, gas mark ¼.

Have ready a baking tray, brushed with oil and flour or covered with Bakewell paper. Mark it with a 20-cm (8-inch) circle.

Whisk the egg whites until stiff and dry, then gradually add the sugar, beating well after each addition. Blend together the vanilla essence, vinegar and cornflour and fold into the meringue.

Spread the meringue carefully to cover the marked-out circle, making the sides higher than the centre so as to give a shell to hold the filling.

Bake the pavlova in the preheated oven on the bottom shelf for about 2½ hours until firm to the touch on the outside, but still soft in the centre. Turn upside down, peel off the paper base and leave to cool.

Whip the double cream until thick or, if using a mixture of creams, first whip the double then gradually whip in the single cream. Stir in the sugar.

Hull, wash and dry the strawberries and halve them, or wipe and prepare any other fruits to be used, and fold into the cream.

Spoon the filling into the gâteau and scatter the toasted coconut over the top. Serve within 2 hours of assembling.

Strawberry and Orange Tart

Serves 6

For the biscuit base

150 g	shortbread biscuits,	6 oz
	e.g. Royal Scot	
75 g	unsalted butter	3 oz
1 level tbsp	sugar	1 level tbsp

For the filling

1	large orange, juice only	1
25 g	cornflour	1 oz
1	egg yolk	1

25 g	sugar	1 oz
	knob of unsalted butter	
250–300 g	strawberries	8–10 oz
2 tbsps	redcurrant jelly (p. 318)	2 tbsps

a 20-cm (8-inch) pie dish or flan dish

Put the biscuits in a polythene bag and crush them with a rolling pin. Melt the butter in a saucepan, remove from the heat and stir in the biscuit crumbs and sugar. Mix well and then press the mixture onto the base of the dish. Leave in a cool place to set.

Squeeze the juice from the orange and make it up to 180 ml (6 fl oz) with water. Place the cornflour in a small saucepan and blend in the orange liquid. Bring the mixture to the boil, stirring constantly until it becomes thick and opaque. Remove from the heat and beat in the egg yolk and the sugar.

Finally, stir in the butter a little at a time until it has been absorbed. Cover the pan with an air-tight seal, e.g. cling-film or a damp piece of greaseproof paper, and leave to cool.

Before the mixture sets, spread it evenly over the biscuit base. Hull and wash the strawberries and cut them in half. Arrange the halved berries over the orange filling to cover the surface completely.

Melt the redcurrant jelly in a saucepan over a low heat and brush the hot jelly over the tops of the strawberries to glaze them. Serve the tart cold with cream.

* The tart is best frozen before being decorated with the strawberries and glaze, as the berries lose their texture when frozen.

Strawberry Snaps

Serves 4–6

100 g	butter	4 oz
100 g	golden syrup	4 oz
100 g	sugar	4 oz
$\frac{1}{2}$	lemon, juice only	$\frac{1}{2}$
100 g	plain flour	4 oz
$\frac{1}{2}$ level tsp	ground ginger	$\frac{1}{2}$ level tsp

For the filling

500 g	strawberries	1 lb
2 tbsps	brandy or Cointreau	2 tbsps
300 ml	double cream	½ pint
	a little caster sugar	

a baking tray
a piping bag with large no. 8 star nozzle attached

Preheat the oven to 180°C, 350°F, gas mark 4.

Melt the butter with the syrup, sugar and juice of the half lemon in a saucepan over a low heat. Remove from the heat and beat in the sifted flour and ginger. Using a teaspoon, drop small balls of the mixture onto a greased baking tray and bake on the centre shelf of the preheated oven for about 10 minutes until golden brown. Allow the tray to cool a minute before lifting the snaps onto a rack to cool, leaving them in their flattened shape. The snaps will now store well in an air-tight container until ready for use.

Hull and wash the strawberries and halve the larger ones. Put them in a bowl and sprinkle with brandy or Cointreau (or any other favourite liqueur, e.g. kirsch). Gently toss to coat the fruit and leave to marinate for several hours.

Lay one snap on a dessert plate and assemble as follows: Beat the cream until thick and spread a little over the flat snap. Place some halved strawberries on top of the cream and sprinkle with caster sugar if desired. Repeat the layers of snap, cream and strawberries until there are two or three layers, finishing with a snap. Place one large strawberry on the centre of the top snap and pipe whirls of cream around it to decorate. Sprinkle the top of the cream whirls with some crushed snaps, using any which may have broken after cooking. Assemble each serving in this way.

Serve immediately, otherwise the snaps will soon become soft.

Strawberry Pancake

Serves 6

6–8	pancakes – 150 ml (¼ pint)	6–8
	pancake batter (see p. 344)	

For the filling

150 ml	double cream	¼ pint
150 ml	soured cream	¼ pint
1 level tsp	icing sugar	1 level tsp
	vanilla essence	
350 g	strawberries	12 oz

Make and cook the pancakes and leave them to get cold before assembling the cake.

Whip the double cream until stiff, then lightly whip in the soured cream. Stir in the sifted icing sugar and a few drops of vanilla essence.

Hull and wipe the strawberries, reserve 8 whole berries and slice the rest. Place a pancake on a flat serving plate, spread a thin layer of cream over it and cover that with a few strawberry slices. Spread a thin layer of cream on another pancake and lay it on top of the first pancake.

Continue the layers until all the pancakes have been used, ending with a pancake spread with cream. To decorate, halve the eight strawberries and lay them on the cream around the edge of the last pancake. Sprinkle a little extra sifted icing sugar over the top and place in a refrigerator to chill. To serve, cut into 6 slices with a large sharp knife.

Strawberry Éclairs

Makes 6–12

1 quantity	choux pastry (see p. 338)	1 quantity
250 g	strawberries	8 oz
150 ml	double cream	¼ pint
1 level tsp	icing sugar	1 level tsp
1 tsp	kirsch	1 tsp
100 g	icing sugar	4 oz
	red colouring	

2 baking trays
a piping bag with no. 8 or 10 plain large nozzle attached

Preheat the oven to 200°C, 400°F, gas mark 6.

Prepare the choux pastry and spoon the mixture into the piping bag. Grease the baking trays and pipe six large or twelve small éclair shapes onto them. Bake on the shelf above the centre of the preheated oven for about 20 minutes until the pastry is lightly browned and well risen. Immediately, remove the éclairs onto a cooling rack, making a small cut in the side of each to let out the steam, and leave to cool.

Wash and hull the strawberries and slice them onto a plate. Whip the cream until it is thick and fold in a teaspoon of icing sugar and the kirsch. Sift the 100 g (4 oz) icing sugar into a small bowl and add enough cold water to mix into a smooth icing of spreading consistency. Add a little red colouring.

To assemble the éclairs: Split them in half lengthways. Spread a spoonful of cream along the base of each éclair and lay sliced strawberries on top of the cream. Close the éclair, leaving a line of strawberries and cream visible. Spread the pink icing over the top of each éclair and serve within an hour.

* The unfilled éclairs can be frozen.

Strawberry Baked Alaska

Serves 5–6

For the sponge

75 g	margarine	3 oz
75 g	caster sugar	3 oz
1	large egg	1
½	orange, grated rind and juice	½
75 g	self-raising flour	3 oz
	pinch of salt	

For the filling

300 g	strawberries	12 oz
1	block of vanilla ice-cream	1
2	large eggs, separated	2
100 g	caster sugar	4 oz

a 20-cm (8-inch) sponge sandwich tin, base-lined and greased

Preheat the oven to 190°C, 375°F, gas mark 5.

Cream the margarine in a bowl and beat in the sugar until the mixture is light and fluffy. Beat in the whole egg plus 1 egg yolk from the separated eggs for the filling (the remaining yolk can be stored, covered, in a cool place for use as a glaze or for mayonnaise, etc.). Fold in the grated orange rind and 1 tablespoon orange juice together with the sifted flour and salt.

Place the mixture in the lined sponge tin, smooth over the surface and bake on the centre shelf of the preheated oven for 20 to 25 minutes until cooked. Turn it out onto a cooling rack and leave to get cold. Turn the oven up to 220°C, 425°F, gas mark 7.

Hull, wipe and halve the strawberries. Have the ice-cream ready and, just before serving, whisk the egg whites until stiff, whisk in half the sugar and then, using a metal spoon, fold in the rest.

To assemble, lay the halved strawberries over the sponge cake and slice the ice-cream block to fit on top. Spread the meringue over the ice-cream and sponge to completely seal the whole filling.

Place on the centre shelf of the hot oven and bake for 2 to 3 minutes until the meringue is beginning to go a light golden brown. Serve at once, otherwise the ice-cream will start to melt.

Strawberry Romanoff

Serves 6

¾ kg	strawberries	1½ lb
1	orange	1
3 tbsps	Cointreau	3 tbsps
3 level tbsps	icing sugar	3 level tbsps
300 ml	double cream, chilled	½ pint
	a few drops of vanilla essence	

6 individual glass dishes

Hull and wash the strawberries, drain them on kitchen paper and place in a bowl. Grate the rind from the orange onto a plate; squeeze out the juice and pour it over the strawberries. Stir in the Cointreau and 2 tablespoons of the icing sugar. Mix gently together and place in the refrigerator (preferably over ice) and chill for at least 1 hour.

Assemble the dessert about 1 hour before serving. Whip the chilled cream until thick and stir in the remaining 1 tablespoon icing sugar and the vanilla essence.

Divide the strawberries and their juices between the individual glasses. Spoon the sweetened cream over them and decorate with a little of the grated orange rind sprinkled over the top. Chill in the refrigerator for an hour before serving.

Note: This makes a delicious, refreshing summer dessert to finish a dinner party.

Strawberry Mille-Feuilles

Serves 6–8

200 g	puff pastry (p. 336)	8 oz
500 g	strawberries	1 lb
150 ml	double cream, whipped	¼ pint
	a little caster sugar	
125 g	icing sugar, sifted	4 oz
	a little cold water	

a baking tray

Preheat the oven to 220°C, 425°F, gas mark 7.

Prepare the puff pastry and leave to rest for 30 minutes.

Roll out the pastry thinly on a lightly floured surface. Put a 20-cm (8-inch) plate or cake tin on the pastry and cut out three rounds. Place on a greased baking tray and bake on the centre shelf of the preheated oven for 10 minutes, remove from the oven and leave to cool on a wire rack.

Hull and wash the strawberries and halve the larger fruits, reserving a few of the best strawberries for decoration. Spread the cream over two layers of pastry and arrange the strawberries on top. Place one layer on top of the other and finally top with the third layer of pastry. A little caster sugar can be sprinkled over each layer if liked.

Mix the sifted icing sugar with a little cold water until it is smooth and thick. Spread the icing over the top of the last pastry layer, leave to set, then decorate with the reserved strawberries.

Serve the dessert like a cake, cutting it into slices.

Note: This dessert lends itself to most firm fruits which do not require cooking. Other favourite combinations, like raspberries, redcurrants and cherries, can be experimented with.

Strawberry Tartlets

Makes 12–14

100 g	*pâte sucrée* (sweet pastry, p. 335)	4 oz
200–250 g	strawberries	8 oz

For the custard

1 rounded tbsp	cornflour	1 rounded tbsp
240 ml	milk	8 fl oz
25 g	caster sugar	1 oz
1	egg	1
¼ level tsp	vanilla essence	¼ level tsp
1 rounded tbsp	redcurrant jelly (p. 318)	1 rounded tbsp
4 tbsps	double cream	4 tbsps

an 8-cm (3-inch) fluted round cutter
twelve to fourteen 6- to 7-cm (2½-inch) patty or bun tins
a piping bag with no. 8 large star nozzle attached

Preheat the oven to 190°C, 375°F, gas mark 5.

Make the *pâte sucrée* and leave to rest. Hull, wash and halve the strawberries.

In a saucepan, blend the cornflour with a little of the milk, then stir in the rest. Bring to the boil, stirring constantly, and cook for 2 minutes. Remove from the heat and beat in the sugar. Lightly beat the egg, beat it into the custard with the vanilla essence and leave to cool for 20 minutes.

Roll out the *pâte sucrée* on a lightly floured surface to a rectangle 23 by 23 cm (9 by 9 inches) and, using the pastry cutter, cut out nine rounds. Re-roll the trimmings and cut out a further four to five rounds. Line the patty tins with the pastry, prick the bases with a fork and leave to rest for 10 minutes in a cool place.

Bake on the centre shelf of the preheated oven for 10 minutes until the pastry is cooked and lightly brown. Leave to cool on a wire cooling rack. (If you don't have enough patty or bun tins, make the tartlets in two batches.)

To assemble the tartlets, fill them almost to the top with the thick confectioners' custard and lay 3 strawberry halves on top of each.

Heat the redcurrant jelly in a pan and brush a little of it over the strawberries to glaze them. Whip the double cream and pipe small swirls in the centre of each strawberry tartlet. Serve them within 3 to 4 hours of making, otherwise the pastry will start to lose its crisp texture.

* Suitable for freezing, but the pastry will lose its crisp texture.

Strawberry Shortbread/Dessert

Serves 8

For the shortbread

150 g	butter, softened	6 oz
75 g	caster sugar	3 oz
150 g	plain flour	6 oz
	pinch of salt	
75 g	cornflour	3 oz

For the filling

350–500 g	strawberries	12 oz–1 lb
300–450 ml	double cream	$\frac{1}{2}$–$\frac{3}{4}$ pint
1 level tbsp	icing sugar	1 level tbsp

2 baking trays
a piping bag with no. 8 large star nozzle attached

Preheat the oven to 180°C, 350°F, gas mark 4.

Cream the butter in a bowl, add the sugar and beat until soft. Sift the flour, salt and cornflour together and gradually add it to the creamed mixture until it is well combined. Divide the shortbread dough into three parts, weighing approximately 175 g (7 oz), 150 g (6 oz) and 125 g (5 oz).

Roll out the largest portion of dough into a circle 23 cm (9 inches) in diameter. Roll out the second largest piece to a circle about 20 cm (8 inches) in diameter and the smallest portion to a circle about 15 cm (6 inches) in diameter. Lay the shortbread circles on the greased baking trays and prick the surfaces with a fork.

Bake on the centre shelf of the preheated oven for about 20 minutes until the shortbread is a light biscuit colour. Remove from the oven and immediately cut the smallest circle into 8 equal pieces. Leave the shortbreads on their baking trays for 5 to 10 minutes to cool slightly before removing them onto a wire cooling rack.

Half an hour before serving, assemble the dessert as follows: Hull and wash the strawberries, reserving 8 of the best for decoration, and cut the rest in half. Whip the cream until thick, then fold in the icing sugar. Place 2 tablespoons cream in the piping bag.

Put the largest shortbread circle on a flat serving plate, spread over it half the whipped cream and put half of the halved strawberries on top. Cover with the second largest layer of shortbread spread with the remaining cream and cover with the rest of the halved strawberries. Finally place the 8 shortbread triangles on top of the filling, leaving them slightly apart to show the strawberries and cream beneath. Decorate each slice with a whirl of cream and place a strawberry in the centre of each whirl.

Note: The cooked shortbreads, without their filling, can be stored in an air-tight tin for up to 1 month.

Strawberry Gâteau

Serves 6

For the sponge

3	large eggs	3
75 g	caster sugar	3 oz
75 g	plain flour	3 oz
1 level tsp	baking powder	1 level tsp
	pinch of salt	

For the filling

500 g	strawberries	1 lb
300 ml	double cream	½ pint
150 ml	single cream	¼ pint
1 level tbsp	icing sugar	1 level tbsp

three 18-cm (7-inch) sandwich tins or an 18-cm (7-inch) round
    cake tin, greased, base-lined and dusted with flour
a piping bag with no. 8 large star nozzle attached

Preheat the oven to 190°C, 375°F, gas mark 5.

Break the eggs into a large mixing bowl, beat lightly and add the sugar. Put the bowl over a pan of simmering water and whisk until the mixture is thick and creamy and the whisk leaves a trail in it when lifted out. Remove the bowl from the heat and whisk for a further minute. (*Note:* If you have a large electric mixer, the sponge can be made without the bowl having to be put over a pan of hot water.)

Sift the flour, baking powder and salt twice onto a piece of paper, then tip it into the beaten eggs and, using a metal spoon, fold it in gently and quickly.

Divide the mixture between the three sandwich tins or spoon it into the large cake tin, smooth over the top lightly and bake on the centre shelf of the preheated oven for about 20 minutes for the sandwich tins and 25 to 30 minutes for the large cake tin. The sponge should be springy to the touch and slightly shrinking from the sides of the tin when cooked. Turn the sponges onto a wire cooling rack and remove the base paper.

Hull the strawberries and wipe them. Reserve 7 whole berries and cut the rest in half.

Whip the double cream until thick, then gradually beat in the single cream, and stir in half the sifted icing sugar. Place 2 tablespoons of the whipped cream in the piping bag.

Slice the whole sponge cake into three layers and lay out flat. Spread the cream equally between the middle and bottom layers. Lay the halved strawberries on top of the two layers of cream, then place the middle layer sponge on top of the bottom one, and the top layer sponge on top of the cake.

Pipe six stars of cream round the edge of the sponge and a whirl in the centre. Sprinkle the remaining icing sugar over the cake, and place a whole strawberry on each star of cream. Leave for 1 hour before serving.

* Suitable for freezing before it is decorated.

Strawberry Ice-Cream

Makes 1 litre (1¾ pints)

500 g	strawberries	1 lb
175 g	granulated sugar	6 oz
300 ml	water	½ pint
150 ml	milk	¼ pint
1	large egg	1
150 ml	double cream	¼ pint

Set the refrigerator to its coldest setting or turn on the fast-freeze section of the home freezer.

Hull the strawberries and rinse under cold water. Pat them dry and press through a sieve or liquidize in a blender. Pour the liquid into a medium-size bowl.

Place the sugar and water in a pan and heat gently until the sugar has dissolved; bring to the boil and simmer gently for about 10 minutes. Leave to get cold.

Heat the milk in a pan almost to boiling point. Whisk the egg lightly in a bowl and pour onto it the hot milk, still whisking. Return to the pan and heat gently until the mixture thickens slightly and coats the back of a wooden spoon, but do not allow it to boil. Leave to cool, stirring occasionally to prevent a skin forming.

Stir the cold syrup into the strawberry purée, then stir in the egg custard. Whisk the cream until thick and fold into the strawberry mixture. Pour into a freezing container and place in the freezing compartment of the fridge or the fast-freeze section of the home freezer.

When the ice-cream has started to set around the edges, turn it into a cold bowl and beat to break up the ice crystals which have formed. Return to the freezer or fridge.

After a further ½ hour, when the mixture has started to set again, repeat the process. Return to the refrigerator or home freezer until the ice-cream is completely set.

Once the mixture is set, remember to turn the refrigerator back to its normal setting or to turn off the fast-freeze section of the home freezer.

Before serving, remove the ice-cream from the freezer for about 10 minutes to allow it to thaw slightly.

Note: This recipe is ideal for using overripe fruit and, if you are a freezer owner, is a useful way of using up a strawberry glut.

Strawberry Sauce

Makes 1¾ kg (3½ lb)

2 kg	strawberries (use slightly overripe or misshapen ones	4 lb
2 kg	granulated sugar	4 lb
160 ml	malt vinegar	¼ pint

a preserving pan or large saucepan

Wash and hull the strawberries. Drain off any excess water and place the whole berries in a large bowl. Stir in the sugar and vinegar, cover and leave overnight, but not longer than 24 hours. Stir occasionally.

The next day, pour the strawberries and their juice into a preserving pan and bring to the boil. Boil rapidly for 15 minutes if using a preserving pan or 20 minutes in a large saucepan. Turn off the heat and leave to stand for 20 minutes.

Stir well, then pour into clean, warm, dry jars. Cover immediately with wax discs and thick polythene and secure well or use screw-top lids. Once a jar has been opened, use within 2 to 3 weeks.

Note: This makes a delicious sauce poured over ice-cream or steamed puddings. It is also a good way of using overripe or damaged fruit.

The following recipes also include strawberries:

Strawberry jam (p. 312)
Bottled strawberries (p. 325)

Try substituting strawberries for the main fruit in the following recipes:

Blackcurrant juice (p. 225)
Cherry and melon coronet (p. 231)
Plum cheesecake (p. 262)
Gooseberry soufflé (p. 240)
Hazelnut meringue (p. 271)
Raspberry sorbet (p. 274)
Raspberry ratafia cream (p. 272)

Part Three: Preserving and Miscellaneous

36 Jam Making

Jam making is one of the best and most popular methods of preserving a bumper crop of fruit. All fruits – and even some vegetables like marrows, tomatoes and beetroot – make good jams. If they have a very mild flavour of their own, like apples and pears, then they can be successfully combined with other fruits or spices to give a better flavoured jam, e.g. blackberry and apple jam or pear and plum jam.

There are several important points to remember before setting out to make your own jam. The golden rules for success are slow, gentle cooking before adding the sugar, complete dissolving of the sugar and then very quick and short cooking afterwards until setting point is reached.

Take care to use slightly underripe or just-ripe fruit which is undamaged and as fresh as possible.

All fruits contain some pectin, but some are much richer in it than others. Cooking apples, currants, damsons, gooseberries and plums are rich in pectin; blackberries, greengages, loganberries and raspberries are fairly rich in pectin; but cherries, pears, strawberries and rhubarb are low in pectin and it is often a good idea to add commercial pectin to these jams during the making to help them set.

A certain amount of acid is also necessary to help jams set. As a rule, fruits low in pectin are usually low in acid as well and so require the addition of extra acid – lemon juice is normally used but citric or tartaric acids may be added instead. When making jam with vegetables such as marrows, tomatoes, beetroot and rhubarb, extra acid must be added to give a good set.

The quantity of sugar added to the jam is important – too much and the jam will be over-sweet and the sugar will crystallize when the jam is stored; too little and the jam will ferment in storage and so not keep. Granulated or preserving sugar are the best sugars to use as they dissolve more quickly. It also helps if the sugar is warmed before being added to the jam as then it will not cool down the fruit so much and hence will dissolve quicker.

Never be tempted to make too large a quantity of jam at one time – 3 kg (6 lb) of fruit should be the maximum. When the sugar has been added to the fruit, the jam should not come further than half way up the sides of the pan. This will allow plenty of room for a rapid boil to reach setting point.

Jam-making instructions

1. Have ready your cooking utensils – a preserving pan is best (a large saucepan with a heavy base may also be used, although the time taken to soften the fruit and to reach setting point will be slightly longer); have also enough undamaged jam jars – clean, dry and just warm to prevent the glass from cracking when the hot jam is poured in.

2. Select slightly underripe or just-ripe fruit – never use overripe fruit as this contains less pectin and the jam will not set so well. Weigh the fruit and have ready the correct amount of sugar and water according to the chart on p. 312. Wash the fruit thoroughly and remove any stalks, hulls, leaves, stones or pips.

3. Put the fruit in the pan with the lemon juice or acid – allow 1 level teaspoon citric or tartaric acid for every 3 kg (6 lb) fruit – and the given quantity of water. Some fruits, like raspberries and strawberries, do not require any extra water as the time taken to soften the fruit is so short.

4. Cover the pan and simmer the fruit gently until it is soft and the skins are tender (see the chart on p. 312 for the simmering times). At this stage the stones from plums, damsons and greengages, etc., will rise to the surface and can be removed, using a draining spoon. If commercial pectin is being used, stir it in at this stage, allowing about 50 to 100 ml (2 to 4 fl oz) liquid pectin or about 1 teaspoon powdered pectin per $\frac{1}{2}$ kg (1 lb) fruit. The amount will vary depending on how much natural pectin is present in the fruit or vegetable. Follow the instructions given on the bottle or packet.

5. When the fruit is soft and the skins are very tender, add the warm sugar. Once the sugar has been added the fruit will not soften any further so, to make sure that it is really soft, press the fruit against the sides of the pan with the back of a wooden spoon and it should disintegrate.

6. Over a very gentle heat allow the sugar to dissolve, stirring occasionally. It is essential that the sugar is completely dissolved before being brought to the boil otherwise the jam will crystallize during storage. A knob of butter can be added at this stage to help clear the jam and prevent a scum forming which might spoil the clarity of the jam when set.

7. Once all the sugar has been dissolved completely, and not before, bring the jam to a rapid boil and boil until setting point is reached,

Jam-Making Chart

Type of Jam	Quantity of Fruit	Extra Ingredients	Water
Apple and Ginger	3 kg (6 lb)	3 level tablespoons ground ginger; 4 lemons, grated rind and juice	1¼ litres (2 pints)
Apricot (fresh)	3 kg (6 lb)	—	650 ml (1 pint)
Blackberry	3 kg (6 lb)	2 lemons, juice only; *or* 300 ml (½ pint) liquid pectin	175 ml (¼ pint)
Blackcurrant	2 kg (4 lb)	—	1¾ litres (3 pints)
Cherry (Morello)	2¼ kg (5 lb)	3 lemons, juice only	—
Damson	2 kg (4 lb)	—	800 ml (1¼ pints)
Gooseberry	2¼ kg (5 lb)	—	850 ml (1½ pints)
Greengage	3 kg (6 lb)	—	500 ml (¾ pint)
Loganberry	3 kg (6 lb)	—	—
Plum	3 kg (6 lb)	—	650 ml (1 pint)
Raspberry	3 kg (6 lb)	—	—
Strawberry	3 kg (6 lb)	2 lemons, juice only; *or* 450 ml (¾ pint) liquid pectin	—

Sugar	Simmering Time	Rapid Boil Time	Approximate Yield
3 kg (6 lb)	30–35 mins.	20 mins.	5 kg (10 lb)
3 kg (6 lb)	20 mins.	20 mins.	5 kg (10 lb)
3 kg (6 lb)	10 mins.	15 mins.	5 kg (10 lb)
3 kg (6 lb)	30–35 mins.	7–10 mins.	5 kg (10 lb)
1½ kg (3½ lb)	30–35 mins.	15 mins.	3 kg (6 lb)
2¼ kg (5 lb)	20 mins.	10 mins.	4 kg (8 lb)
3 kg (6 lb)	30 mins.	10 mins.	5 kg (10 lb)
3 kg (6 lb)	20 mins.	15–20 mins.	5 kg (10 lb)
3 kg (6 lb)	15–20 mins.	5 mins.	5 kg (10 lb)
3 kg (6 lb)	15–20 mins.	15 mins.	5 kg (10 lb)
3 kg (6 lb)	15–20 mins.	5 mins.	5 kg (10 lb)
3 kg (6 lb)	10–15 mins.	10–12 mins.	5 kg (10 lb)

according to the times given in the chart on p. 312. Unnecessary stirring during the rapid boil time should be avoided, although it may be necessary if the jam starts sticking to the base of the pan.

8. To test whether the jam has set, turn the heat off under the pan and place a teaspoonful of jam on a cold saucer. Leave for a few minutes to cool, then, using a fingertip, gently push the surface and if it wrinkles, setting point has been reached. Another method is to use a sugar thermometer. It should read 104°C, 220°F, although jams not so rich in pectin may require a slightly higher temperature (105°C, 222°F).

9. When the jam has reached setting point, use a perforated spoon to remove any scum from the surface. Leave the jam to stand for 10 minutes (especially jams using whole fruits) to prevent the fruit from rising to the surface when potted. Do not stir the jam as this will cause bubbles to become trapped which will spoil the clear appearance of the jam in the jars.

10. Pour the jam into the prepared jars and fill almost to the brim. The less air between the jam and the cover, the less chance there will be of a mould forming on the top.

11. Place the wax discs immediately, wax side down, onto the hot jam to give an air-tight seal which again will help prevent any mould forming during storage. Cover with a cellophane cover dampened on one side, stretched over the jar, damp side uppermost, and secured with a rubber band. If preferred, the cellophane covers can be put on when the jam is completely cold.

12. Label the jars with the type of jam and the date, and store, when cold, in a cool, dry place. If stored near steam in the kitchen, mould may form on the top of the jars.

The following, more unusual, jam recipes can be found in their individual chapters:

37 Jelly Making

Introduction

The same basic principles apply to jelly making as to jam making – the quality and freshness of the fruit, the amount of pectin and acid present, and the amount of sugar used are just as important.

A good jelly should be clear, of a good colour, and well set but not too solid. It should also have a good flavour of its fruit.

Not all fruits make good jelly – the best are those rich in pectin and with their own distinctive flavour, e.g. redcurrants and blackcurrants, crab apples and quinces.

When making the fruit juice, a jelly bag will give the best results, but do not be tempted to let the jelly drip longer than overnight as the more exposure the juice has to the atmosphere, the more the quality of the pectin will be spoilt. A good rule is that the jelly should be made within 24 hours, from the preparation of the fruit to the storage of the finished jelly.

Fruits rich in pectin, such as blackcurrants and redcurrants, damsons and quinces, can be simmered with water, strained through a jelly bag, and then the pulp can be returned to the pan with more water and boiled for a second time. The pulp and water are then put back into the jelly bag to strain. This method will increase the extract of pectin from the fruit, thus giving a larger yield of jelly from the same quantity of fruit. The usual amount of water added is 1¼ to 1¾ litres (2 to 3 pints) for the first extract and then a further 600 ml (1 pint) for the second extract.

The amount of sugar added to the fruit juice varies according to the type of fruit used, but as a rule the pectin-rich fruits take up to 600 g (1¼ lb) granulated sugar or preserving sugar per 600 ml (1 pint) fruit juice, whilst most of the other fruits take up to 500 g (1 lb) of sugar per 600 ml (1 pint) of juice.

The rapid boiling to reach setting point should not take longer than 10 minutes for jelly making. Longer boiling than this will start to spoil the colour of the jelly and will not give such a good set. Do not stir the jelly unnecessarily during its rapid boil as this will cause bubbles to form and therefore the jelly will not be so clear when set.

The jelly, once setting point is reached, is always poured immediately into warm, clean, dry jars – never left to stand or else a skin will start to form on the surface of the jelly in the pan, thus spoiling its consistency. Once potted, it is stored in the same way as jam.

Instructions

1. Have ready a preserving pan or large saucepan with a heavy base, and enough jam jars for the yield of jelly given in the recipe.

2. Select the fruit – preferably slightly underripe – and wash thoroughly. There is no need to remove the hulls or pips or to top and tail berries. Neither is there any need to peel and core apples and pears for jelly making. Large fruits such as apples and pears, however, should be cut into fairly small pieces.

3. Place the fruit in the pan with the given quantity of water (see the chart on p. 318) and any acid such as lemon juice. Cover the pan and simmer gently for about $\frac{1}{2}$ to 1 hour until the fruit is quite soft and the skins and fruit disintegrate when pressed to the sides of the pan with the back of a wooden spoon.

4. Have ready a jelly bag which has been scalded with boiling water. Suspend the bag over a large bowl (a large piece of muslin suspended over a bowl can be used instead). Pour the fruit into the jelly bag and leave for 3 to 4 hours until it has almost stopped dripping. If a second extract is to be obtained, return the pulp to a clean pan with half the original amount of water and simmer for $\frac{1}{2}$ hour. Pour the juice and pulp into the jelly bag and allow it to drip for about 1 hour. The two extracts can be mixed together in the pan.

5. Measure the juice into the clean preserving pan and bring to the boil before adding the sugar. Allow approximately 500 g (1 lb) granulated or preserving sugar per 600 ml (1 pint) of juice (see the chart on p. 318 for the exact amounts).

6. Allow the sugar to dissolve completely over a low heat before bringing to a rapid boil. (See chart on p. 318 for boiling times.)

7. To test that setting point is reached, turn off the heat below the saucepan, place a teaspoonful of jelly on a cold saucer and leave for a few minutes to cool. Then, using a fingertip, gently push the surface and, if it wrinkles, then the jelly has set. Alternatively, a sugar thermometer can be used, to read 104°C, 220°F.

8. Once setting point has been reached, the scum should immediately

be removed from the surface, using a perforated spoon. The last traces of scum can be removed with a little kitchen paper. Remember not to stir the jelly.

9. The jelly should then be poured at once into warm, clean, dry jars, which should be filled almost to the brim. To prevent bubbles becoming trapped in the jelly, tilt the jars slightly and pour the hot jelly in down the side of the jar.

10. Put on the wax discs, wax side down, cover the jars with dampened cellophane, either at once or when the jelly is cold, and secure with elastic bands.

11. Label the jars with the date and the type of jelly, and store when cold in a cool, dry place.

Jelly-Making Chart

Type of Jelly	Quantity of Fruit	Extra Ingredients	Water
Apple or Crab apple	2 kg (4 lb)	1 lemon, peeled rind and juice	To cover fruit – 1½–1¾ litres (2–3 pints)
Blackberry	3 kg (6 lb)	3 lemons, juice only	600 ml (1 pint)
Blackberry and Apple	2 kg (4 lb) 1 kg (2 lb)	—	1¼ litres (2 pints)
Blackcurrant	2 kg (4 lb)	—	To cover fruit – 1½–1¾ litres (2–3 pints)
Damson	3 kg (6 lb)	—	1¾ litres (3 pints)
Elderberry and Apple	1½ kg (3 lb) 1½ kg (3 lb)	—	To cover fruit – 1½–1¾ litres (2–3 pints)
Gooseberry	2 kg (4 lb)	—	To cover fruit – 1½–1¾ litres (2–3 pints)
Mint and Apple	2 kg (4 lb)	3 lemons, juice only; bunch of fresh mint; few drops green colouring	To cover fruit – 1–1¼ litres (1½–2 pints)
Quince	2 kg (4 lb)	—	2¾–3 litres (5 pints)
Redcurrant	3 kg (6 lb)	—	To cover fruit – 1½–1¾ litres (2–3 pints)

Sugar	Simmering Time	Rapid Boil Time	Approximate Yield
500 g for every 600 ml juice (1 lb for every 1 pint)	1 hr	7–10 mins.	2½ kg (5 lb)
500 g for every 600 ml juice (1 lb for every 1 pint)	30 mins.	7–10 mins.	3½ kg (7 lb)
500 g for every 600 ml juice (1 lb for every 1 pint)	45 mins.	7 mins.	3½ kg (7 lb)
600 g for every 600 ml juice (1¼ lb for every 1 pint)	30 mins.	5 mins.	2½ kg (5 lb)
500 g for every 600 ml juice (1 lb for every 1 pint)	30 mins.	5 mins.	3½ kg (7 lb)
350 g for every 600 ml juice (¾ lb for every 1 pint)	1 hr	7–10 mins.	3½ kg (7 lb)
500 g for every 600 ml juice (1 lb for every 1 pint)	30 mins.	7 mins.	2½ kg (5 lb)
350 g for every 600 ml juice (¾ lb for every 1 pint)	40 mins.	10 mins.	2–2½ kg (4–5 lb)
500 g for every 600 ml juice (1 lb for every 1 pint)	1 hr	5–7 mins.	2½–3 kg (5–6 lb)
600 g for every 600 ml juice (1¼ lb for every 1 pint)	45 mins.	3–5 mins.	3½ kg (7 lb)

38 Vegetable Bottling

We had intended to include a section on vegetable bottling, since this is an obvious way in which the amateur gardener could store excess vegetables, but recent research has indicated that pressure fluctuations, which are likly to occur with home vegetable bottling, will allow harmfull enzymes to survive and therefore could be dangerous. *We do not recommend, therefore, that you attempt home bottling of vegetables.*

39 Fruit Bottling

Introduction

Bottling is an ideal way to preserve any variety of surplus fruit. The object of bottling fruit in preserving jars is to kill the yeasts and moulds present in all fruits. This is done through heat and the air-tight sealing of the bottles to prevent re-infection.

Fruits to be bottled should not be overripe, underripe or damaged. The only exception is windfall apples, which are peeled, cored and sliced, any bruised parts having been removed.

The best and most easily available jars are Kilner jars which can be re-used, although it is advisable to buy new seals. These are sold at most ironmongers' shops.

Before processing, always check that your jars are not cracked or chipped, and inspect the seals on the tops. Usually these tops can be used a couple of times provided that the rubber seal is not damaged or broken. The jars must be clean, preferably sterilized with boiling water, before being filled with fruit. The fruit slips into the jars more easily if the latter are a little damp inside.

Fruit can be bottled in either sugar syrup or water. Sugar syrup is preferable for obtaining the best results in flavour and colour. However, the drawback to using syrup is that it can cause the fruit to rise to the top of the jars during processing, which is less attractive.

The usual proportions for making the syrup are 250 g (8 oz) granulated sugar per 600 ml (1 pint) water. If you prefer the syrup to be sweeter, add more sugar to suit your taste. The above quantity will give enough syrup for 1 to $1\frac{1}{2}$ kg (2 to 3 lb) bottled fruit.

Golden syrup or honey can be used instead of sugar for a different flavour. A pinch of ground cinnamon added to the syrup will give a slightly spicy flavour. Red wine syrup for bottling pears or cherries is also delicious. For this, use 300 ml ($\frac{1}{2}$ pint) water and 300 ml ($\frac{1}{2}$ pint) red wine to 250 g (8 oz) sugar, with a cinnamon stick, 2 cloves and a pinch of ground nutmeg. Dissolve the sugar in the water, bring to the boil and

322 *Part Three: Preserving and Miscellaneous*

boil for 2 minutes. Add the red wine and spices and simmer for a further 5 minutes. Leave to stand for ½ hour and then strain.

Pack the jars as fully as possible without squashing the fruit down. Use the long handle of a wooden spoon to help pack down the fruit.

Any of the three methods given below for processing can be used. If only a small quantity is to be bottled it is more economical to use the water bath or pressure cooker method.

1. *Water bath method:*

A deep saucepan is necessary. The jars must not come into direct contact with the base of the pan. A thick wad of newspaper or thin wooden slats will do the trick. Fill the jars of fruit to the brim with cold water or syrup, then fit the covers and screw-bands, tighten them and then release them by one quarter turn. Place the jars in the pan of cold water, completely covering them. Now heat the water in the pan to 74°C, 165°F, taking 1½ hours to do so, and follow our chart of processing times.

2. *Pressure cooker method:*

If you have a large enough pressure cooker, this can be used for bottling. However, follow the manufacturer's instructions carefully. Our chart gives average pressure times but your particular model may vary slightly. Usually for pressure cooker processing, 2½ kg (5 lb) pressure is required.

The jars should be placed on a trivet and enough water added to the pan to cover the trivet and the base of the jars (again this quantity varies according to the make). Fill the jars with fruit and boiling syrup or water almost to the brim; cover the jars and tighten the screw-bands, then release them by one quarter turn. Place the bottles in the pressure cooker and bring to the correct pressure quickly. Maintain pressure according to the manufacturer's instructions or else according to our chart on p. 323. Always leave the cooker off the heat to cool for 10 minutes before opening. Tighten the screw-bands if necessary.

3. *Moderate oven method:*

To bottle a large quantity of fruit, the oven method is best. Again, the jars are filled with fruit and then boiling syrup or water, almost to the brim. The covers are placed on top, but NOT the screw-bands. Place the jars on a baking sheet lined with a thick wad of newspaper to absorb any liquid spilt during processing. Up to 5 kg (10 lb) can be processed at one time. (*N.B.* The jars are usually ½ kg, 1 kg or 2 kg/1 lb, 2 lb or 4 lb. Take this weight for the chart not the weight of the fruit being processed.) Follow the chart for the processing times.

Remove the jars from the oven, put on the screw-bands and tighten them. Leave on wooden boards overnight to get cold.

Test all your jars to make sure that they are sealed properly. Remove the screw-bands and lift by the tops. If you can do this, they have sealed properly. Another sign that the bottles are sealed is that the tops become concave. Now label and store your jars in a cool, dry place. They will store well for at least 1 year.

Fruit-Bottling Chart: *Preparation and Processing*

	1. Water Bath	2. Moderate Oven	3. Pressure Cooker
	Method: Slowly heat water from cold to 74°C, 165°F, taking about 1½ hrs. Maintain temperature as given below.	*Method:* Preheat oven to 150°C, 300°F, gas mark 2. Process for length of time given below.	*Method:* Fill cooker up to two thirds full only. Process times according to the manufacturer's instructions. Allow to cool for 10 mins. before opening.
Fruit and Preparation	*Syrup or water:* Cold syrup or water added before processing.	*Syrup or water:* Boiling syrup or water added before processing.	*Syrup or water:* Boiling syrup or water added before processing.
Apples Peel, core and slice; immerse in cold, salted water – 1 level tbsp salt per 1¼ litres (2 pints) water – to prevent discoloration. Rinse before bottling.	Maintain temperature at 74°C, 165°F, for 10 mins.	½–2 kg (1–4 lb): 30–40 mins. 2½–5 kg (5–10 lb): 45–60 mins.	Maintain pressure for 4 mins.

Fruit-Bottling Chart: Preparation and Processing – cont.—

Fruit and Preparation	1. Water Bath	2. Moderate Oven	3. Pressure Cooker
Blackberries Remove any hulls and leaves. (If mixing with apples, prepare apples and pour boiling water over them, leave to soften for 3 mins., then drain.)	Maintain temperature at 74°C, 165°F, for 10 mins.	½–2 kg (1–4 lb) 30–40 mins. 2½–5 kg (5–10 lb): 45–60 mins.	Maintain pressure for 1 min.
Blackcurrants Remove from stalks and rinse if necessary.	Maintain temperature at 74°C, 165°F, for 10 mins.	½–2 kg (1–4 lb): 30–40 mins. 2½–5 kg (5–10 lb): 45–60 mins.	Maintain pressure for 1 min.
Cherries Remove stalks and stones. Reserve any juice.	Maintain temperature at 82°C, 180°F, for 15 mins.	½–2 kg (1–4 lb): 40–50 mins. 2½–5 kg (5–10 lb): 55–70 mins.	Maintain pressure for 1 min.
Gooseberries Top, tail and snip the berries to allow the syrup to penetrate during processing.	Maintain temperature at 82°C, 180°F, for 15 mins.	½–2 kg (1–4 lb): 40–50 mins. 2½–5 kg (5–10 lb): 55–70 mins.	Maintain pressure for 1 min.
Pears, dessert and cooking Peel, halve and core. Put in cold water with 1 level tbsp salt and 2 level tsps citric acid per 1¼ litres (2 pints) water, to prevent discoloration. Rinse before bottling.	Maintain temperature at 90°C, 190°F, for 30 mins.	½–2 kg (1–4 lb): 60–70 mins. 2½–5 kg (5–10 lb): 75–90 mins.	Maintain pressure for 5 mins.
Plums and Damsons Remove stalks, rinse in cold water (wipe bloom off dark varieties). Best results are achieved when plums left whole.	Maintain temperature at 82°C, 180°F, for 15 mins.	½–2 kg (1–4 lb): 40–50 mins. 2½–5 kg (5–10 lb): 55–70 mins.	Maintain pressure for 3 mins.

Fruit and Preparation	1. Water Bath	2. Moderate Oven	3. Pressure Cooker
Raspberries and Logan-berries Remove hulls and any damaged or overripe fruits. Do not rinse or wash the berries.	Maintain temperature at 74°C, 165°F, for 10 mins.	½–2 kg (1–4 lb): 30–40 mins. 2½–5 kg (5–10 lb): 45–60 mins.	Maintain pressure for 1 min.
Redcurrants Remove from their stalks and rinse if necessary.	Maintain temperature at 74°C, 165°F, for 10 mins.	½–2 kg (1–4 lb): 30–40 mins. 2½–5 kg (5–10 lb): 45–60 mins.	Maintain pressure for 1 min.
Rhubarb Cut off leaves, trim base and wipe the stalks. Cut into 3–5 cm (1–2 inch) lengths. A little red colouring added to the syrup or water helps to preserve the colour.	Maintain temperature at 74°C, 165°F, for 10 mins.	½–2 kg (1–4 lb): 30–40 mins. 2½–5 kg (5–10 lb): 45–60 mins.	Maintain pressure for 1 min.
Strawberries Choose medium-sized fruits. Remove hulls and rinse in cold water. A little red colouring added to the syrup or water helps to preserve the colour.	Maintain temperature at 74°C, 165°F, for 10 mins.	½–2 kg (1–4 lb): 30–40 mins. 2½–5 kg (5–10 lb): 45–60 mins.	Maintain pressure for 2 mins.
Tomatoes Choose medium or small, even-sized tomatoes. Remove stalks and rinse in cold water. Process in brine – 1 level tbsp salt per 1¼ litres (2 pints) of water, with ¼ tsp citric acid per 500g (1 lb) tomatoes.	Maintain temperature at 90°C, 190°F, for 30 mins.	½–2 kg (1–4 lb): 60–70 mins. 2½–5 kg (5–10 lb): 75–90 mins.	Maintain pressure for 5 mins.

40 Pickling Vegetables and Fruits

Introduction

Most vegetables and fruits can be preserved by pickling, but, as with all preserving, they must be young and fresh to give the best results.

Vegetables are usually pickled in spiced vinegar and fruits in a sweet spiced vinegar. Most vegetables, after cleaning and preparing, are first steeped in brine for 24 to 48 hours to help preserve them. However, marrows, courgettes and cucumbers are usually layered in dry block salt and left for 24 hours to extract some of their moisture.

After soaking in brine, the vegetables are drained, washed well and then dried thoroughly. They are then packed into clean jars with screw tops and the cold spiced vinegar poured over to cover them. The jars should be sealed well to prevent evaporation of the vinegar.

It is best to leave the vegetables for 2 to 3 months before using, to allow the vinegar to penetrate them thoroughly and give a good flavour. Pickled vegetables can be served either as an hors d'œuvre or as a salad to accompany cold meat.

A different method, using spiced syrup (this is spiced vinegar with sugar added to it), is used to pickle fruits. After the fruits have been washed and prepared they are then cooked in the syrup until tender. The pickled fruits are then packed into clean jars and covered with the boiling spiced vinegar. The jars are sealed and can be used after a week, but better results can be achieved if they are left for at least 1 month to mature.

These fruits make a delicious if rather rich dessert and are most successful served with roast meats, especially lamb and turkey.

Spiced Vinegar

1¼ litres	malt or white vinegar	2 pints
50 g	whole pickling spice	2 oz
	or	

> 1 level tbsp whole cloves,
> 1 level tbsp allspice
> berries, 1 level tbsp
> mustard seed, 1 cinnamon
> stick, 4 peppercorns
> and 1 blade of mace

Place the vinegar and all the spices in a bowl and stand in a saucepan of water. Cover the bowl with a plate to prevent the vinegar losing its flavour. Bring the water in the pan slowly to the boil, then remove from the heat and leave the bowl standing in the water for about 2 hours.

Strain the vinegar to remove the spices and pour it into a clean bottle (the empty vinegar bottle is ideal); seal and label the bottle and store until ready for use.

Method for pickling vegetables

1. Select young, fresh vegetables and prepare (see the chapters on each individual vegetable).

2. Either place the vegetables in cold brine (250 g/8 oz salt to 2¼ litres/4 pints water) or layered in dry salt. Leave for 24 to 36 hours, according to the instructions given for each vegetable in the recipes following.

3. Remove from the brine or salt and rinse well in cold water. Drain thoroughly.

4. Have ready clean jars with screw lids which have a plastic coating inside, e.g. some makes of jam jars, used chutney jars or Kilner jars.

5. Pack the vegetables, but not too tightly, in the jars to within 3 cm (1 inch) of the top.

6. Any water collecting in the jars after packing should be poured off before the jars are filled with cold spiced vinegar (opposite) to within 1 cm (½ inch) of the top, to cover the vegetables completely.

7. Cover the jars tightly with screw tops to prevent the vinegar evaporating, though a little evaporation will take place if the vegetables are stored for any length of time.

8. Store the labelled jars in a cool, dark place. Although the vegetables can be used immediately, it is usually best to leave the jars for 2 to 3 months before use. Most pickles will store for up to 1 year.

Beetroots

Small beets are pickled whole, larger ones are either sliced or diced after cooking.

Wash the beetroots well and place in a saucepan of cold salted water. Bring to the boil, cover and cook for 1½ to 2 hours, depending on the size of the beets. Drain and leave to get cold, then remove the skins, the tops and the roots. Slice or dice the larger vegetables and pack them into clean jars, but not too tightly. Add a little salt, if liked, to the spiced vinegar and pour it over the beetroots to cover them. Seal tightly, label and use fairly quickly. For longer storage, over 3 months, cover the beets with boiling spiced vinegar and seal tightly at once. The diced or sliced beets are better for longer storage than the whole beets.

Red Cabbage

Remove any damaged outer leaves, halve and remove the centre core. Shred the cabbage finely, place in a bowl and layer with dry salt. Cover and leave for 24 hours. Remove from the salt, rinse under cold water and dry thoroughly. Pack the cabbage into clean jars, pour over it cold spiced vinegar to cover, seal and store for a week before use. This pickle is best used within 3 months as the cabbage starts to lose its crispness.

Cauliflower

Cut the cauliflower into florets and wash well. Place in a bowl and cover with brine. Put a plate over the bowl and leave to stand for 24 hours. Drain the cauliflower well and pack it into clean jars. Pour over it the cold spiced vinegar, to cover. Seal, label and store the jars for 2 to 3 months before use.

Courgettes and Cucumbers

Wipe the courgettes or cucumbers and trim off the ends. Cut into 1-cm (½-inch) slices, place in a bowl, layer with dry salt and cover with a plate. Leave to stand for 24 hours. Remove the slices from the salt, rinse under cold water and dry thoroughly. Pack them into clean jars and pour over them the cold spiced vinegar, to cover. Seal, label and store for at least 1 month before use.

Marrows

Although marrow can be pickled on its own, it is usually combined with other vegetables to make a mixed pickle. Peel and cut off the top and stalk. Cut into 3-cm (1-inch) rings and remove the centre seeds. Cut the rings into fairly small cubes, place in a bowl and layer with dry salt. Cover and leave to stand for 24 hours. Remove the marrow cubes from the salt and rinse under cold water. Dry them thoroughly, pack them in clean jars, then pour over them the cold spiced vinegar, to cover. Seal, label and store.

Mushrooms

Wipe and trim the mushrooms and leave whole. (Small button mushrooms are the best for pickling.) Layer the mushrooms in a casserole with a little salt. Pour the spiced vinegar over them, to cover, put on the lid and bake in a moderately cool oven, 160°C, 325°F, gas mark 3, until the mushrooms are tender – about 1 hour. Drain from the vinegar and pack into clean jars. Bring the vinegar to the boil and pour over the mushrooms. Seal at once, label and store when cold. This pickle makes a good first course, either on its own or as part of an hors d'œuvre.

Onions

Small pickling onions are best for this. Peel the onions, leave whole and place in a bowl. Cover with brine, then leave them covered for 24 to 36 hours, depending on the size of the onions. Drain thoroughly from the brine and pack into clean jars. Pour the cold spiced vinegar over them, to cover; seal, label and store for at least 3 months before use. If yellow spots appear on the onions after a few months' storage there is no need to worry as this is quite harmless and the onions can still be used.

Onion and Apple Pickle

Use any type of onion and sour apples in equal quantities. Peel the onions, peel and core the apples and slice both thinly. Pack into clean jars. To every 1¼ litres (2 pints) spiced vinegar used add 1 level tablespoon salt. Pour the *hot*, salted spiced vinegar over the onion and apple, to cover, then seal at once; label and store. This pickle is ready for use when cold but can be stored for several months.

Mixed Pickle

Choose a selection of vegetables – usually sprigs of cauliflower, onions, French beans, cucumbers, marrows or courgettes. The quantities of each do not matter. Peel the onions, but it is only necessary to slice, dice or cut the other vegetables into even-sized pieces. Place the prepared vegetables in a bowl and layer with salt. Cover with a plate and leave for 36 hours. Remove from the salt, rinse in cold water and dry thoroughly. Pack them into clean jars, then pour cold spiced vinegar over them, to cover. Seal, label and store for 1 month before use.

Method for pickling fruits

1. Choose fresh firm fruits and prepare them as given in the chart on p. 332.

2. Place the spiced vinegar in a medium-sized saucepan, add the sugar (for quantities see the chart on p. 332) and heat gently to dissolve. Bring to the boil for 1 minute.

3. Add the prepared fruits to the spiced syrup and simmer gently until the fruit is tender but not breaking up.

4. Have ready clean jars with screw lids which have a plastic coating inside, e.g. some makes of jam jars, used chutney jars or Kilner jars.

5. Drain the fruit from the syrup and pack into the jars to within 3 cm (1 inch) of the top.

6. Return the spiced syrup to the pan and bring to the boil. Boil rapidly until it has thickened slightly and reduced in quantity by a third.

7. Pour the hot thickened syrup over the fruits in the jar to cover the fruits completely and to within 1 cm (½ inch) of the top of the jar.

8. Seal at once with the screw lids, label and leave to get cold before storing in a cool, dark place.

9. Any extra syrup should be kept in a sealed jar, as you may find that the level of the syrup in the jars will go down during storage and any extra syrup can be used to top up the jars to the original level.

Pickled Fruit Chart

Fruit	Preparation	Quantity	Vinegar
Apples	Wash and prick small ones. Peel, core and thickly slice large ones.	1 kg (2 lb) small or crab; 1¼ kg (2½ lb) large ones	600 ml (1 pint) spiced vinegar
Blackberries	Rinse and hull; drain well.	2½ kg (5 lb)	600 ml (1 pint) spiced vinegar
Cherries	Wash, stone and leave whole.	2 kg (4 lb)	600 ml (1 pint) spiced vinegar
Pears	Peel, halve and core.	2 kg (4 lb)	600 ml (1 pint) white vinegar
Plums and Damsons	Wash, halve and stone.	1½ kg (3½ lb)	600 ml (1 pint) malt vinegar
Rhubarb	Wipe, trim both ends and cut into 3-cm (1-inch) pieces.	1½ kg (3 lb)	650 ml (1 pint) spiced vinegar

Additions	Sugar	Cooking Time
—	1 kg (2 lb)	10 mins.
—	1 kg (2 lb)	5 mins.
A few drops of red colouring added to the syrup before thickening	¾ kg (1½ lb)	10 mins.
6 cloves 2 cinnamon sticks	1 kg (2 lb)	Gently dissolve the sugar in the vinegar, add spices and simmer for 10 mins. Add pears and cook for 15–20 mins.
1 level tsp mixed pickling spice; 4 cloves; 2 cinnamon sticks; pinch of ground nutmeg; ½ lemon, grated rind only	1½ kg (3½ lb) demerara sugar	Gently dissolve the sugar in the vinegar, add spices and lemon rind and simmer for 10 mins. Add plums and cook for 5 mins.
—	1 kg (2 lb)	5 mins.

Baking Blind

Sometimes it is necessary to cook a pastry flan or pie case before putting in the filling. This is known as baking 'blind'.

Line the pastry flan or pie case with a piece of crumpled tissue paper or greaseproof paper. Half fill the case with dried beans or rice to keep the paper down and help the pastry keep its shape during cooking (the beans or rice can be kept, stored in a screw-top jar, and used again and again for baking blind).

If making tartlet cases it is only necessary to prick the bases with a fork and line the inside with a piece of kitchen foil. Beans or rice are not needed.

Bake the pastry case on the centre shelf of a preheated oven at 200°C, 400°F, gas mark 6, for about 15 minutes. Remove the paper and beans (or, if making tartlets, the foil paper) and bake for a further 5 to 10 minutes until cooked and a light golden brown.

Shortcrust Pastry

Makes 200 g (8 oz)

200 g	plain flour	8 oz
	pinch of salt	
50 g	margarine	2 oz
50 g	lard	2 oz
	cold water to mix	

Sift the flour and salt into a bowl. Cut the margarine and lard into pieces, add to the flour and, using the fingertips only, rub the fats into the flour until the mixture resembles fine breadcrumbs.

Add just enough cold water to mix to a firm but not sticky dough, using a palette knife or round-bladed knife. The less you handle the pastry, the lighter it will be when cooked.

Cover the pastry and leave in a cool place for 20 minutes before using.

* The pastry may be frozen at this stage.

Sweet Shortcrust Pastry

Makes 200 g (8 oz)

200 g	plain flour	8 oz
	pinch of salt	
50 g	margarine	2 oz
50 g	lard	2 oz
50 g	caster sugar	2 oz
1	large egg yolk	1
	cold water to mix	

Sift the flour and salt into a bowl. Cut the margarine and lard into pieces, add to the flour and, using the fingertips only, rub the fats into the flour until the mixture resembles fine breadcrumbs. Stir in the sugar.

Mix the egg yolk with a little cold water, and bind the mixture together to give a firm but not sticky dough.

Cover and leave in a cool place for 20 minutes before using.

* The pastry may be frozen at this stage.

Pâte Sucrée

Makes 100 g (4 oz)

100 g	plain flour	4 oz
	pinch of salt	
50 g	softened butter	2 oz
50 g	caster sugar	2 oz
1	large egg, yolk only	1
a few drops	vanilla essence (optional)	a few drops
1 dsp	cold water	1 dsp

Sift the flour and salt onto a clean working surface. Make a well in the centre and put in the softened butter and the sugar, egg yolk, vanilla essence and water. Using the fingertips of one hand, pinch together the centre ingredients, gradually working in the flour from the sides until it is well blended into a smooth, soft dough. Knead lightly for a moment, and leave to rest for about 45 minutes before using.

Note: The traditional *pâte sucrée* does not have vanilla essence in it, but the addition of the essence enhances the flavour.

* Can be frozen at this stage.

Puff Pastry

Makes about 200 g (8 oz)

200 g	plain flour	8 oz
½ level tsp	salt	½ level tsp
200 g	butter, chilled	8 oz
½ tsp	lemon juice	½ tsp
approx.	ice-cold water	approx.
150 ml		¼ pint

Sift the flour and salt into a bowl. Rub in about 25 g (1 oz) of butter, using the fingertips only.

Place the remaining butter between two pieces of greaseproof paper and flatten it out with a rolling pin into a square about 1 cm (½ inch) thick. Add the lemon juice and ice-cold water to the flour and mix to a firm but pliable dough.

On a floured surface, roll out the dough to a rectangle a little wider than the slab of butter and twice as long.

Place the slab of butter on one half of the dough and fold over the other half. Seal the edges with a rolling pin, cover and leave the parcel in a cool place for 15 minutes.

Give the pastry a quarter turn and roll out into a rectangle the same width as before, but three times as long as the folded parcel. Fold the bottom third up and the top third down over it. Seal the edges and give a quarter turn. Take great care when rolling that the butter does not break through the dough. If it should, sprinkle it with a little flour. Roll and fold again in the same way, cover and leave in a cool place for 15 minutes.

Repeat the process – rolling, folding, turning, rolling, folding and resting for 15 minutes – until the pastry has been rolled six times in all.

Then leave the pastry in a cool place for a final 20 minutes before using.

* The pastry may be frozen at this stage.

Rough Puff Pastry

Makes 200 g (8 oz)

200 g	plain flour	8 oz
	a good pinch of salt	
150 g	butter	6 oz
	or	
100 g	butter ⎱ blended together	4 oz
50 g	lard ⎰	2 oz
½ tsp	lemon juice	½ tsp
approx.	ice-cold water	approx.
150 ml		¼ pint

Sift the flour and salt into a bowl. Cut the butter or blended butter and lard into pieces the size of walnuts and stir them gently into the flour. Add the lemon juice and the ice-cold water and, using a palette knife or round-bladed knife, gently mix together to give a fairly soft, elastic dough. Be careful not to break up the pieces of fat.

Place the dough on a floured surface and roll out into a rectangle about 45 by 15 cm (18 by 6 inches) wide. Fold the bottom third of pastry up and the top third down over it. Give a quarter turn and seal the edges. Roll out the pastry again to a rectangle and fold as before.

Repeat this process four times in all, by which time the pastry should be smooth and the fat evenly distributed throughout.

If possible, leave the pastry to rest in a cool place for 15 minutes between the second and third rolling and folding. Cover the pastry with polythene and leave for 20 minutes before using.

* The pastry may be frozen at this stage.

Flaky Pastry

Makes 200 g (8 oz)

200 g	plain flour	8 oz
	a good pinch of salt	
75 g	margarine	3 oz
75 g	lard	3 oz
1 tsp	lemon juice	1 tsp
	cold water to mix	

Sift the flour and salt into a bowl. Blend the margarine and lard together on a plate, using a palette knife, and divide the mixture into four equal portions.

Rub one quarter of the blended fats into the sifted flour, using the fingertips only, until the mixture resembles fine breadcrumbs. Stir in the lemon juice and enough cold water to mix into a soft dough. Turn the dough onto a lightly floured surface and knead until smooth. Put it onto a plate, cover and leave for 15 minutes.

Roll out the dough into a rectangle about 60 by 20 cm (24 by 8 inches) and cover the top two thirds of the pastry with little pats of butter from the second portion of blended fats. Fold the unbuttered third of the dough over the middle and the top buttered third over that.

Seal the edges with a rolling pin and give the dough one quarter turn. Roll out and fold again, this time without adding any fat. Then leave to rest, covered, for 15 minutes.

Repeat the whole process twice more, using the remaining two portions of blended fats, and rest it for 15 minutes in between. After the final rolling and folding, cover the pastry with polythene and leave in a cool place for ½ hour before using.

* The pastry may be frozen at this stage.

Choux Pastry

Makes 10–12 éclairs or 1 gougère

65 g (4 rounded tbsps)	plain flour	2½ oz (4 rounded tbsps)

	pinch of salt	
50 g	margarine	2 oz
150 ml	water	¼ pint
2	large eggs	2

Sift the flour and salt onto a piece of paper. Put the margarine and water into a medium-sized saucepan and heat gently until the margarine has melted, then bring to the boil. Remove from the heat and immediately tip the flour into the pan. Beat quickly, using a wooden spoon, until all the flour has been absorbed into the liquid. Continue beating until the mixture is smooth and leaves the sides of the pan clean.

Cool slightly; lightly mix together the eggs and beat a little at a time into the mixture in the pan, beating well between each addition. The pastry should be glossy and thick enough to hold its shape when piped.

If the pastry is not to be used immediately, cover with a piece of damp greaseproof paper to prevent it drying out.

Basic White Sauce

Makes 300 ml (½ pint)

	margarine or butter	¾ oz
3 level tbsps	plain flour	3 level tbsps
300 ml	milk	½ pint
	salt and freshly ground pepper	

Melt the margarine or butter in a saucepan. Stir in the flour, mix together to make a roux (i.e. a paste) and, over a gentle heat, cook for a minute.

Remove from the heat and gradually blend in the milk, using a wooden spoon. Season with salt and pepper and return the pan to the heat. Stirring constantly, bring to the boil and cook for 2 minutes before serving.

Note: To make a *coating sauce* use 25 g (1 oz) margarine or butter and 25 g (1 oz) plain flour.

To make a *binding sauce* use 40 g (1½ oz) margarine or butter and 40 g (1½ oz) plain flour.

Béchamel Sauce

Makes 300 ml (½ pint)

300 ml	milk	½ pint
1	small onion	1
1	small carrot	1
4–6	peppercorns	4–6
1	bay leaf	1
1	blade of mace	1
20 g	margarine or butter	¾ oz
3 level tbsps	plain flour	3 level tbsps
	salt and freshly ground pepper	

Pour the milk into a saucepan. Peel the onion and carrot, cut both in half and add to the pan of milk. Add the peppercorns, bay leaf and mace, bring very slowly to the boil, turn the heat off at once and leave on one side for ½ hour to let the seasonings flavour the milk. Strain the milk into a jug and discard the vegetables and spices. Rinse out the pan and melt the margarine or butter in it. Stir in the flour, mix together to make a roux and cook for a minute over a gentle heat. Remove the pan from the heat and gradually stir in the strained milk, using a wooden spoon. Season with a little salt and pepper.

Return the pan to the heat and, stirring constantly, bring to the boil; cook for 2 minutes before serving.

Note: To make a coating or binding béchamel sauce, see note at foot of basic white sauce recipe (p. 339).

Cheese or Mornay Sauce

Makes 300 ml (½ pint)

300 ml	basic white sauce (p. 339) or béchamel sauce	½ pint
50–75 g	cheese, grated	2–3 oz

Prepare the basic white or béchamel sauce, then remove the pan from the heat and stir in the grated cheese. Stir until the cheese has melted,

but do not return to the heat or the cheese will start to cook and so
spoil the sauce.

Cream Sauce

Makes 300 ml (½ pint)

300 ml	basic white coating sauce (p. 339) or béchamel sauce (p. 340)	½ pint
150 ml	single cream	¼ pint

Prepare the basic white coating sauce or béchamel sauce, remove from
the heat and stir in the cream. If necessary the sauce can be gently re-
heated, but take care not to boil. Check for seasoning before serving.

Egg Sauce

Makes 300 ml (½ pint)

300 ml	basic white sauce (p. 339) or béchamel sauce (p. 340)	½ pint
1	hard-boiled egg	1

Prepare the basic white or béchamel sauce.
Shell the egg, chop finely and stir into the cooked sauce. Return to
the heat for a further minute before serving.

Parsley Sauce

Makes 300 ml (½ pint)

300 ml	basic white sauce (p. 339) or béchamel sauce (p. 340)	½ pint
1 rounded tbsp	fresh parsley, chopped	1 rounded tbsp

Prepare the basic white or béchamel sauce, stir in the chopped parsley
and keep on the heat for 1 minute before serving.

Hollandaise Sauce

Makes about 150 ml (¼ pint)

2 tbsps	wine vinegar	2 tbsps
2	egg yolks	2
50 g	butter	2 oz
	salt and pepper	
	a few drops of lemon juice	

Put the vinegar in a small pan and boil until reduced by half. Leave to cool.

Mix the cooled vinegar with the egg yolks in a basin over a pan of simmering water. Using a balloon whisk, stir gently until the sauce begins to thicken. Whisk in the butter a little at a time, making sure that each piece is worked in before adding the next. Take care that the sauce does not boil.

Now add the seasonings and the drops of lemon juice, and serve hot, immediately.

Note: If during the making the sauce separates, this can be rectified by beating in a tablespoon of cold water.

Mayonnaise

Makes 300 ml (½ pint)

2	egg yolks	2
300 ml	olive or cooking oil	½ pint
1 level tsp	dry mustard or French mustard	1 level tsp
	a good pinch of caster sugar	
	salt and freshly ground pepper	
1–1½ tbsps	vinegar	1–1½ tbsps

The eggs and oil should be at room temperature.

In a bowl, mix the yolks with the seasonings – mustard, sugar, salt and pepper. Pour the oil into a jug and, using a wooden spoon, beat it a drop at a time into the egg yolks. After about a third of the oil has been added, the mayonnaise will begin to thicken. At this stage the oil can be added more quickly. When it is really thick, add the vinegar and the remaining oil. Check for seasoning, then store the mayonnaise in a screw-top jar in the refrigerator and use as required.

Note: It will store for at least a month in the refrigerator. If you have a liquidizer, whole eggs can be used. All the ingredients, except the oil, are put into the blender and then, on a fast speed, the oil is added in a steady trickle.

French Dressing

Makes about 150 ml (¼ pint)

6 tbsps	olive or cooking oil	6 tbsps
2 tbsps	wine or malt vinegar	2 tbsps
	pinch of dry mustard	
	salt and freshly ground	
	pepper	
1 tsp	caster sugar	1 tsp

The best way to prepare French dressing is to make it in an empty screw-top bottle, e.g. a sauce, vinegar or tonic water bottle.

Pour the oil into the bottle, add the vinegar, seasonings and sugar. Put the top on the bottle and shake well until emulsified.

Before using, shake the bottle well as the vinegar and oil will separate out during storage. This dressing will keep indefinitely.

Note: Lemon juice may be used instead of vinegar and, for those who like garlic, a little garlic salt may be added instead of the ordinary salt. If you are making a larger quantity of dressing, a crushed clove of fresh garlic may be used if preferred.

Fritter Batter

Makes about 12 fritters

100 g	plain flour	4 oz
1	large egg	1
150 ml	milk	¼ pint
½ level tsp	baking powder	½ level tsp
	oil for frying	
a deep-fat frying pan		

Sift the flour into a bowl (if making savoury fritters, add a pinch of salt; for sweet fritters, add 1 level tablespoon caster sugar), make a hollow in the centre and break in the egg. Using a wooden spoon, gradually beat the flour into the egg, adding the milk a little at a time to give a smooth batter. Beat for a further minute and leave to stand for 15 minutes.

Just before using the batter to coat the vegetables or fruits, stir in the baking powder. Once coated, fry in hot, deep oil or fat for a few minutes on each side.

Pancake Batter

Makes about 12 pancakes

125 g	plain flour	4 oz
	pinch of salt	
1	standard egg	1
150 ml	milk ⎫ mixed together	¼ pint
150 ml	water ⎭	¼ pint
	a little oil for frying	

Sift the flour and salt into a bowl, make a hollow in the centre and break in the egg. Using a wooden spoon, gradually beat the flour into the egg, adding the milk and water at the same time to give a smooth batter. Beat well for a minute and pour into a jug. Leave to stand for 15 minutes.

Heat a little oil in an omelette pan or small frying pan, drain off any excess and pour in a little batter, swirling the pan so that it coats the base. Cook briskly for a minute until set and the bottom of the pancake is a light brown. Toss and cook the other side.

Have ready a cooling rack covered with a tea towel and place the pancake in the towel to keep warm whilst cooking the other pancakes. Keep warm until ready to use.

Note: Pancakes can be made the day before, wrapped in kitchen foil and kept in the refrigerator. To heat through for serving, place them, still wrapped in foil, in a warm oven (160°C, 325°F, gas mark 3) for 15 minutes.

* Pancakes freeze well.

Index

More About Penguins and Pelicans

*Penguin Handbooks offer an enormous range of practical guides to help
you with cooking, drinking, sewing, knitting, gardening, sports, hobbies,
child care, the law – all these and many more. Some of them are listed on
the following pages.*

Cookery and Wine

THE FARMHOUSE KITCHEN
Mary Norwak

A bevy of recipes, with notes on their history, which includes all
the traditional country occupations of bread-making, pickling
and brewing as well as delicious and time-honoured meals.

VEGETABLE COOKERY
Nika Hazelton

An A-Z of vegetables, both fresh and dried, with their history, ways
of keeping and preserving them, their nutritional value, and a host of
exciting recipes.

LEAVE IT TO COOK
Stella Attenbury

Slow cooking makes food tastes better and saves time. Here are
recipes for meat, fish, soups, casseroles, vegetables, sweets and
savouries that you can leave for up to eight hours and only improve
the taste.

HERBS FOR ALL SEASONS
Rosemary Hemphill

In four parts, one for each season, this book gives instructions for
planting, growing and drying each plant, with a variety of recipes to
suit all tastes and a fascinating collection of herbal remedies and
beauty aids.

Cookery and Wine

ENGLISH FOOD
Jane Grigson

'Jane Grigson is perhaps the most serious and discriminating of the younger generation of cookery writers, and *English Food* is an anthology all who follow her recipes will want to buy' – Pamela Vandyke Price in the *Spectator*

THE PENGUIN BOOK OF JAMS, PICKLES AND CHUTNEYS
David and Rose Mabey

'An excellent book; practical, personal and suggestive, every recipe's clearly the result of real experience and written with great charm' – *The Times*

COOKING WITH WINE
Robin McDouall

You'd be surprised at the number of delicious ways you can disguise Calvados, sherry, Champagne, beer, cider – and, of course, wine. . .

THE PENGUIN BOOK OF HOME BREWING AND WINE-MAKING
W. H. T. Tayleur

Here is all you need to know about beer and wine, liqueurs and cider, perry and mead: how to make them, bottle them, store them and serve them. You'll know how to drink them!

THE PENGUIN GUIDE TO REAL DRAUGHT BEER
Michael Dunn

Mike Dunn tells us how real draught beer is made and served, how it has survived the mass-market bright beers, who makes it, and where you can get it.

Making and Doing at Home

THE PAUPER'S HOMEMAKING BOOK
Jocasta Innes

This book is directed towards those people who are setting up
home in earnest, who have lots of energy and ideas, and – after paying
out mortgage or rent – almost no cash.

SIMPLE CLOTHES AND HOW TO MAKE THEM
Kerstin Lokrantz

Some of these garments for men, women and children are
traditional; all are functional, extremely easy to make and hardwearing,
and the instructions are clear and detailed.

SELF HELP HOUSE REPAIRS MANUAL
Andrew Ingham

Given sufficient practical information, almost anyone can do basic
electrical, plumbing, glazing and carpentry repairs. Here is the
information.

POTPOURRIS AND OTHER FRAGRANT DELIGHTS
Jacqueline Hériteau

An entertaining guide to the old-fashioned art of preserving the
fragrance of herbs, flowers and spices, with over a hundred recipes.

LOUISA CALDER'S CREATIVE CROCHET
Louisa Calder

Cheap and cheerful designs and patterns can make you an expert
creator of hats, belts, ties, cushions, gloves and many other crochet
items.

Gardening

THE WELL-TEMPERED GARDEN
Christopher Lloyd

'I cannot remember when I enjoyed a book so much, and no matter what your special interests may be, I cannot recommend it too highly' – Ron Hay in *The Times*

THE PIP BOOK
Keith Mossman

'The perfect present for the young enthusiast, *The Pip Book* should ensure that even the most reluctant avocado puts down roots and sends up shoots' – *The Times*

ORGANIC GARDENING
Lawrence D. Hills

The author gives detailed instructions for growing a wide range of fruits and vegetables by organic principles, many of them varieties no longer available from shops.

TOWN GARDENS TO LIVE IN
Susan Jellicoe and Marjory Allen

Here is a book about creating the kind of garden *you* want to live in: formal, naturalistic, or just plain easy to keep.

THE NEW VEGETABLE GROWER'S HANDBOOK
Arthur J. Simons

Practical and exact instruction combined with sound scientific explanation make this one of the most reliable 'green-finger' manuals on sale.